STANDARD LOAN

NAPIER COLLEGE LIBRARY
SIGHTHILL
Sighthill Court
Edinburgh EH11 4BN
Tel 031-443 6061
Ext 307

This book is due for return on or before
the last date stamped below

1 2 FEB 1984	2 2 JAN 1988	
2 0 FEB 1984	2 9 NOV 1988	
2 2 MAR 1984	2 7 APR 1989	
1 2 DEC 1984		
1 0 APR 1986		
1 6 FEB 1987		

STATE INTERVENTION IN INDUSTRY

a workers' inquiry

Coventry
Liverpool
Newcastle
N. Tyneside

Trades Councils

SPOKESMAN

First published in 1980 by:
Coventry, Liverpool,
Newcastle and North Tyneside
Trades Councils,
5 Queens Street,
Newcastle-upon-Tyne

Second (revised) edition 1982 published by:
Spokesman
Bertrand Russell House
Gamble Street
Nottingham

ISBN 0 85124 363 0 Pbk
ISBN 0 85124 367 3 Cloth

Cover: Tony Fry, Collective Design/Midland
Printed by the Russell Press Ltd., Nottingham.

Contents

Preface to second edition   4

Preface   5

Introduction   9

1. Party policies   19

2. Government policies   33

3. Expectations . . .   47
    Nationalisation   50
    The National Enterprise Board .   54
    Planning agreements and government aid   64
    The co-operatives   71

4. . . . And realities   77
    Nationalisation   78
    The National Enterprise Board   80
    Planning agreements and government aid   99
    The co-operatives   112

5. Opposition   121
    Silence   121
    Resistance   127

6. Conclusions   141
    At Congress House and Walworth Road   141
    Learning the lessons in the localities   162

Appendices   187
I   The NEB's performance   187
II   Members of the NEB and their other interests   190
III   Chart of NEB acquisitions and disposals   197
IV   Attendance at national stage of the inquiry   208
V   Coventry Trades Council Joint Activities Sub-committee   209
VI   Bibliography   213

Preface
to second edition

We have rewritten the conclusions for the second edition mainly in order to emphasise and drive home the lessons to be learned from the experience of workers in our areas under the last Labour government. We feel that the industrial policies now coming from the leadership of the trade unions and the Labour Party reflect too complacent an assessment of the industrial policies of the last Labour government. We also see our conclusions as a contribution to developing a new approach to economic and industrial planning; an approach which builds mainly on the perceptions of current social need and wasted resources, and the potential power of people organised in their workplaces and localities.

Many people have made useful comments on the original report of our enquiry and we have used many of these insights in rewriting the conclusions. We would like to thank especially: members of the Conference of Socialist Economists, particularly Richard Disney and Robin Murray; members of the Socialist Environment and Resources Association, particularly Victor Anderson, John Bradbrook, Dave Elliott and Stan Rosenthal, and finally Bob Rowthorn, all of whom made the effort to write long and helpful letters or papers. Hilary Wainwright wrote the draft of the conclusions which were discussed, amended and thrown into the dustbin at several meetings of representatives from all the trades councils involved. Responsibility for what follows is therefore a collective one.

November 1982

4

Preface

It is amazing how easily the policies of Labour governments take on a rosy hue when we are in the gloom of Tory rule. Already the industrial policies of the last Labour government are being written up as a major success story. Take for instance the TUC's 'Campaign for Economic and Social Advance'. One of their propaganda sheets has an article headed 'The Enterprising NEB'. It goes on:

> 'The National Enterprise Board has been a major success story. The track record proves the NEB has been able to look after the national interest and to be truly enterprising.'

After the experience of the NEB's activities in Tyneside, Merseyside and Coventry we would not agree. We feel it is time we said so, before people forget what actually happened under the last Labour government and what effect its industrial policies had on working people in these and other areas.

But our purpose is not simply to remind people of what 'really happened'. Our four trades councils agreed to work together on this inquiry in November 1978 when there was still a Labour government. Our intention then was to use the inquiry to add to the pressure on the government to change its disastrous policies.

When the Tories won the election in May 1979 we wondered at first whether we should drop the idea. There is always a very strong pressure once the Tories get back not to think through the criticisms and alternatives which occur to us when Labour governments begin to go wrong. The atmosphere after Thatcher's victory was no exception. There was a strong feeling around that we had to throw ourselves into defensive action alone.

But we felt it was important, at the same time as campaigning against the Tories, to spend some extra effort learning from the experience of the last Labour government.

For many of our weaknesses in the rank and file of the trade union movement come from a failure to look thoroughly into why Labour governments have not lived up to the expectations working people have of them. *For this has happened not just once, but again and again;* every time in fact. The result has been an accumulated cynicism not just about Labour politicians — as about all politicians — but about *any* form of political action, any collective effort to change things.

5

We have carried out this inquiry in order to achieve, instead, an accumulation of lessons and experiences through which to strengthen and to politicise our workplace and community organisations.

We say 'politicise' because the one conclusion which comes most clearly from the inquiry is that *never again can we leave politics to the politicians.* Socialist politicians do not have the power to carry through socialist policies by parliament alone. Shop stewards committees, linked with public sector workers and with community based groups, through trades councils and other local organisations, need *themselves* to organise and campaign on a broader, political front. Tony Benn said something similar in his Granada Guildhall lecture on May 15th 1980:

> 'the trade union movement in particular has to rethink its own vision of itself in much bolder terms, if it is to widen its appeal to those beyond its own ranks.'

In the way that it has been organised, this Inquiry is itself a small illustration of trade union organisations taking on a wider, bolder role.

The *Introduction* describes this in more detail. It highlights the principles which underlay the way in which we organised the Inquiry; for we believe that the process involved in a collective piece of work like this is as important as the end product.

Chapter One then explains the origins of the new industrial policies, that is, of the NEB, planning agreements and the emphasis on industrial democracy. It describes the impact of the failure of the 64-70 Wilson governments in which so many people placed their hopes, and it looks at the radicalising effect of the campaigns over Upper Clyde Shipbuilders (UCS) and other closures.

Chapter Two is a blow by blow account of the Cabinet and civil service manoeuvres, the CBI and City pressures, and the long silences from the TUC which, together, led to the defeat of the Labour Party's manifesto policies. This chapter, in itself, shows how revealing this case study is of the kind of ruling class we are up against.

Then, in *Chapter Three,* we move away from London, from national conferences and national committees, to the needs and expectations of workers in our four areas. We describe the problems that workers faced in the early 1970s in each of the industries directly affected by state intervention. Shop stewards explain what they hoped for when sympathetic ministers were in the Department of Industry and when manifesto policies were, as they saw it, becoming legislation.

Next comes the reality: how the policies actually operated; the closures, the deals, the aid without strings, the myth of industrial democracy. This, in *Chapter Four,* was the meat of the Inquiry, bringing together all the local information.

Why was all this allowed to happen? That's the focus of *Chapter Five.* It looks in detail at the TUC's support for Wilson. It asks why Benn and Heffer never resigned to lead a campaign from the back benches, and why few people outside parliament and the TUC really knew what was going on. It examines the inadequacies of existing trade union structures in specific cases; it highlights the lack of accountability of trade unionists on the board of the NEB. Finally, on a more optimistic note, it draws some lessons from those campaigns which did win some victories, however precarious, like the campaigns of workers at Parsons and at Lucas Aerospace.

Finally, in *Chapter Six,* we draw some conclusions for discussion. We describe the lessons which the MPs who supported the original policies draw from the experience. Their emphasis is on getting the party structures right so that next time the policies *will* be implemented. Consistent with this view, the majority view within the Labour Party NEC in 1980, is strongly to reaffirm the original policies of the 1973 programme with an additional emphasis on control of foreign trade.

We, on the other hand, are very much more critical of the policies themselves. We argue that they contain contradictions that make them vulnerable to the same pressures of international competition and corporate power as were Wilson's industrial policies. In other words, we consider that the industrial policies of 1973 do not provide us with a 'transitional' strategy; for insofar as they are consistently pursued, they come up against the same kind of resistance as a more full-blooded socialism. And they come up against the same problems of winning support to counter that resistance at a time when 'socialism' and 'nationalisation' have lost the vision of liberation and new possibilities which used to be associated with them.

So we are back to the problem of how to convince people that socialism is not just about replacing a boss working for private shareholders with a boss working for the government; that socialism is about destroying bosses altogether, about management being accountable to workers and about workers having control over the purpose and the conditions of their work.

In our conclusions, therefore, we do not evaluate possible socialist industrial policies so much in terms of their consistency as a programme for government, as if the government really has the power to control private capital. Rather, we evaluate policies in terms of whether they provide a focus for and a means of building the political power of workers' industrial and community based organisations, and of preparing those organisations to take control.

We end, therefore, with a discussion of the ways we might strengthen our workplace and community organisations. How, for example, we can extend the scope of trades councils and combine committees to fight for control over the private and public planning decisions which, locally and nationally, shape our lives, but are taken regardless of our needs. How, at the same time as extending the political scope of our trades councils, shop stewards committees, tenants and women's groups, we can deepen the support for these organisations among the people they represent. Finally, we consider what kinds of policies will unify working class people and provide a focus for building the power of our local and shop floor organisations. In this way, the first chapters begin with 'high' politics while the last chapters conclude with a discussion of day-to-day struggles and the ways of organising which develop them politically. We hope this inquiry will itself contribute to this process.

Acknowledgements

We would like here, on behalf of our four trades councils, to thank all those who have helped us with the Inquiry. In addition to those trade union organisations listed at the front of the Report, we would like to acknowledge particularly the work of our drafting committee: Hilary Wainwright (Newcastle), Paul Field and Slim Hallett (Coventry) and Eddie Loyden (Liverpool). We would also like to thank the Lucas Aerospace Combine Committee for enabling Hilary Wainwright to spend several months of her research with them on the writing up of this report.

A number of other people gave us valuable assistance and advice during the Inquiry and the writing of the Report. In particular: Norman Ginsburg; Keith Hodgson of the Trade Union Studies Information Unit; Mike George from the Centre of Alternative Industrial Systems; George Osgerby and George Blazycka. We would like also to thank Coventry Workshop and the Open University for providing the facilities needed in the drafting of this Report; Ivy Ternant for typing the Report; James Swinson for designing the cover; and many others, especially delegates of the four trades councils, who have read and made useful comments on earlier drafts.

Coventry Trades Council
Colin Lindsay — President
Jack Gould — Secretary
31 Stepney Road,
Coventry

Newcastle Trades Council
Ken Ternant — President
Colin Randall — Secretary
199 Hugh Gardens,
Benwell,
Newcastle 4

Liverpool Trades Council
Barry Williams — President
Alex Doswell — Secretary
70 Victoria Street,
Liverpool 1

North Tyneside Trades Council
Stan Brett — President
John Foster — Secretary
25 Roxburgh Terrace,
Whitley Bay,
Tyne and Wear

8

Introduction

This inquiry began as an inquiry into the NEB. But as interest in it grew, its brief was extended to cover state intervention in industry more generally. The inquiry was extended in this way because shop stewards and trades council delegates felt that the NEB was just one instance of a more general problem: the problem that state intervention in industry, which has always been a major part of any socialist programme, has failed to live up to people's expectations.

In Britain, at least, socialism has usually been associated in most people's minds with increased state intervention. Many socialists have also emphasised workers' control and popular power but this emphasis has never been strongly enough supported or practically enough worked out to shape the popular image of socialism.

Measures taken in the first years of the 1945 Labour government strengthened this popular equation of state intervention with socialism. Important nationalisation measures were carried through and the basis of the welfare state was laid. But it was not long before the forms which nationalisation took began to cloud the popular vision of socialism. Two particular features of this were the subordination of the nationalised industries to the requirements of private industry and the absence of any change in the relation between managers and workers.

In the 50s and early 60s the notion of socialism as primarily a matter of increased state intervention contributed to a weakening of the influence of socialist politics: paradoxically, against the background of a growing trade union militancy. The intensity of the cold war and the experience of state socialism under Stalin is part of the explanation. But perhaps a more important part of the explanation lies in the bargaining power provided by full employment: with this new bargaining power many workers found they could win improved living standards through their shop floor strength alone. An increase in state intervention in industry — that is an increase in 'socialism' — did not seem to many active trade unionists to have the relevance which it had, for instance, in the 30s. But, as the strength of support for Nye Bevan and his programme for social ownership indicated, state intervention still had considerable credibility.

The Wilson administration's use of the state further eroded the credibility of

Labour Party Conference 1975.

socialism. The Industrial Reorganisation Corporation (IRC) further enhanced the power of the major corporations at the cost of thousands of jobs. As the boom collapsed and, from 1973 onwards the economy plunged deeper into recession, working class experience of the state became increasingly ambiguous under Labour as much as under the Tories. The state provided a health service, but a service which was, and is, rapidly deteriorating and over which working class people have no control. The state nationalised collapsing private companies only to carry out massive redundancy and rationalisation plans without creating alternative employment. While in the 50s and 60s few working class people considered the state to be 'their' state, they were at least more likely to believe in its neutrality. After the experience of the 1974-79 Labour government, such a belief was more difficult to hold. The state was increasingly seen as responsible for declining living standards and a growing sense of powerlessness. Proof of this lies partly in the resonance of Thatcher's anti-state election campaign in important sections of the working class.

The Tory Offensive

Tory propaganda played very effectively on this alienation of many working class people from the state. Their promises and their rhetoric gave the impression that a reduction in state intervention would mean an unleashing of new sources of prosperity, choice and opportunity for everyone. In fact, of course, the idea of dismantling an interfering and oppressive state has proved to be a cover for a *more rapid erosion* of the social provisions of the state, to meet the needs of crisis-ridden British capitalism. Profitable state-owned industrial assets, suitably relieved of their more burdensome parts, have been sold to private shareholders. Expenditure on the welfare state has been cut while finance to private industry has increased through generous tax relief as well as direct aid. Direct state control has still proved useful in continuing to rationalise what is left of Britain's diminishing manufacturing base for the present and future benefit of private capital. And finally, through the Employment Act, the powers of the state are being strengthened to destroy the power of workplace trade unionism.

So far, it has proved difficult to generate mass resistance to this Tory offensive. This is partly because people are not confident about the alternative, however angry they are about the Tories.

Shopfloor power and the new industrial policies

Under the last Tory government, shop floor organisations faced with attacks on their living standards were confident enough to take matters into their own hands and create their own alternatives in the short run, through work-ins, occupations and strikes with strong political overtones. This had a major influence on debates about industrial policy within the Labour Party. In particular, it produced a new emphasis on workers' control. As a result, the new industrial policies of 1973 did not rely entirely on state intervention as the basis for socialism.

Trade unionists who had put most of their energies through the 50s and 60s into building up their shop floor and local strength, placed considerable faith in these industrial policies, in their leading advocates and in the possibility of these policies being implemented by the 1974 Labour government. After all, that Labour government came in partly as a result of the industrial strength of the miners and after the workers at UCS and elsewhere had forced humiliating reversals on the Heath government. The electoral position of the new government may have been fragile but the Tory leadership had, because of these defeats, lost all authority. Now was the time for the Labour Party not just to extend state intervention but, in the famous words of the 1974 Manifesto to:

"bring about a fundamental and irreversible shift in the balance of wealth and power in favour of working people and their families."

Yet, as it turned out, far from extending working class power, the effect of the last Labour government was in many ways an erosion of the *real power* of workers' organisations, (even if it led to an increase in the *status* of trade unions). The shattering of the expectations which trade unionists had of that government is one of the factors which have led to an erosion of the industrial strength and confidence of those who led the powerful resistance to the last Tory government.

The origin and purpose of this inquiry

We see this inquiry, the process of discussion involved in it, the new links and contacts created through it, the report itself and the final conference, as

11

part of our present struggle against the Tories. It is not simply a post mortem. It is a contribution to building up the confident belief that there *are* alternatives to Thatcherism and the dole; alternatives which we as workers and as members of local communities must play a role in creating.

In our discussions with those stop stewards committees directly affected by the Labour government's policies, we have found bitter disappointment, confusion and anger at what actually happened. In three cases at least — British Leyland (Speke), Tress Engineering (Newcastle) and Alfred Herberts (Coventry) — the contrast between Labour's initial promises and the eventual policies seemed so scandalous that workers and local researchers produced their own reports. In the case of BL Speke and Tress Engineering, the stewards demanded an inquiry.

In May 1978 at Speke, the T&GWU 6/612 branch called on the T&GWU executive to initiate an inquiry. The motion was supported by the regional T&GWU. It was passed at the executive itself, but then nothing more was heard of it. Throughout the late summer of 1978 the stewards at Tress won the support of several constituency Labour parties and of the County Association of Trades Councils for a demand to the Labour Party National Executive Committee (NEC) that it should conduct an inquiry. But the majority view on the NEC was that for the Labour Party NEC to organise an inquiry into government policy or into the activities of a quasi-governmental organisation was quite unprecedented, and that there was not the machinery or the resources to carry it out.

At a local level however, interest was growing in the issue of Labour's industrial policies, in what had gone wrong, in what were the alternatives and in how they could best be fought for. It was an interest which grew out of bitter experiences.

On Tyneside, workers in shipbuilding saw their proposals for industrial democracy by-passed by Gerald Kaufman at the Department of Industry along with management and national union officials. Their jobs were being rationalised into a place in the dole queue.

Workers in power engineering were, at the same time, fighting to hold off the government's plan to use the NEB to reorganise the industry under the control of GEC. While the NEB was in this way actively concerning itself with *rationalisation* on Tyneside, it proved unable, or unwilling, to carry out the original task of *expansion* and job creation. Another part of Tyneside's heavy engineering industry, Vickers Engineering, was receiving millions of pounds from the government but none of it went to halt the run-down and eventual closure of the Scotswood works in West Newcastle.

Amidst all this, a Regional NEB was created. Its creation was announced as if a good fairy had arrived to create jobs and rebuild the area's industry. But its funding was negligible compared to the investment required. Moreover, its criteria were so strictly commercial that most of its annual income in 1978 remained unspent.

12

Newcastle Upon Tyne.

On Merseyside, the experiences were similar. The campaign of the Speke stewards for some form of inquiry struck a chord with other workers in the area. Workers at Dunlop, also on the Speke estate, had experienced the closure of their plant. The government had given millions in aid and deferred taxation to Dunlops over the years but it did not have the powers to intervene to stop the loss of 2,400 jobs in an area where unemployment was already over 13%.

The workers at Lucas Aerospace Victor works in Liverpool had also suffered as a result of the Labour government's alliance with the captains of industry. After threatening to sack 1,800 workers, Lucas Aerospace negotiated a deal with the government whereby, in exchange for £8 million, it agreed to make 'only' 900 workers redundant. (So far, trade union resistance in Lucas Aerospace has blocked all but 100 of these redundancies.)

Workers in shipbuilding on Merseyside were also disappointed at the reversal of Labour Party promises. The running of the yards – and the closure of the yards – seemed little different from the way they were run by private management.

Perhaps the workers at the Kirkby co-operative felt the most disappointed. It was they who had had the highest hopes, because they had benefited directly, before the Manifesto's industrial policies had been finally ditched.

When members of the Newcastle Trades Council talked with trade unionists on Merseyside the idea of a Trades Council inquiry seemed a natural way to

13

start a debate that would improve on policies for the future and strengthen rank and file contact across industries and between localities.

When trade unionists in Coventry heard of the idea they too found that it related closely to their experiences. They had special problems with the NEB. At least 12 major factories in Coventry are or were owned by the NEB, employing 13% of Coventry's total workforce.

In Coventry, like Liverpool, there had been high hopes for the policies, especially when they delivered some goods, as in support for the Meriden Co-op. These hopes had been shattered, not only at Meriden but at Alfred Herberts, Chrysler and British Leyland, to name those companies most directly involved.

This then is the background to our inquiry. This is how the inquiry came to be organised at a rank and file level, by trades councils with the backing of shop stewards committees, rather than at a national leadership level.

The brief for the inquiry, which was agreed by full delegate meetings of Coventry, Liverpool, Newcastle and North Tyneside Trades Councils in November and December 1978 was as follows:

> "It was agreed that this would be a Workers' Inquiry, and that it would take as its focus the National Enterprise Board. Other aspects of State Intervention would inevitably arise and these would also be considered by the Inquiry. In particular:
> — Nationalization
> — Planning Agreements
> — State Aid and Government Orders to Private Industry
> — Workers' Co-operatives
> The Workers' Inquiry will consider:
> — What has been the record of state intervention
> — Why the results have been so unsatisfactory
> — Why the labour movement has been unsuccessful in preventing these unsatisfactory results
> — What alternative strategies are required."

3. Organisation of the inquiry

Stage 1 The Local Inquiries

The inquiry has been organised in three stages. First the local stage; each trades council organised this differently according to local conditions. In Coventry, members of the Trades Council unemployment sub-committee with research and organisational help from Coventry Workshop, a local trade union and community research and information centre, organised lengthy discussions with shop stewards at Alfred Herberts, British Leyland (Canley), Meriden, Rolls Royce and Chrysler. In most cases there was more than one discussion. Close contact was maintained from the first discussion, as stewards

14

searched for additional information and further discussions were held over a period of about six months.

On Tyneside, the Trades Councils sent out the aims of the inquiry plus in some cases a detailed questionnaire to shop stewards and office committees in the shipyards, NEI Parsons, Vickers and the ex-shop stewards from Tress Engineering. This was followed up by discussions and further documentation. The Trade Union Studies and Information Unit, the Tyneside Socialist Centre and the West End Resource Centre helped to provide some of the back up analysis. The Trades Council's Centre for the Unemployed played a major part in organising the local inquiry. All this led up to a Saturday morning meeting at which shop stewards presented the local evidence for the inquiry to the presidents and secretaries of North Tyneside and Newcastle Trades Councils.

John Sturrock — Report.

Liverpool.

In Liverpool, the Trades Council, with Eddie Loyden, the ex-MP for Garston, had lengthy discussions with the ex-stewards from the BL Speke No.2 plant. This was followed by a meeting with representatives from the Kirkby co-operative and Dunlop. At the Lucas Aerospace plant on Merseyside and the Dunlop Speke plant, the shop stewards had already conducted their own investigations which were contributed to the Trades Council Inquiry.

Stage 2 The National Tribunal

The second stage was a national tribunal in the House of Commons. There,

15

the four Trades Council Presidents questioned MPs and ex-ministers involved in formulating and trying to implement the original party policies. The questioning was based on the issues raised in the course of the local inquiries. (See Appendix 4.)

A drafting committee was set up consisting of four of the twelve or so Trades Council representatives responsible for organising the inquiry. This committee produced a first draft at the end of February for discussion, comment and amendment by all the shop stewards committees involved as well as the delegates to each of the Trades Councils. On Tyneside, the two Trades Councils organised a meeting of representatives of all the shop stewards committees involved. In Coventry and Liverpool, the Trades Councils organised separate discussions with the shop stewards committees.

In May, a second draft was written incorporating all the comments and amendments made during these discussions. This second draft was again circulated to all the shop stewards committees involved, inviting them to a joint meeting in Leeds. Further comments were sent in by shop stewards from Alfred Herberts, from Chrysler, Meriden and the shipyards on the Tyne. Representatives from Rolls Royce, NEI Parsons, ex-Dunlop, Speke, ex-British Leyland, Speke, ex-Tress Engineering, Lucas Aerospace and Vickers attended the meeting in Leeds. This meeting discussed final amendments and came to general agreement about the conclusions. In this way the workers whose experiences form the main basis of this report have been closely involved at every stage of the report. But the final analysis and writing has been the responsibility of the four Trades Councils. It is they who are the 'we' in all that follows.

Stage 3 The Coventry Conference

This report leads into the third stage of our inquiry: a delegate conference to discuss socialist industrial policies and the most effective ways of organising for them. Coventry Trades Council has taken the initiative to organise this locally. But it is to be supported by the other Trades Councils as well as the stewards committees who have been involved in the inquiry. We hope that through this conference the vital issues raised by our local experiences in Coventry, Merseyside and Tyneside will be discussed on a far broader level. We know that our experiences are not unique. We also hope that through these discussions links and contacts will be made which will strengthen our organisations and our policies for the future.

At frequent intervals throughout this three stage process, beginning in June 1979, representatives from the four Trades Councils have met at the Leeds Trades Club to discuss the local inquiries, plan and evaluate the national tribunal and discuss drafts of the report.

A Workers' Inquiry

We have highlighted the process by which this inquiry has been organised, especially the local dimension, in order to show how such a co-operative

16

Coventry.

venture between trades councils, and between trades councils and shop stewards can open up fruitful and sustained forms of political discussion, closely related to the practical problems of building up the grass roots strength of the socialist movement. We have, for example, explicitly referred to the local organisations who have helped with the inquiry because the existence of local research/educational/political centres has been important in enabling this sort of sustained discussion to take place. Throughout the inquiry we have stressed the importance of extending the discussion, of giving enough time for shop stewards committees to get involved. Sometimes this has been at the cost of 'getting the report out' quickly and smoothly, but then the production of a report was not for us the be all and end all of the project. The following report, then, is not an expert economists' assessment of the Labour government's policies, nor a journalistic account of 'what happened'. Rather it has been and, we hope, will be, a focus for political discussion 'from below', through which to extend both the democracy and the political consciousness of our movement.

venture between states. Thought this sphere was under attack and also
betrayed was equally fruitful and sustained forms of political discussion
closely related to the practical problems of building up the present-day
of the present movement. We have, for example, explicitly referred to the
local organisations who have helped within the party because they are good
[...] test on radical [...] represented as [...] important to establish
the soil of sustained discussion to take place. Throughout this history we
have stressed the importance of extending the discussion, of giving enough
time for our surveys committed to get involved. Sometimes this has been
partly a matter of getting the results out quickly and smoothly and thereby
encouraging a sort of spontaneous interest in the art and so on of the project.
The following is a form, in part, not just pure economic reasons or of the
labour government business, they collaborate about it. What they want
Rather than that end, we hope, will be a fresh and impolitical description from
below. Through which to extend both the democracy and the political
consciousness of our movement.

1.
Party policies

In spite of all Wilson's boasting about leaving a balance of payments surplus of £7m, the 1964-'70 Labour government failed to fulfil even the minimum aims expected of a Labour government by most of its supporters. In particular, it failed to maintain full employment. By 1970 unemployment was over ½m and going up; the job situation in traditional industrial centres like Merseyside, Clydeside and Tyneside was getting worse in spite of all sorts of regional grants and aid.

It was not just a large number of traditional Labour supporters who judged the policies of this government a disaster, and stayed at home when its survival was at stake. The majority of the Labour Party NEC shared this sense of failure, for which they were partly responsible. The NEC further recognised that new industrial policies had to be developed if ever the Labour Party was to have a chance of being elected to power again. In 1971 the NEC document arguing for such a rethink concluded:

"*A new economic policy is needed*, based on full employment, steady growth in selected regions of the country and sectors of the economy, precise policies (announced, and agreed *in advance*) to deal with obstacles to growth, radical programmes for manpower, a massive extension of democracy in industry . . ."

So from 1971 until the conference of 1973, the NEC industrial sub-committee organised numerous study groups and working parties of Party and trade union leaders, and co-opted experts within the Party, to work on just such a new economic policy.

Top heavy decision making

It is important to note at this stage the top-heavy nature of the policy making machinery through which this work was carried out (as with all Labour Party policy). Of course the rank and file membership have the chance to debate NEC proposals at conference and they have the opportunity to put forward motions for alternative policies. But they are in a very much weaker position if they have not been involved in any of the prolonged debates and systematic work which is necessarily involved in formulating new policies.

At no point during the two years work which went into formulating the vital

19

1973 Programme were there any attempts to organise industrial policy discussions and debates involving the shop stewards and local Labour Party members who would be directly affected by, and expected to fight for the new industrial policies. In 1973, for example, the NEC's report on the past year's political education does not include one single school or weekend conference specifically on industrial policy. And the report of the Research Department is no more encouraging: all the industrial policy discussion went on in the NEC industrial policy sub-committee and its various specialist working groups. No one on that sub-committee was directly involved in the shop stewards combine committees (though there was informal contact in several cases) or in the local trade union and community organisations which were to be given — in theory at least — such an important role in the final proposals.

Yet the creative, though thwarted, responses of shop stewards during the first months of Labour's industrial policies (see Chapter 3) and the evidence presented to this inquiry, both bear witness to the fact that these rank and file activists had plenty of ideas, criticisms and arguments. These ideas and criticisms would have improved and sharpened the policies themselves and helped to build the fight for their implementation.

A new consensus — a common enemy

The policy discussions (of the early '70s) led to an important shift in the traditional divisions and alliances within the Labour Party. Temporarily, on the surface, it led to a new (or to put it more accurately, recurrent) consensus between the Tribunite left and the centre leadership. It also reflected a genuine radicalisation of some of those who had been more associated with the centre. The most notable here were Tony Benn and Stuart Holland.

One of the reasons for this was that a new enemy was identified — one on which most could agree, at least while in opposition. The new, or rather newly recognised, enemy was the multi-national corporation. The growth of powerful multi-nationals is the resilient fact of economic life which, it was argued, lay behind past failures. Corporate power is such, went the analysis, that governments can no longer rely on indirect methods of planning the economy by, for example, stimulating demand to achieve full employment without inflation, or regional incentives to ensure an even growth rate, and so on. Many multi-nationals can give two fingers to government plans with one hand, while taking the incentives in the other. They could and did manipulate prices and fuel inflation, regardless of the government's taxation and monetary policies. They could and did cause havoc with the balance of payments, through the movement of capital and transfer pricing. The need to find a solution to the problem of the multi-national corporations was the main impetus behind the new policies.

The new industrial policies, then, were presented and argued for primarily as a solution to the problem of the economic power centred upon the multi-national corporations. This is made clear on the first page of the industrial

"The new giants do not rely for investment on savings within Britain, nor on reinvestment of profits earned within Britain. They borrow on the world money market, particularly in the Eurodollar market. Their priority policies use the convenient mechanisms of transfer pricing between plants in Britain and plants overseas. Their industrial location policies are largely determined by international factors. Almost by definition their decision-making is susceptible to world economic forces, and not influenced by the comparatively small beer of British Treasury techniques of demand management. If the Chancellor deflates or reflates, it is now only a minor factor: pricing policies, expansion or contraction policies, are determined within an economic context . . . which is no longer national but multi-national in character. As for hopes of regional job creation, and the ending of the social injustice which has blighted Scotland, Wales and the North for so many generations — forget them, unless we do what needs to be done."

Judith Hart —*Guardian* — 1st July 1975.

and economic section in the '73 programme. After spelling out the programme's objectives — full employment, control of inflation, rising living standards for all — it goes on:

"Yet if we are to meet even these limited objectives — and especially if we are at the same time to contain inflation — we must adopt a number of radical and socialist policies. For a major transformation has taken place in the economy: first, the economy is now completely dominated by a hundred or so giant companies. Fifty years ago the 100 largest manufacturing companies produced 15 per cent of net manufacturing output. By 1950 their share was still only 20 per cent. But since then the pace of concentration has quickened — and their share by 1970 had risen to as much as 50 per cent. Yet even this is not the end of the process. For by 1980 — just seven years away — those 100 giants are likely to account for no less than two-thirds of net output in manufacturing. What does this mean? It means that the next Labour Government will preside over an economy where the power of decision will rest with a small number of leading companies in the private sector . . .

. . . The interests of these huge private companies cannot be expected to coincide with the interest of the national economy: for if it is in their interests, for example, to go multi-national rather than multi-regional, then they will go multi-national.

We cannot, therefore, afford to rely on indirect measures to control the economy — whether these be fiscal or monetary measures, or generalised hand-outs, and tax concessions. Instead, we must act directly at the level of the giant firm itself.

The policies we outline below on price controls, on new public ownership, on economic planning, and on new industrial powers are designed to make this possible." (Our emphasis.)

This was the argument for giving a Labour government the power to make planning agreements with 100 or so major corporations, and to create a State Holding Company, the NEB, with the power of acquiring majority shareholdings — or indeed the complete shareholding — in major profitable companies and also of setting up new public enterprises.

Partial nationalisation: a transition to socialism?

Most of the Labour left were pleased with the new industrial policies. They felt that they brought the issue of extending public ownership out of the ice-box, in which it had been shut since the left's symbolic 'Clause 4' victory over Gaitskell in the late '50s. The takeover of at least 25 major profitable companies — which the '73 programme proposed — may not be socialism, but it seemed a considerably greater stride towards the commanding heights than anything put forward by the NEC as practical policy in the last ten years. Some Tribunites like Ian Mikardo saw the NEB as the only available route to the commanding heights:

"When you talk about social ownership, it is the big companies you want, not every little ten man engineering workshop; and it was the big companies that these proposals were talking about. It was obvious we should support the NEB and so on: there was nothing else." (Evidence to the inquiry.)

Others like Eric Heffer saw it as second best but at least a step towards the best. At the national inquiry he described himself as:

"very old fashioned in a sense. I think we should simply designate the major industries and take them over. I've always accepted Connolly's statement that socialism is nationalisation plus workers' control. I was brought up on that and I've never changed my mind. But if the sort of Industry Act that Tony Benn is talking about had been implemented, I'd have got a lot of what I want anyway."

There was surprisingly little criticism of the new proposals from the Tribunite left. We say surprising because, in the '50s, many of them had fought hard against proposals for a state holding company and 'competitive state enterprises', when they were proposed by Tony Crosland and others as an alternative to direct nationalisation. Maybe this background to the proposals is one reason why the right wing of the Party embraced them with almost equal enthusiasm as the left.

Wilson lashes out at the multi-nationals

The parliamentary leadership, Wilson, Callaghan, Healey and the rest could, at the time, fairly easily incorporate all the new analysis in order to create a much needed new political identity. In a sense they had to. After the hopeless mess of 1969-'70, from the point of view of the labour movement at least, their only hope of political survival lay in becoming the enthusiastic champions of the new industrial policy. Wilson played the leading role in this with a remarkable performance at the 1973 Party conference. He launched into an emotional attack on the multi-nationals, summoning up the memory of Chile:

"Multi-national corporations, or more truly supra-national corporations, owing fealty to no state or community, but capable in their remote boardroom fastenesses* of closing down whole communities, imperilling the monetary reserves and threatening the currencies of free nations — yes, and remembering President Allende, of seeking to subvert elected Governments."

He spelt out the powers which a new Industry Act would have in order to control these corporations:

"powers to *seek agreement* with companies over a wide range of industrial matters including prices, profits, investment programmes, overseas trade, industrial relations and industrial democracy, and if necessary *in the national interest* to issue directives on any of these subjects. Power to invest in individual companies or to purchase them outright — by agreement with the company concerned if practicable — or by statutory instrument subject to the approval of Parliament where *the national interest so requires*...

... All the powers of the Industry Act will apply to multi-national companies operating in this country in the same way as British-owned firms." (our italics.)

Aggressive sounding stuff at first sight, but what power is there in the 'power to seek agreements', and who will have the power to define the 'national interest' when investment funds are still in private hands?

Alongside these new powers there must, he proclaimed, be an extension of public ownership into the pharmaceutical, machine tool construction, road haulage, shipbuilding and aircraft industries. He firmly dismissed doubts on this sensitive point:

"In past years, the case for the public ownership of steel, for example, however clear to Socialists, has sometimes rung with an uncertain sound in the ears of the electorate — nor were we always helped by the faint hearts of apostatists within our own midst. But there is no argument in the Party now about that."

And he topped it all off with an irrelevant tirade at the Stock Exchange:

"With prices where they are, it is an outrage that people should be making money, accumulating fortunes, by buying food grains, cocoa, coffee, sugar — or for that matter, materials essential to industry, to employment — not on the basis of need, or use, or want, but as a means of getting rich quick. It is an outrage that prices are sent rocketing by people who will never see, touch, taste, or handle the commodities in which they are dealing."

He sounded so convincing that some sections of business and the City got a bit frightened — those, that is, who were not familiar with Wilson's sensitivity to the anxieties of businessmen like themselves, or to his slippery rhetoric.

*For those unfamiliar with Wilson's literary flourishes — we had to look it up too — the dictionary tells us that 'fastenesses' means 'stronghold, fortress, castle'.

Gerald Scarfe.

REVERSIBLE TURN COAT

A blurring of differences

At the time, the consensus in the Party might have seemed a good thing — even a victory for the left. In one sense that is true. The success of these proposals within the Party was to a large extent due to the stony silence of the right, who lacked any alternative theoretical analysis or practical proposals.

However, in the course of this inquiry we have found it necessary to question the advantage of this consensus and to argue that there was a blurring of the issues throughout the debates on new industrial policies. This made it very much easier for Wilson to emasculate the original proposals when in government.

For example, the need for more investment in domestic manufacturing industry, and the necessity of the state to ensure that this investment was carried out, was stressed by both sides. This was seen by both left and right as a means of rebuilding the competitive position of British industry *and* a means of overcoming regional employment problems. There was rarely any explicit recognition by the left of a possible conflict between the competitiveness of British industry, employment and other social priorities. As a result, issues concerning the criteria of state investment decisions, the compatability of even long term, national, competitive criteria with social needs were never adequately thought through.

Did the apparent consensus, then, indicate inconsistencies and ambiguities which became important later? After all, we should not forget that the proposal for the NEB was not *defeated*, but *transformed*. What was it about the original proposals which made this transformation possible?

The state capitalist model and the corporate state

The first relevant point which struck us here is that both key components of the new industrial strategy, a state holding company and a planning agreements system, were already an established part of the state machinery in different forms in Italy and France. Neither economy could be said to be in transition between capitalism and socialism!

In Italy especially, interventionist industrial policies seemed to have evolved as part of a highly centralised, easily corruptible corporate state, with strong authoritarian tendencies. Perhaps we had better define what we mean here because the term 'corporate state' is likely to figure quite a bit in our discussion of government intervention in industry.

The sort of danger we are pointing to by referring to a corporate state is this: the state's increasing involvement in industry can produce a cosy relationship between employer's organisations, the trade union leadership and the government; a relationship which could strengthen the power of the employers over employees and weaken the ability of trade unions to be a counter power in the interests of their members and the wider working class community.

All this could take place with arguments and justifications using the same terms as those used to justify socialist policies: e.g. national planning and the need to control the multi-nationals to bring them in line with national interests and government policies.

The bringing together of these three leading groups could sometimes lead to changes in company policies. It has done so in Italy and France. Furthermore, the changes achieved could often be in the short run interests of the majority of people. After all, governments do have to win votes and maintain some sort of consensus and social peace.

At the inquiry's national tribunal, Stuart Holland pointed to some of the achievements of the state holding company, (IRI) in Italy: for instance, the modernisation, re-equipping and rationalisation of Italy's shipyards with no compulsory redundancies.

"But", as one of the Trades Council presidents at the national inquiry pointed out, "this was in conditions of an expansion of world shipping, the period of boom following the destruction of shipping during the war. These were the times when workers' employment needs and employers' requirements for a profitable return on investment could coincide. What happens in periods of recession, when markets are scarce and if profits are to be maintained and government expenditure saved — cutting the wage bill, throwing workers out of their jobs?"

Stuart Holland's answer was that:

"We intended that the NEB should have an important counter-cyclical and a growth creating role; by which I mean that when there is a recession in private investment and redundancies would be created, then the public sector, provided its investment is on a sufficiently broad range of companies and it is not putting all its money into just one company as it actually is now with 90% of its money in British Leyland, you would be able to have a broad wave of investment to counter the effects of different cycles. You can also bring investment forward in state enterprises with similar effects. This counter-cyclical advance planning in the public sector would be backed up by planning agreements with the private sector."

A nice idea perhaps, but such measures would not come naturally during a deep recession — far worse than the cycles which the IRI had to ride — to a corporate group of employers/government and trade union leaders. During a recession, the only conditions, if any, under which investment might — for a period — be brought forward in this way is if this corporate state is under great pressure from the workforce and the affected communities. Those who advocated the new policies recognise this. Their conversion to the need for popular pressure led them to make industrial democracy central to their industrial policies.

The role of shop floor action

The conversion of Labour MPs like Tony Benn to the importance of working class pressure was itself a result of such pressure. The work-in at UCS was the decisive influence, but the general growth of shop floor power throughout the 1960s was also influential. Benn describes this influence himself:

"This (a rejection of the corporatist idea of public ownership planned from the top) must be attributed entirely to what was being done on the shop floor during that period, and if those events had not occurred when they did and in the form they did, the Labour manifesto of 1974 would not have reflected any aspirations beyond the traditional Morrisonian approach to public ownership." (*Arguments for Socialism*, Tony Benn.)

We can see the impact of 'what was being done on the shop floor' on the ideas of the Labour left most vividly in Benn's own development.

In 1969, Tony Benn did not see workers' action as a positive political force. On the contrary, he is reported as viewing occupations to defend jobs as negative and self destructive. This was the view he took over the occupation

26

threat by 3,000 workers at GEC's Napier factory in Liverpool, who were facing closure in the autumn of 1969. Benn warned against militant action:

> "The image sometimes projected of 'wild men who will greet you with a beard and a bomb' could be immensely damaging, he said, 'It would be a grave danger that might hinder the future flow of jobs to the unemployment blackspots of Liverpool'." (*Daily Mirror* Sept. 18 1969.)

Upper Clyde, Govan shipyard.

The *success* of industrial action in saving jobs at UCS changed his mind. At the 1971 Labour Party Conference, Benn went out of his way not just to praise the UCS shop stewards but to draw out the lessons for the Labour party. In summing up the debate on industrial policy, he draws lessons by describing how John Davies:

> "forgot the workers on the Clyde on whose rock solid strength his plan could and must really founder. He thought, and the Cabinet thought that the decision on Upper Clyde Shipbuilders would be a mini day wonder that would be quickly forgotten. And they were wrong, and it is *very important for this conference that we understand why they were wrong and the significance of the fact that they have been proved wrong.*" (our emphasis.)

The implications he drew from this marked a challenge not only to the parliamentarians of the right, but also to those of the left who limit their radicalism to demands on the parliamentary party:

> "the changes we contemplate cannot be made by parliamentary action alone, it requires the active work of the industrial movement. These men are fighting to survive because they have no alternative. They are generating

a new leadership at shop floor level and, above all, they are creating a climate, not only to carry Labour to power, but to sustain us as we carry through the changes which they know need to be made. And without the support of the industrial Labour Movement we cannot succeed, and without us they are left in a blind alley."

This train of thought led in two directions as it permeated the policy-making machinery of the Party.

It led to the Social Contract which strengthened and consolidated the idea of trade union support for the Labour government, in exchange — in theory — for union and employment protection legislation, an increase in various social benefits, more interventionist industrial policies and an extension of industrial democracy.

Secondly, it led to a stronger notion of industrial democracy than had ever before been proposed in official Labour Party policy statements.

The one thing it did not lead to, as we shall see in Chapter 5, was 'the active work of the industrial movement . . . to sustain us as we carry through the changes which they know need to be made' if, by 'the changes', Benn meant the industrial policies he was supporting in this speech.

Failure to prepare for power

While the most notable theme in this important speech is the recognition that parliament cannot carry through socialist policies alone, that the industrial power and action of the working class is a vital part of the political weaponry of the labour movement, there is also a notable absence from the speech. There is no mention of the powers which the industrial movement will have to sustain radical policies *again*. As a result, the preparation for the 1974 Labour government consisted almost entirely of discussion of *policies* to the exclusion of the *strategy* and the *means* of carrying these policies through. Paradoxically, *the Labour left identified the power of the corporations, but did not prepare to meet that power.*

The new policies for industrial democracy illustrate very well this combination of a real appreciation of workers' industrial power with an extraordinary naivety about the employers' response.

On the one hand, Benn and others welcomed sit-ins, occupations and other shop floor initiatives as challenges to the unaccountable economic power of shareholders and managers. They recognise that political democracy is not sufficient to control this power. Workers need an industrial franchise as well as a political franchise:

"What we are determined to ensure is that those who have devoted their lives to industry shall not be excluded because they are not shareholders in the firms which they work in, from exercising the right to shape and plan the work they do and the re-equipment of the firms in which they work and to secure for themselves, their children and the communities in which they live, greater security than they can achieve under the unacceptable face of capitalism." (Tony Benn in Parliamentary Debate on the Industry Bill.)

They further argue that nationalisation by itself would not achieve this extension of democratic rights. It would replace the power of the shareholders by the power of government ministers. Benn was after a more direct form of democratic control:

"We reject as a party and as a movement the idea that one worker on the board is industrial democracy. We reject co-ownership. We reject the phoney works councils not rooted in the strength and structure and traditions of the trade union movement.

All these are window dressing, designed to divert the demand for democratic control into utterly harmless channels. We are talking about the transfer of power within industry and we will not accept the existing pattern of nationalisation as a form for the future. We have had enough experience now surely to know that nationalisation plus Lord Robens does not add up to socialism, and that is the message we are sending out . . .

It is the extension of the industrial franchise that really lies behind our concept of this shift of power, not the transfer of power from management to ministers *but the sharing with those who own.*" (our emphasis.) (1973 Labour Party conference speech.)

But, as this final quote illustrates, there is the assumption that power can be shared with the shareholders; that planning proposals based on social needs can be *agreed* with corporate management.

Some of the speeches made by backbench left MPs in the Standing Committee of the Industrial Bill (which went on from January to July 1975) illustrate the same optimism. For instance, Brian Sedgemore moved an amendment for compulsory planning agreements to be included in the Industry Bill. Compulsory powers would, he believed, ensure that companies 'contribute to national needs and objectives' and, as if it was only a matter of forcing these companies to see reason, he argued:

"It would only need planning agreements with half-a-dozen or so companies in each sector to enable a model to be drawn up and to get some sensible planning . . . In finance we could draw up planning agreements with a view to channelling institutional funds into manufacturing industry. The Secretary of State himself is anxious to do that, and it would need only an agreement with a few of the main financial institutions for a significant contribution to be made to that end . . . (in the construction industry) one could draw up planning agreements between the government, building societies and the construction industry and make some sense out of that sector."

There could be some opposition of course but the whole point of making planning agreements compulsory would be to overcome that, as Sedgemore continued:

"It is clear that in all those sectors there are companies which would not co-operate with the Government unless the measures were compulsory. It is a tragic commentary on the way our society is governed that the CBI

29

has almost openly invited the bulk of British industry to thwart and frustrate the Bill's objectives. That in itself makes an amendment of this kind essential. In a reasonable society, one might not need it. There might be voluntary co-operation."

Sedgemore explained this unreasonable behaviour in terms of the attitude of the CBI. He contrasts this with the more reasonable attitude of businessmen on the continent:

"In France we have seen far more voluntary co-operation on the subject of planning agreements than the Government would hope to get in this country.

As a result of the leadership – or the lack of leadership – of the CBI, a number of large firms have made perfectly clear that they are not anxious to enter into planning agreements with the Government."

Behind all this confident talk of the effectiveness of compulsory powers – of being able to plan companies which are neither controlled nor owned by the government – is the assumption that the government could, with these powers, get *agreement* with the companies to create jobs and establish industrial democracy in spite of or as well as improving their competitive position. Ironically it was Michael Meacher – forced as a minister to argue against Sedgemore's amendment even though personally he supported compulsory power – who brought out this assumption of genuine agreement even behind compulsory powers, when he said:

"One can take a horse to water, but one cannot make it drink. One can force a company in a planning agreement to sign a document but whether it can be forced (by government) to make changes in the manner it undertakes its economic activities and its relations with its employees is another matter . . . it is a question of new attitudes on both sides of industry that in our view cannot be legislated for."

Compulsory powers or not, planning agreements require from management a 'change in attitude', because it is·management which carries out the plans, and controls the investment funds, so long as they remain in private hands. No amount of formal signatures will make any difference unless either management are prepared to carry them out or unless the workforce force them to. In which case, it is the workforce rather than the government which has the vital power. But the exercise of this requires preparation and self confidence. *How far can such preparation and political self confidence be achieved with the Labour Party's industrial policies of 1973 and, now, of 1980?* This is one of the central questions of this inquiry.

In spite of these ambiguities and weaknesses, the ruling class reacted to the industrial policies of the 1973 Party programme and the February 1974 manifesto as if they *did* pose a threat to the 'freedoms' which private owners and managers of wealth have always considered to be their natural rights. What, to sum up, were the vital features of the new industrial policies which thus gave rise to businessmen's fears and workers' hopes?

1. NEB and government policy

The NEB would have compulsory powers to acquire shares including a majority or a complete shareholding in whatever companies it chose. Its criteria for acquiring shares and exerting control would be based on government policy as regards employment needs, economic growth, regional planning, diversification possibilities, price control and the amount of government money received by the company.

2. Planning agreements and financial aid

The original idea of planning agreements was that the minister for industry would have the power, with parliament's agreement, to require unwilling companies to become involved in planning agreements. These planning agreements would enable the Department of Industry to bring the company's plans more into line with government (and latterly trade union plans, although trade unions would have only a consultative role). This power could apply to all companies requiring financial aid from the government.

3. Parliament and the nationalised industries

The new policies proposed that nationalised industries would, via the minister of industry, be directly accountable to parliament. The minister would have greater powers to intervene in the activities of the nationalised industries on behalf of parliament.

4. Industrial democracy

In all three cases: the NEB, planning agreements and the nationalised industries, the proposals were for the creation of shop floor based forms of democracy, organised through trade union channels. The forms that this should take were not spelt out but they included wide ranging proposals for the disclosure of information.

In conclusion

The only other time that such a radical threat was posed to the private owners of potentially productive wealth was in 1945. Then, as in 1974, the policies were double edged. The legislation for nationalisation of unprofitable, infrastructural industries had its uses for private capital as well as for working class people; similarly with the extension of the Welfare State. Then, as in 1974, there was a groundswell of militant support for the radical interpretation of the policies promised in the manifesto of the incoming government. But in neither period did this popular pressure shape the policies which the government finally adopted. The next chapter will explain why.

2.
Government policies

"I presume, Secretary of State, that you don't intend to implement the industrial strategy in the Labour Party's programme" said Sir Antony Part, testily, as he greeted Tony Benn on Benn's first day at the Department of Industry. (Sir Antony Part was Permanent Secretary at the Department of Industry – he is now on the Board of Directors of Lucas Industries, and Debenhams, and EMI, and Metal Box and Savoy Hotels, among others.)

Little cause for concern

Whether this now well known quote is mythical or real, it sums up accurately the wary, but cynically unperturbed response of industrialists and civil servants towards the Party's industrial policies during the first weeks of the new government. Tony Benn might indulge in dangerous rhetoric, they reasoned, but they were well used to Jekyll and Hyde qualities in Labour politicians, and anyway the majority of the cabinet were sufficiently moderate to keep even a Mr Hyde under control. As the *Times* put it in their leading article on the new Wilson administration – a leader which showed no signs of anxiety beyond a few warnings about trade union militancy and inflation:

> "This will not by any means be a government of wild men . . . The Labour administration will include people of the highest ability; even (!) among its more left wing people . . . Mr Benn has proved himself a capable administrator, however little sympathy one may have with the speeches he makes on broad political issues." (*Times* – March 5th 1974.)

As if the speeches, the ideas, can be ignored (as so often they can) so long as the 'chap' in charge is a good administrator and of 'the highest ability'; then he will soon realise the way things should be run, as they always have been run, with a few sensible reforms perhaps.

At first, the CBI's response too was cool, hedged with qualifications and muted warnings, but not hostile. They hoped that consultation could lead to agreement. They could even see elements of the policies which might improve relations between industry and government. For instance, in response to Benn's request to see representatives of Britain's leading hundred companies to discuss planning agreements, Sir Michael Clapham, President of the CBI, is reported to have seen ". . . no harm in the Department of Industry's becoming aware of the plans of the major industries; many companies already informed the Department". (*Times* March 21st, '74.) And when in early May the *Times* reported the growing opposition of the CBI the report contrasted this with ". . . previous statements on the so-called planning agreements with the top 100 companies (when) CBI officials have taken a much less strong line, suggesting that they did not believe these agreements would involve such intervention".

This lack of initial opposition was confirmed by MPs who had contact with leading industrialists. Brian Sedgemore, commenting on a meeting he had with industrialists early on in the new Parliament, told us that:

"Industrialists I talked with felt resigned to the introduction of planning agreements. They just wanted to know more about them and take the necessary precautions."

Tony Benn had received a similar impression. In the course of describing, at this Inquiry's national tribunal, how his initial draft White Paper was watered down he said:

"I believe that if this (watering down) had not taken place we could have had planning agreements with all the 100 major companies. I say this because we got it with the oil companies − though we stayed up all night until they gave way. And we could have got it with the other main companies. Some leading industrialists had seen how they worked in other countries and told me they saw no problem in principle."

The *Financial Times* also looked enviously to the continent and at Japan. In an article entitled 'Where Planning Agreements Really Help', the *Financial Times* writer argued that there could be some value in planning agreements as one, though not the only 'way of achieving a government-industry partnership'; a way of improving industry-government relations as in France and Japan, 'where the two sides enjoy a real sense of partnership'.

As with planning agreements, similarly with the NEB: at first industrial commentators did not see it as anything very threatening. The *Times,* for example, commented that:

"The striking thing is not that an NEB would be a radical new departure but that it seems to be a logical extension of what has gone before, under both Labour and Conservative governments."

The writer went on:

"Indeed, Benn could establish an NEB on the lines of the Green Paper,* with only the most minor modifications to the existing Walker legislation."

He ends up with a warning that:

"The rub lies, not in the power, for here the changes would be marginal. The key is how these powers would be used in practice."

Such a view runs through all the otherwise bland responses. A watchful eye was kept on ministers at the Department of Industry, by industrialists and civil servants alike.

*The green paper on the NEB was prepared as a discussion paper while the Labour Party was on in opposition. White Papers are papers laying out for discussion and consultation the basis of the government's legislative intentions.

But the dominant belief was that ministers were unlikely to be taking the manifesto promises literally. Apart from this initial cynicism, the CBI had other more immediate battle fronts to attend to; the repeal of the Tory Industrial Relations Act was going through smartly, along with the introduction of the Employment Protection Act to extend picketing rights, support the closed shop and strengthen protection against unfair dismissal. The introduction of seemingly tough price controls was another issue over which the CBI had to defend its members' interests. Moreover, Wilson, concerned above all to stay in power, had made it clear that nothing so potentially controversial as industrial policies would be legislated on during the first parliament. The CBI's initial approach to the Department of Industry then was to wait and see.

Benn means business

By early May, their contacts in the civil service were warning them that the waiting must end. Benn meant business. CBI leaders went to see Mr Benn and, as the *Times* reported:

". . . confirmed for themselves that the Department of Industry is deeply engaged in proposals for implementing Labour's pre-election ideas for reforming private industry." (*Times* May 3rd.)

Further confirmation that Sir Antony Part had been over presumptious, came when Tony Benn produced a public report on progress made in implementing Labour's pre-election programme. This report was initially delivered in Benn's report to the TUC-Labour Party Liaison Committee, as an individual member of that committee.

The report reaffirmed, and in some ways made more specific, the Labour Party programme for '73. The NEB was to have power, subject to 'going through the full parliamentary process', to extend public ownership by acquiring leading manufacturing companies; it was to operate 'in line with longer term public need rather than short term market considerations'. This included, among other things, using its power to invest in order to create a more regionally balanced location of investment. Planning agreements were not made obligatory as some of the pre-'74 Party documents had argued; but they were to be the condition on which financial aid would be granted to the 100 major companies. Moreover, the conditional agreements 'will need to be on a tripartite basis with the unions involved from the outset'. This union involvement in planning agreements would be part of a radical change in the relation between the unions and the Department of Industry so that 'the same close relations as now exists between this Department and management will exist with the unions as it does already with the Department of Employment'. In matters of aid to industry the books will be opened 'so that discussion can be held free from charges that secrecy is being used to prevent a full consideration of the alternatives'.

Finally, the report argued that all this should be backed up by 'a major campaign of public explanation and discussion about the problem which the policy is designed to overcome and the outlines of the policy itself'. The basis of this campaign would be a Green Paper produced by a working party within the Department (made up entirely of supporters of the party programme; Eric Heffer, Stuart Holland, Frances Cripps, etc.). The report ended on this campaigning note:

> "As soon as the Green Paper is published we shall undertake a series of meetings in major cities throughout the country at which we would hope to meet local trade union officials, representatives of local employers associations, local authorities, shop stewards and gatherings of working management whose support is essential if our policies are to succeed."

Chris Davies – Report.

The disappearing Green Paper

As we shall see, this Green Paper was never to see the light of day, let alone the eyes of shop stewards, local authorities and countrywide meetings.

The report was responded to as if it was a declaration of war. For a start, it went against a traditional principle of cabinet government which normally protects the cabinet from undue party or popular pressure, that once a government is elected the policy slate is in theory wiped clean until the cabinet formulates its own policies and then campaigns for them through the parliamentary processes. Yet here was an attempt by a *government department,* or rather the ministers thereof, to campaign for policies – party policies in fact – before the cabinet had decided upon *its* policies. This sort of thing had to be stopped. Harold Wilson saw to it that it was stopped, with the more or less tacit support of the rest of the Cabinet and leading civil servants.

Wilson takes charge

Wilson took over the chairmanship of the cabinet sub-committee which covered industrial matters. From then on he made sure that he was in effective charge of all the vital aspects of industrial policy. Once Wilson was allowed to take charge directly, the original industrial policies were as good as dead for as Tony Benn said very clearly at the beginning of his evidence to the national tribunal of this Inquiry:

> "The majority of the cabinet did not understand or support the policies on which we were elected. It would be absurd to say that they did. Harold Wilson certainly had the idea that the NEB would be another IRC and virtually said so. Therefore the first problem was that although we had the support of conference and through the manifesto the electorate, we did not at any stage have the support of the cabinet for the manifesto's industrial policies. This became clear when we put our Green Paper to the cabinet sub-committee and the paper was rewritten with the crucial elements of our policy (as spelt out in the earlier report) left out."

This view of what happened is confirmed by Wilson's description of the same event:

> ". . . it was essential that both sides of industry should know exactly where they stood, within what it was vital to emphasise was to continue to be a mixed economy. It was not until late July that the Department of Industry's draft White Paper emerged. As I had feared, it proved to be a sloppy and half-baked document, polemical, indeed menacing, in tone, redolent more of an NEC home policy committee document than a Command Paper. One basic weakness was that it appeared to place more emphasis on the somewhat amorphous proposals for planning agreements than on the NEB. A special committee of senior ministers was set up under my chairmanship to mastermind its re-drafting, which quickly decided that the document should be re-written. The final draft owed a great deal to Michael Foot, writing within the parameters we laid down. The section on planning agreements was cut down to size . . .
>
> The role and powers of the NEB were strictly defined; above all it was to have no marauding role." (Wilson's autobiography *The Final Term*.)

Wilson's control over the cabinet sub-committee, his stamping down on Benn's attempts at a popular campaign and, finally, the production of the new White Paper 'The Regeneration of British Industry' written so that it could mean all things to everyone ("that's why Footy was brought in, he's a master of words, but knows little about industry" observed one Labour MP in the course of this inquiry) — these were the first decisive blows in the defeat of the original policies.

After this Benn, Heffer and Meacher were merely Wilson's messengers in the standing committee, defending legislation which Edward Heath could have supported, against the hysterical opposition of Tories like Heseltine.

The games they play

A brief sketch of the scene in Standing Committee, at the point when the issue of compulsory purchasing powers for the NEB was raised, will illustrate this. On March 25th 1975, backbench Labour MPs moved that a clause be added to the Bill so that "the power of the NEB to acquire property, securities or a share in any enterprise shall, with the consent of the Secretary of State be exercisable compulsorily".

On the same afternoon the Tories were pushing an amendment emphasising, yet again, that any involvement of the NEB had to be by agreement only. The Tory game was to make things as difficult as they could for Benn and Heffer by forcing them to provoke the Left MPs, but the game was of the ministers' own making once they had decided to pilot Wilson's Industry Bill through the House. Bound as they were by cabinet responsibility, they had to play the game that the Tory schoolboys – led by Headboy Heseltine – had arranged for them.

Heffer was presenting the Bill during that afternoon. Again and again Tory speakers said they felt that the government was not clear enough on the issue of whether NEB acquisitions could only be by agreement. So Heffer had to reassert the fact that, as he quoted from the White Paper which replaced his own draft:

> ". . . all holdings in companies, whether 100% or in part, should be acquired by agreement.

> This is absolutely clear. It is not only in the White Paper, it is in statements made by my Right Hon. Friend the Secretary of State, by me and by the Prime Minister . . . the government's attitude has been spelled out very clearly. That is what my Hon. Friends (Wise, Sedgemore, et al, in their amendment for compulsory powers) are worried about. That is the whole point of their amendments."

Heffer then had to turn on his old allies and defend those who defeated him. Not surprisingly, the arguments are not very convincing:

> "Whilst I could well be tempted to enter into an interesting philosophical discussion about the right or wrong way to advance the concept of public ownership, I do not think I should be loved by anyone, particularly the Whips, if I were to enter into such a discussion. I want to confine myself to Amendment No.521 . . .

> I must tell my Hon. Friends that the government could not accept either the drafting of the amendment because it is very untidily drafted, or the basic point in it."

Then, after further questioning by Audrey Wise, he went on:

> "If it is essential that we move into a certain sector, involve ourselves by taking over a large company in that sector, and we cannot find a willing seller because all manner of obstacles are put in the way even though the most generous offer is made, this is something which we must have a look at . . .

> The NEB, like any private company, will be able to take over because it

will have money. The National Enterprise Board will have up to £1,000 million pounds, and that is not to be regarded lightly; it is a considerable amount of cash.

It will therefore have exactly the same power in that sense as the private sector companies. But I cannot go beyond that and give a definite answer at this stage."

Audrey Wise was not satisfied:

"I am sorry that the Minister suggested that we might have spent too long on this series of amendments. I submit that the principle involved is extremely important and that what we are seeking is not simply a philosophical discussion to which he also referred, but a discussion on whether the Bill will have any bite.

My Hon. Friends and I are not at all reassured by his reply. He suggests that there might be a sort of technical aspect and that he will look at our proposition as though it is a small, narrow point. He tells us that the Government will not accept the principle of compulsory acquisition when necessary and yet he expects us to believe that somehow the Government can find some way of dealing with the situation where there are no willing sellers . . .

My mind boggles at the suggestions that there is any third way. They are either willing sellers or they are in compulsory acquisition. I have obtained from the Minister no clarification of a third way."

Just as Audrey Wise was no clearer, neither were the shop stewards and other Labour supporters who had been inspired by the rather clearer speeches of Benn and Heffer in the early days at the Department of Industry. Wilson had not simply defeated their policies, but he had managed to do so without their supporters outside parliament being fully aware that a defeat had taken place.

Why so easy?

Why did Wilson get away with it so easily? Why did no one resign? There were protests from left wing MPs. But not a sound, at least not an audible one, from the TUC. Yet those 'radical industrial policies' were part of the government's side of the social contract. And what of the TUC-Labour Party Liaison Committee? Had not they agreed to the campaign proposed by Tony Benn? What prevented them from carrying it out under their own auspices? Had any campaign been carried out by anyone in support of the new industrial policies?

These are questions we shall try to answer in Chapters five and six.

What was the CBI worried about?

To return however, to industrialists' responses to the fact that Industry Ministers were treating the Party programme seriously. What was it about these policies which made them anything more than an attempt to bring together management, government and trade union leaders into the more harmonious corporate partnership which many far sighted industrialists favoured?

The Labour Party's policies contained two main sources of anxiety for major industrialists and financiers. First, top management and large shareholders would, with the NEB's compulsory powers and planning agreements tied to financial aid, lose much of their control over the movement of their company's capital. The power or 'freedom' to move funds in search of the highest return on investment is fundamental to the way in which companies make competitive profits and accumulate further capital and, with it, further powers. As Campbell Adamson, Director-General of the CBI put it:

> "There has been criticism in recent months, that the Government-CBI-TUC discussions had in them the makings of a corporate state. I do not believe this. The real danger, which we need to fend off with all our strength, is that increasing government intervention and direct control of industry will so weaken the market economy that our economic freedom will be lost . . ." (*Times* – May '74.)

Disclosure of information

The second cause for concern was that the proposals on disclosure of information would enable workers to gain information, and government support, to challenge the last remaining management prerogatives. Moreover, the encouragement which shop stewards were getting from Tony Benn was in danger of producing a generally more militant and confident mood towards management. The strength of feeling about disclosure of information was made very clear to a group of Labour MPs on the Industry Bill Standing Committee who were asked to meet the CBI. Brian Sedgemore told us what happened:

> "They took far more exception to the disclosure of information proposals than anything else. Admittedly by that time all the proposals had been watered down considerably. Against the disclosure of information provisions the Director General had two main arguments. First he said that it's happening anyway. Management are already giving their workers the information they need. I answered that this wasn't happening in Luton, in Vauxhall, in Chrysler, Brown Boveri or anywhere else I knew of. Then he switched his argument and said that if the government allow trade unionists to get this information by law, the companies would refuse to give it. So we put it to him, that wasn't this tantamount to breaking the law? He replied:

> 'Well, it's human nature that if you try and make people do things they don't do them'."

The *Guardian* gained a similar impression of the CBI's hostility to the disclosure of information provisions and commented:

> "The CBI regards the disclosure provisions of the Bill as even more damaging to industry than the provisions for increased nationalisation."

It seems, then, that industrialists have a far greater fear of any measure which could increase the power of shop floor trade unionists than they do of any increase in state intervention (so long as it is in the right hands).

Everything to everyone

By the time the White Paper had been rewritten, they had nothing to fear from increased state intervention. Except in the unlikely event of parliamentary debate and decision upsetting the compromise arrived at outside. For the White Paper made it quite clear, first on planning agreements that 'There will be no statutory requirement upon a company to conclude on Agreement; not even as a condition for receiving financial assistance; for financial assistance under the Industry Act 1973, including regional development grants, will of course continue to be available for companies not covered by Planning Agreements'. That is, the £7m and more a day given to private industry would continue without any statutory accountability. What is more, if a company did enter into a planning agreement, while the government would have no rights to enforce the company to meet its side of the agreement, the agreement would be given sufficient recognition 'by statute to enable the company concerned to rely on the assistance promised under it'.

Secondly, on the NEB: at one point it proclaims that the NEB's main strength 'will come through the extension of public ownership into profitable manufacturing industry by acquisitions of individual firms in accordance with paragraphs 30-33 below'. But when we turn to paragraphs 30-33 it says 'The intention is that all holdings in companies, whether 100% or in part, should be acquired by agreement'. Has there ever in the history of capitalist production been a leading profitable company whose shareholders and top management have agreed to public ownership?

Mutual understanding

For the CBI and leading industrialists to achieve these initial guarantees was not difficult. It does not require any conspiracy theory to understand how this happened. Neither did it require any massive exertion of pressure to make it happen. The channels of communication, the relationships of mutual understanding, the institutions for bargaining between the state — both government and civil service — and leading industrialists have been painstakingly built up and improved over decades of facing common problems, be it war, social unrest or economic depression. Increasingly from the First War onwards, with occasional upsets, legislation on industrial matters has been shaped more by consultation with the CBI and its predecessors and, to a slightly lesser extent, with the TUC than with the party (and this applies with differing emphasis to both parties) in government.

Tony Benn's remarks in his speech during the guillotine debate on the Industry Bill unintentionally illustrate the extent to which this consultation/bargaining process with the CBI and the TUC in determing the final content of legislation was taken for granted:

"He (Benn) promised that the Government would hold further talks with the CBI and TUC about the Bill's provisions. He had told the House that the Government would consider any representations from both sides of industry at these talks and, if necessary, amend the Bill." (*Financial Times* 14th May.)

The price of unemployment.

The CBI's campaign

The CBI and individual industrialists organised a lobbying campaign to create a favourable atmosphere as far as the media and 'public opinion' were concerned and thereby add to the pressure on the cabinet. Just prior to publication of the government's proposals, the CBI announced that it "regarded as non-negotiable any attempt to subject the leading 100 companies to a planning agreement system". It then produced a document 'Industry and Government' which widened the attack in similar terms. This was backed up with campaigns run by individual companies. Sir Jack Callard, Chairman of ICI, spoke out even against the final White Paper proposals. ICI spent £60,000 in writing to its 800,000 shareholders, 132,000 employees and 43,000 pensioners explaining why ICI should not be allowed to become one of the big private sector firms which might be bought by the NEB.

The CBI and other industrialists kept up their pressure, especially on Wilson and, via him, on the cabinet sub-committee and therefore, given collective responsibility, on Benn, Michael Meacher and, until he resigned over the common market, Eric Heffer, right until the Act was passed. The Bill received a hostile response from industry. It was, they said, in 'stark contrast' to the 'warm assurances they had received from Mr Wilson during their last talks at Downing Street'. The CBI President, Ralph Bateman, had evidently found these talks 'very delightful'. Wilson had to be pressed further, especially on the disclosure of information clauses in the Bill. So, sure enough, only a few days after the Bill was published, a five-man delegation was back at Downing Street talking as if they had some effective veto over the content of the final Act:

> "The Confederation of British Industry told the Prime Minister last night that he would have to consider changes to some totally unacceptable parts of the Industry Bill if there was to be a common approach to tackling the current economic crisis." (*Financial Times* 1st Feb. '75.)

Wilson reacted as if 'of course if they say so' then the Bill must be looked at again and further more detailed discussion could be arranged:

> "The CBI told Mr Wilson that the Bill seemed to go further against private sector interests than the original White Paper on the regeneration of industry, but the Prime Minister emphasised that it was the White Paper which was the 'master document' and it was to this that legislation would have to bear the closest relation. If this was not apparently the case, then a closer look would be necessary.
>
> After the meeting, Mr Bateman said neither side had reached any final decision on any of the points raised concerning the Bill but conceded that there were 'some genuine misunderstandings'. He continued 'we will be meeting again and until then we do not know how many of our anxieties will remain and how many can be removed'. Further discussions are to be held before the committee stages of the Bill are reached." (*Financial Times* 13th Feb.)

CBI rules!

These last minute consultations, backed up then and earlier by a sustained and effective campaign with the Civil Service, must explain the peculiar goings on within the Standing Committee on the Industry Bill. One MP on the Standing Committee describes what went on:

> "I had not seen an operation quite like this before. Here was this Bill which was a watered down version of a White Paper which was a watered down version of a watered down manifesto commitment. And then the three ministers on top of this kept bringing what were really wrecking amendments."

In this way the CBI successfully achieved the amendments it wanted to the offending parts of the Bill. The disclosure of information clauses were transformed from one page of fairly clear provisions, by which trade unionists would have a good chance of obtaining information which companies would otherwise withhold, to six pages of qualifying clauses that turned the provisions into a farce. Motions would have to go through the House of Commons and the House of Lords and could be annulled by either.

Furthermore, notice would have to be served allowing a period of at least three months before an order could be served on the company – by which time the needs for which the information was required might well have passed. And, in any event, the process is so weighted against trade unionists that few, if any, would ever succeed.

The CBI backed by concerted efforts within the civil service similarly got rid of the final problem – the minister himself. Joe Haines describes some of this in his first hand report of the pressures on Downing Street in the first two years of the government, and Wilson's response: 'the whispers from the Treasury's contacts grew stronger. Only if Tony Benn was sacked, it was said, would the confidence of British industry be restored. If confidence was restored then (so it was argued) industrial investment would begin again'. Wilson, sensitive as ever to the requirements of 'business confidence', duly obliged. Once the left was defeated at the Referendum, Benn could be sacked from Industry without much danger of significant opposition within the Party.

In conclusion

Through this combination of extra-parliamentary pressure, and the opposition of the Parliamentary Party leadership, the radical industrial policies were turned into little more than 'a source of finance for manufacturing industry' and 'a means of rationalising and reorganising British industry' in response to the pressures of international competition.

It is worth noting the extra-parliamentary power and influence of an organisation like the CBI, backed up by the Civil Service. This was at a time when the common complaint of the media was (and is) the extra-parliamentary strength of the unions. Maybe, if the unions had exerted more of this supposed power, democratic processes might have had a greater chance.

One reason why there was so little labour movement resistance was that trade union leaders believed, and gave others to believe, that union leaders *were* exerting power by their presence in discussions with the Cabinet on economic strategy, on the board of the NEB, on numerous other quangos connected with industry, and in all the negotiations over major rationalisations (British Leyland, Chrysler, Lucas Aerospace, Power Engineering etc.). In this way, as we shall see, they tied their members to industrial policies to which the members had never given their assent.

Moreover, trade union members often thought the original policies *were* being implemented. After all the names were the same: 'NEB', 'planning agreements', 'Industry Bill'; Tony Benn was still in government; the Tories and their press had attacked the Bill viciously throughout its passage through parliament. There were very few public signs of the changes that had gone on behind the scenes. It was only when workers were personally hit by government policy, by an NEB closure, by the refusal of the government to impose a planning agreement when giving out millions of pounds in industrial aid, that trade unionists caught a glimpse of what had been going on. So, an important part of the story is the expectations which people had of these policies. An important explanation of the way workers reacted to the final policies lies in the way that the original policies were sold to them. This will be the subject of the next chapter.

3.
Expectations...

In all three areas there were high expectations of the new policies. It was not so much the specific policies which gave workers hope. Few trade unionists knew the details of the planning agreements and NEB proposals. It was more a general impression which the Labour Party had given that the big corporations would be brought under social control — in some cases under social ownership; and that both the old and the newly nationalised industries would, this time, be democratically organised.

No industrial pressure

In general, there was no organised industrial pressure for the Labour Party's industrial policies. The assumption was, as it always has been on account of the initial burst of loyalty to a new Labour government, that the government could and would carry out the policies with which they won the election. On Tyneside though, there was an important attempt to bring together shop stewards to discuss and press for the new industrial policies.

An exception: Tyneside

In January 1975, while the Industry Bill was going through the committee stage, shop stewards committees at Vickers (a multi-plant, multi-national engineering company with several plants on Tyneside) and at Swan Hunters (the Tyneside based shipbuilding company) set up 'The Tyne Stewards Conference'. Its regular meetings — every month or so until the autumn of 1975 — involved between 60-90 shop stewards, representing around 35 of the major corporations based on Tyneside. These meetings discussed planning agreements, workers' control, combine committees, the NEB and nationalisation. The resolution agreed at the first meeting of over 90 delegates gives an indication of the confidence and optimism which existed at the time:

1. A working party to be elected to co-ordinate the shop stewards committees in Tyneside to exert pressure for workers' control. Its functions to be:

To co-ordinate with the shop stewards committees of the large companies on Tyneside and surrounds in:

a. the distribution of information on the Industry Bill and documents and

Laurie Sparham – International Freelance Library.

Vickers Scotswood, Newcastle.

proposals on workers' control and participation; and to publicise these issues and organise any necessary meetings.
b. to draw up proposals for industrial democracy in our companies and industries for discussion by the workers in the companies affected.
c. to press for the implementation of the Industry Bill proposals as contained in the report of the National Executive of the Labour Party and not the watered down version before Parliament at present; and to this end to support the setting up of a National Conference and organisation of Combine Committees.

One of the items which shop stewards brought up again and again was their members' lack of awareness of the political and industrial situation and the lack of any information coming from union central offices. The conference put education and information high on their list of priorities. It also organised studies of the different industries and co-ordinated shop stewards' proposals for workers' control.

The possibilities for 'workers' control with management participation', as one proposal put it, was the aspect of the new industrial policies which most caught the Tyne shop stewards' imagination. It was the issue of structure and forms of control rather than substantive proposals for the industry – investment, products, hours, technology etc. – which dominated the discussions and activities of the Tyne Shop Stewards Conference. This was partly because trade unionists had not fully realised the extent and speed of the crisis and run-down of industrial production. They felt there was time to get the

48

structure right, *then* defend jobs. It was also because of the encouragement which Tony Benn, the Secretary of State for Industry, gave to initiatives on industrial democracy. For example, a statement he made in a speech to the GMWU in Gateshead was widely quoted in the Tyne Shop Stewards' literature:

> "I see it as the role of Government, and of the Organising Committee and the Board (of the NEB) and the Unions themselves to stimulate and encourage and support moves by workers in industry to hammer out their own proposals for the structure of the industry and the injection of a genuinely democratic element into the management pattern."

With this sort of encouragement, this feeling that they had allies in government, a source of political power over their managements, shop stewards in, for example, Vickers, Swan Hunters, Thorns and Charles Churchill, believed that here was a new opportunity to win control over the company's decisions, as a means of guaranteeing job security for the future. The assumption was that workers could prepare their own proposals and then win the backing of the Department of Industry. At one meeting of the Tyne Shop Stewards Conference some workers asked 'what if management refused to discuss these proposals?' Tony Banks, from the AUEW research department and closely involved with the formulation of the industrial policies, replied that they should then discuss their proposals direct with the government.

Events proved that many of the stewards who organised the Tyne Shop Stewards Conference underestimated what they were up against and overestimated the power that well intentioned politicians might have over the cabinet, multi-national corporations and their own civil service. Most of these proposals got no further than the paper they were written on.

This chapter will be full of similar proposals, formulated with high expectations during the first months of the Labour government, to be knocked back once the socialist ministers at the Department of Industry had been brought under control. Under each heading of the new industrial policies, we will look at the industrial problems which workers faced in the mid 70s; at the ways in which shop stewards expected Labour's new policies to solve these problems; and at the ways that shop stewards prepared and campaigned for such solutions.

49

Section 1:
Nationalisation of Shipbuilding

As we have just seen, the shop stewards committees at Swan Hunters were involved in regular discussions about the new industrial policies with shop stewards from other companies on Tyneside. Partly as a result of these discussions, partly as a result of the strong feelings in the yards, they set up the 'Nationalisation Committee'. It was elected by some 300 shop stewards to formulate and press for proposals for workers' control of the newly nationalised industry. The proposal it produced in early '75 was the one referred to above with the confident title "Workers' control, with management participation". This reflected the belief of active trade unionists in the yards that nationalisation would make a difference. They were aware of the disillusionment of the miners and the steel workers. But it seemed the Labour Party was recognising its mistakes. This time, nationalisation would be different. As Norman Laffey from the Swan Hunter yard in Hebburn put it:

"Under private industry you were nothing more than a number, a man who came into the gate, drew his time card, reported to his place of work and that was it. With nationalisation Mr Benn encouraged us to forward our views. That's one reason why we formed the Nationalisation Committee. The whole object of the exercise was to say to the government: these are our views which we have kept close to our chests all these years because being just a number we've never had the chance to express them."

What were the views which shipbuilding workers had kept to their chests?

"Well, besides our views on workers' control, investment and diversification were the main things. If people saw the tools of our trade here they'd wonder how we made a ship, so much of our machinery is that old. Swan Hunters never put much back in, not in the last ten years anyway. Any new investment was always government financed, like the new dock in Hebburn several years back. Another strong feeling we had about the old shipyard owners was the way they never highlighted the social consequences of what they did. They dominated the community but they never really cared enough about the people who lived there. They let industry decline without diversifying. We thought nationalisation would make it easier to press for diversification with a view to the social consequences."

But in thinking that they could get a structure of workers' control through which to press these views, they turned out to be too optimistic.

As Jimmy Johnson, Convenor at George Clark's (now Clark Hawthorns), a marine engineering company, put it:

"We knew nationalisation had turned sour in other industries. But we really believed that things would be different for us. Shipbuilding had been through quite a boom then, and the effects of the oil crisis in '73 had not quite hit us. I think that made us over-confident."

Swan Hunter shipyard, Wallsend.

By mid '75, as the order book grew emptier, some stewards expressed doubts about the emphasis on industrial democracy. They felt the new urgent issue of jobs had to be tackled more directly, as Ted Cuskin, a shop steward from Clellands shipyard in Wallsend, put it:

"We've got to secure jobs, stop closures and block further rationalisation, and that means building up our defensive strength, building up the combine committee before we start talking about industrial democracy. Otherwise we'll get bogged down in all sorts of phoney committees and the like."

In the next chapter we will see how the harsh realities of nationalisation forced the stewards to direct their attention away from proposing structures for workers' control towards building combine wide organisations to fight for jobs.

On Merseyside, too, shipyard workers had high expectations. But the threat of run-down and redundancies loomed large. As a result they put stress on policies which could achieve job security, such as greater government control over ship owners, or even nationalisation of shipping, to ensure that employment needs were taken into account in ship ordering.

The Merseyside shipyard shop stewards too were concerned to prepare for nationalisation, to get it implemented on *their* terms.

At Western Ship Repair Yards, in particular, the shop stewards showed considerable interest in creating a committee to achieve some control over the nationalised industry. One of the Merseyside MPs, Eddie Loyden, raised the idea of a committee mainly in order to make sure that the ship repair yards were fully included in the nationalisation legislation. They started a committee, but their first problem came from the District CSEU (not a problem on Tyneside where the District CSEU gave the Swan Hunters' initiative its support). One steward from Western Ship Repair told us how:

"the secretary of the district Confed. came to find out what we were doing when he heard Eddie had been down talking about the problems of nationalisation. It was the first time the Confed. secretary had come for *two years*."

The CSEU clearly was not too happy about a political initiative outside of their control. The Confed. secretary wrote to Harold Wilson complaining about the involvement of MPs like Eddie Loyden and Eric Heffer with the shop stewards. Though this did not stop either the MPs or the stewards from organising a committee to press the case of the Western Ship Repair Yards.

At Cammell Lairds too, though without success, the shop stewards set up a committee. But again it could not get very far. The CSEU kept preparations

and consultations for nationalisation firmly in the hands of a few national officers. There was not a single lay representative of the shipbuilding workers on the joint working party of the TUC, the Labour Party and the CSEU which drew up proposals for nationalisation. The only 'lay' discussion which the CSEU organised was a single conference.

These, then, were some of the problems and expectations in an industry which was definitely to be nationalised. What about other industries, where redundancies were threatened but nationalisation was not an immediate issue?

Section 2:
The National Enterprise Board

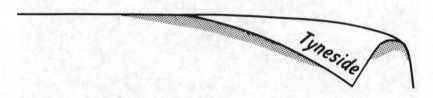

Tress Engineering and the NEB: A Fairey Story

In 1977, the Fairey corporation went bankrupt, mainly as a result of a risky project in Belgium which backfired. A small valve producing subsidiary of Fairey's on Tyneside, Tress Engineering, faced the threat of closure.

At first, the stewards representing the 350 Tress workers considered the possibility of a co-operative. The shop stewards even went as far as asking the company if they could buy the factory from the company at a nominal price. The company refused. The fact that they would have to fight to establish a co-operative led the stewards to think twice about it:

> "We talked to a lot of people about it, we looked at the experience of the Leadgate Engineering Co-operative at Consett. It seemed to us that they'd had to drop all the normal protective trade union practices in order to survive. They'd worked unpaid overtime, they kept the workforce to a minimum, they gave up all demarcations. It seemed to us that, like them, we'd be on our own. It would be going into the jungle. And anyway, what we expected of NEB control at the time was that it would be like a co-operative but with government support and a chance of survival."

So they turned to the NEB. The Trafalgar House Investments Group was hovering like a vulture around the carcase of Fairey, hoping to take it over. The Tress stewards were convinced that this would have been quickly followed by a ruthless asset stripping operation which would have put them on the dole. In the face of this sort of threat, the NEB seemed like the safest ally. The stewards were not sure of the details of the NEB but as Alec McFadden, the ex-AUEW convenor, put it to us:

> "We remembered the government's promises on jobs in areas of high un-employment, like Tyneside. We thought the NEB was set up to safeguard jobs, to control the profit hungry corporations. That's the impression we got at the time. We never realised, until too late, how much the original

intentions had been watered down. The NEB's guidelines said that it would be an instrument through which the government would operate directly to create employment in areas of high unemployment. The way some people in the Labour Party had been talking that is what we thought it was."

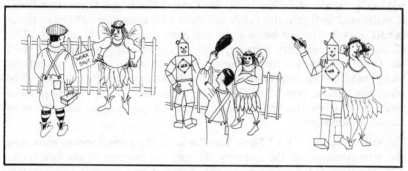

Fairey Story.

The shop stewards decided to *campaign* for the NEB to take over Fairey. The shop stewards in different Fairey plants had already been in contact with each other over pensions and wages. Now was the time to step up the organisation. They lobbied MPs, they argued with the Receiver and they threatened to occupy all sixteen Fairey factories. By January 1st 1978, Trafalgar House was beaten back and, in spite of opposition from the city and the Tory Press, the NEB took control. The shop stewards were fairly confident that this would lay the basis for a secure future. Alec McFadden again:

> "Basically we thought that it would maintain employment, secure our future, it would invest, and provide backing for alternative products to stabilise the company in the face of fluctuations in the petro-chemical industry. Management there must have been the worst on the river. We hoped that would change. We hoped that we'd get to know more about what was going on. The future plans and so on. We were pretty confident that this is what the NEB would mean."

The stewards at Tress had had no previous direct experience of state intervention in their industry from which to draw lessons and arrive at a more cautious view. In the power engineering industry on Tyneside however, some lessons had been learned.

Power Engineering and the NEB: an alternative to Weinstock

Because of the problems facing their industry, workers in the power engineering companies on Tyneside — Reyrolle Parsons, C.A. Parsons and Clarke Chapmans — had had enough direct experience of Labour governments to make them sceptical of the NEB. Still, they did consider the NEB to be the lesser of two evils. The other evil was takeover by GEC and "chopper" Weinstock — as Weinstock was called because of the vast numbers of jobs he has destroyed.

55

To understand their attitude to the NEB and the role they hoped it would play, we should explain the problems faced by workers in the power engineering industry.

The immediate problem facing management was over-capacity because there was no prospect of orders from the Central Electricity Generating Board (CEGB) until well into the 1980s and there were increasing difficulties in the export market. The last home order had been placed in 1973 and, by 1976, all parts of the industry were approaching a grave crisis. Management in all the firms concerned were talking of 'imminent redundancies'. Against the background of this impending crisis, the Labour government in May 1976 asked the "Think Tank" (the Central Policy Review Staff, CPRS) to produce some thoughts on the options open to the UK power plant industry, with utmost possible speed.

The main proposal of the "Think Tank" was for the government to encourage the rationalisation of the industry through the merging of the two boiler manufacturers (Clarke Chapman with Babcock and Wilcox) and the two turbine manufacturers (GEC with Parsons) to create two new companies. The CPRS also recommended that the CEGB should place an early order for the Drax B power station and commit itself to a steady ordering programme to maintain the industry's long term viability.

The Power Engineering Trade Union Committee, which had been created in late '76 to co-ordinate trade union activity throughout the industry, welcomed the last two recommendations. But they were totally opposed to the sort of restructuring which the CPRS report recommended. They remembered the effects for the workforce of the mergers encouraged by the Industrial Reorganisation Corporation in 1967; especially the merger involving GEC. Between 1967 and 1976, at least 64,000 jobs were lost at GEC, almost half through direct redundancies and closures. A merger with GEC was the last thing which the Power Engineering Trade Union Committee wanted. It seemed, however, that this was the solution favoured by the government. One of the TASS representatives on the trade union committee sums up the pressures they faced:

> "The pressures upon the Committee to accept the monopoly merger were enormous and came from Government Ministers, Government Departments, GECB, NEB, NEDO, the whole of the media, GEC and even some trade unionists."

In particular, the government were trying to make the bringing forward of Drax B contingent on acceptance of the recommended rationalisations. The committee argued, instead, that Drax B should be ordered in advance, with no strings attached; the government should give more favourable support in the export market; and that it should have a steady home ordering programme and give help in developing a full range of machines and boilers, and diversification into other allied products.

Full nationalisation was the stated long-term objective of the Power Engineering Trade Union Committee. But with the weak position of the Government

North East Photographers Co-operative.

in parliamentary terms, and the lack of political pressure in support of complete nationalisation, a short term solution was necessary. But in the politically tense atmosphere following the publication of the CPRS report, with its central proposal for mergers, the unions had argued tactically that, at the very least, the NEB should be fully involved in any merger arrangement in the hope that this would help to safeguard jobs.

Shop stewards argued that if the NEB took a majority share of a new company, with GEC and Parsons each holding a minority share, that would at least prevent a GEC takeover and wholesale rationalisation in traditional Weinstock style. According to Matty Straughan (Chairman of the Power Engineering Trade Union Committee and AUEW Convenor at C.A. Parsons):

> "We are prepared to accept the NEB as an alternative to what was being suggested. The Government were proposing a complete takeover by GEC which, as the largest company, would inevitably take complete control. We made it clear that the only way we would have accepted merger would be with NEB involvement as we saw this as the lesser of two evils."

Don Brown, a TASS representative from Clarke Chapman's, expressed a similar view, although the Clarke Chapman-Babcock and Wilcox merger had got as far as a preliminary agreement, with trade union support:

> "Originally we were happy with the proposed merger for technical reasons and we had a ballot of the membership in which nearly 70% voted in favour of a merger with NEB involvement. We thought NEB involvement would not have necessarily been long term, but we believed another party would step in to fill its place if it dropped out, thus maintaining the crucial 'balance' between the two companies. We felt NEB involvement would at least create a social climate which would prevent the government giving the industry wholesale to one of the two private enterprise companies.

Many people felt that sooner or later a company in such a 'balance' would inevitably lead to full nationalisation."

A step in the right direction, a move towards full nationalisation, that was a common attitude towards the NEB in the evidence brought before this inquiry.

The NEB and British Leyland: a planned car industry under democratic control?

As for the workers at Parsons, mergers or the effects of them, were a problem to workers at the British Leyland plants involved in this inquiry, at Speke on Merseyside and at Canley, Coventry. Mergers had produced a wasteful and, at times, farcical managerial structure, which was one of the factors behind British Leyland's chronic state of crisis — a crisis which was usually blamed on the workforce. Besides the chaotic managerial structure, the other, deeper, problem had to do with the level of investment. Between 1970 and 1974 British Leyland had invested only about £250 in new capital equipment for every one of the workers it employed. The other major European owned corporations invested twice as much.

In 1974, in the face of the growing vulnerability of British Leyland, the Department of Industry initiated an inquiry into the company's affairs. The shop stewards' combine committee's evidence to this inquiry — the Ryder inquiry — pressed the demand for a "planned capital investment programme supported by public funds" and "full democratic control" through joint union, management and government committees — one third representation of each. The problems facing British Leyland workers at this time have been well documented (see bibliography), so this inquiry will not go over them.

When the NEB took over British Leyland, shop stewards at Speke thought that now they had a chance to achieve what they were pressing for through Ryder. Frank Banton, Secretary of the T&GWU branch at the Speke Standard Triumph No.2 plant, summed up the optimism with which workers at both the two British Leyland plants regarded the NEB takeover:

"We considered that the NEB was on our side and that it would make a difference. There'd always been government money available, but in an airy fairy sort of way, you know. We thought that with the NEB the government would be more directly involved; it would take more responsibility, be more knowledgeable about what was going on and be more accountable. We also assumed that the NEB was set up partly to save jobs through more investment."

The problem of investment figures centrally in stewards' expectations of the NEB. We will see it stressed again in relation to the machine tool industry.

Under-investment and the need for state directed investment was also an important part of the analysis behind the Labour Party's proposals for the NEB. As we shall see however, it is important to separate the *explanation* for the poor *competitive position* of the company — which indeed does, in the case of the British motor and machine tool industries, lie in under-investment relative to profits — and the *solution* from a *socialist standpoint,* that is, to meet social needs. From this point of view, the amount of investment is, of course, important; more important are the *criteria* and *purposes* for which it is invested. An acceptance of competitive criteria mixed with workers' employment needs understandably underlies many of the views expressed by shop stewards in this chapter. One of the central questions of this inquiry is how far competitive and social criteria *can* co-exist, especially in a period of deepening recession. If they cannot, then what kind of policies can be fought for which are formulated on social criteria alone? And what does this require of Labour movement organisations nationally and inter-nationally?

Just as these questions are raised by the case of British Leyland, so they are of Alfred Herberts and most of the succeeding cases and sections.

British Leyland, Speke.

Mike Tomlinson — International Freelance Library.

Alfred Herberts and the NEB: the hope of high investment and genuine worker participation

Workers at Alfred Herberts, the machine tool company, also had high hopes that NEB control would be different from the sort of government involvement they had suffered in the past. Governments had by no means neglected the machine tool industry. At every stage and in every aspect of its development the industry had been surrounded by state agencies offering money and advice in a bewildering variety of forms. Although there has been a huge *quantity* of state intervention, it was not of a kind to either save jobs or improve the long term technical efficiency of the industry. For instance, the government made no direct attempt to get the owners of the industry to *invest.*

The company reports and accounts between 1965 and 1970 illustrate the problem; during that period, Herberts gained only £8.7m in profits but *distributed £9.2m in dividends.* Similarly, from 1967 to 1970 B. Elliot — the other giant UK machine tool organisation — obtained £3.6m in profits and gave out £1.3m to its shareholders. In the later '60s, the Labour government did make some attempt to improve the rate of investment in the industry by proposing a planning board and by making a limited investment in advanced technology firms like Herbert-Ingersoll and Kearney and Trecker, Marwin. On the first proposal, the government gave in to hostile pressure from employers' associations and scrapped the idea. On the second initiative, they failed to exert sufficient control over the firms in which they invested, in order to use these companies as pace setters, and to impose investment and employment standards on the rest of the industry. For instance, the government limited their investment in these companies to a 15½% share of the equity and two government nominees on the board.

When Alfred Herberts went bankrupt in 1974 and the workers were encouraged by the Labour ministers at the Department of Industry to draw up their own plans for running the company, there was a strong feeling that this time government involvement could be different. It could strengthen the security, the work conditions and the confidence of the workforce rather than supply a cushion for the employers.

Since 1965, workers at Alfred Herberts had seen numerous attempts at reorganisation, at pushing the company in 'new directions', at bringing in this or that 'bright and persuasive man who knew from long experience what needed to be done' (as Richard Young, managing director at Tube Investments, was described when given the chairmanship in '65) or yet another 'new, tough, managing director' (as Neale Raine was described when he came in 1970). They had seen 'drastic' plans, and a succession of accountants and 'productivity experts'. Finally, they were presented with a five year plan which the *Sunday Times* described as "clearly a desperate exercise in survival" and went on to predict "as such will probably be successful" (*Sunday Times* 30.4.72). Two years later, the same paper had to report that management's problems had only deepened. 1974 was:

> "supposed to be the company's annus mirabilis . . . instead it was a year in which Sir Richard resigned, Sir Halford retired, seven senior executives suffered heart attacks, and Raine went begging for more money."

One member of the stewards committee summed up a common feeling after all this:

> "All that these men have done, and you can quote Neale Raine, Buckley, Young; all they've done is come for a short period, help increase the losses, reduce the labour force, and go out with a golden handshake. It's been left to the men, with 40 or 50 years experience, to pick the bits up.
>
> I'd never been one, to tell you the truth, for worker ownership, but this was a clear case of where the working man couldn't have done any worse and probably done a lot better."

Ownership by the NEB would, they thought, give 'the working man' a chance to prove that he could run production better and with different, wider purposes in mind than just building up Alfred Herberts as a company. They thought that production plans at Herberts would be part of a wider plan for the whole machine tool industry. They talked about the kind of plans they would like to see implemented. One steward described an idea they had for the Herbert Ingersoll plant at Coventry:

> "We were thinking about how the NEB could best serve the industry. One thing we talked about was the idea of having Herbert Ingersoll taken over as a Research and Development Centre for the whole industry. Then they could approach any part of the car industry or the machine tool industry and ask what machines they needed. Then the Centre could have designed and developed them and distributed production of them to plants that needed work. It would have been a way of doing something useful rather than producing the same old candlesticks which fewer and fewer people want."

John Sturrock — Report.

Benn encouraged the Herberts' workers to develop these ideas. He encouraged them to set up joint worker-management site committees in order to agree a 'new corporate plan'. We shall see the results of this in the next chapter.

Rolls Royce and the NEB: business as usual

Representatives of the joint shop stewards committee at Rolls Royce, Parkside, in Coventry, placed a similar emphasis on social and industrial planning when they talked about their hopes for the NEB. Rolls Royce had been taken into public ownership by the Tories in 1971 following the collapse of the company; so they had been working for the state for three years. They did not think of state intervention in itself as anything to do with socialism or workers' interests. At the time of the collapse, they knew the government would support the firm because of its importance for defence:

"The Tory government had no choice but to nationalise us in 1971."

Rolls Royce stewards did not feel that the NEB could achieve a complete change in the nature of state intervention. But they felt that if it had stuck to the original Green Paper and the Labour Party manifesto it could have made a move towards a new sort of *social* planning. As one steward said:

"Planning exists in all countries of the world. In itself this was not what we needed. What we needed was an integrated social plan. The NEB did not look like being based on a complete plan, it was piecemeal; the original idea would have been a step in the right direction and there would have been a lot of support for it in the trade union movement."

The AUEW-TASS members had even lower expectations of the NEB. They too recognised that state takeover had been inevitable even under a Tory government:

"To allow Rolls Royce to close would be like pulling down the Union Jack over Buckingham Palace".

But they did not think the NEB would mean a qualitative change in the nature of state control of Rolls Royce. All they could see happening under the NEB was a continued process of rebuilding Rolls Royce so that it would be attractive to private finance. They feared that the NEB would provide an additional propaganda instrument for the government with which to "batter" the unions into accepting wage restraint.

Besides wages, conditions and control, the other issues on which the TASS representatives placed a lot of emphasis was the social use and purpose of their work. Rolls Royce management were the "Undershafts"* of the Aero-Engine business, selling defence equipment to whoever was prepared to pay: South Africa, Chile, Rumania, Yugoslavia, the US, Iran. Morals and ethics played no part. NEB control would not change this, the TASS representatives predicted. They argued that:

"Neither the NEB, nor any extension of state involvement, so long as it is

*Mr Undershaft was a character in George Bernard Shaw's *Major Barbara*; he was the salesman for an arms company.

62

dictated by the parameters of the market economy, will alter the fundamental relationships of the Rolls Royce workforce and management."

So there were mixed expectations about the NEB depending partly on workers' past experiences of the state, and partly on the political traditions which had built up over the years in their workplace and locality.

Section 3:
Planning Agreements and Government Aid

Lucas Aerospace: Workers' plans not management plans

Another group of workers who were sceptical about both the new industrial policies and traditional forms of nationalisation were the workers at Lucas Aerospace. The Victor works of Lucas Aerospace in Liverpool was one of the plants contacted during this inquiry. Here, and throughout the company (at plants in Burnley, Willesden, Bradford and Hemel Hempstead), this feeling that government intervention was not in itself a solution led to a new initiative: a workers' plan for socially useful production.

The stewards at all these different plants were part of a national shop stewards' combine committee, which has always had nationalisation as one of its objectives. The government, however, was not intending to include Lucas Aerospace in its nationalisation plans for the aerospace industry. Tony Benn at the Department of Industry had made it clear to the shop stewards that he would be sympathetic to whatever other proposals they put forward. He implied, for instance, that he would not allow financial aid to be given to Lucas Aerospace without these proposals being taken seriously and the shop stewards being consulted. In spite of government support for other proposals, it was clear that if Lucas Aerospace shop stewards were to push for nationalisation they would really need to have full support in the plants.

The combine committee had a long discussion about this, taking up at least two sessions of their regular weekend meeting at Wortley Hall. The representatives from the different plants reported that they did not think there would be sufficient support for a campaign for nationalisation in their plants. After the experience of coal and steel, people did not see nationalisation as a solution to the insecurity of their jobs.

Yet most of the delegates stressed that there was a need for some alternative to management's rationalisations. People began to talk about getting more involved in the company's investment decisions, about putting forward their own alternatives, and so on. The problem with that, the discussion went on, would be that workers' representatives would start to look at things the way that management did. "We would be taking on board *their* problems, their *system*" as one delegate put it. Yet the idea of putting forward their own proposals for the industry to safeguard jobs and to win support for the objective of nationalisation seemed an important advance on nationalisation as a policy on its own. The problem was to work out the *basis* of the workers' proposals so that they would be in the interests of working people rather than helping management to carry out its reorganisation.

One delegate began talking about the social needs that existed side by side with redundancies; the old people dying of hypothermia while heating engineers were being thrown on the dole; the blind and the crippled with primitive aids, while highly skilled designers were told that their services would no longer be needed, and so on. The solution became obvious: "we should fight the dole by claiming the right to work on socially useful products", concluded a representative from Burnley. So, in 1975, the Lucas stewards began to draw up their alternative plan. They began by assuming they could get government backing or perhaps a compulsory planning agreement, but they also stressed the way the proposals depended ultimately on their own resources, on the creativity and industrial power of workers on the shop floor and in the offices. The next chapter will describe the response of the government to their plan. Chapter Five will summarise the history and some of the lessons of their struggle.

Chrysler: Workers open the books

Shop stewards and office staff at Chrysler (Stoke, Ryton, Whitley and Linwood) similarly felt it important to put forward their own proposals, rather than rely on the government. In 1975, Chrysler was facing a financial crisis which was all too often blamed on the workforce. A joint committee of shop stewards and staff representatives decided to investigate what was really behind the crisis. They found, first, a failure to invest sufficiently. Their report described how:

> "the Stoke plant has been allowed to become a museum of antiquated machinery."

and they went on to spell out details of the age of the machinery. Further evidence of lack of investment was the fact that Chrysler's fixed assets per worker were lower than all other European car firms except British Leyland and Vauxhall. Finally, the annual report expenditure since 1970 of £15 per worker did not even cover the cost of depreciation and repair. No wonder Chrysler (UK) was in a state of crisis!

Secondly, the committee discovered that this under-investment was not through lack of central funds on the part of the Chrysler corporation. Rather they found pretty damning evidence that Chrysler's policy on acquiring the Rootes Company in 1967 was to systematically strip the assets of this UK subsidiary: its machines and its tools; its design and its technical expertise and its profits. The committee reports that:

"Between 1970 and 1973 the fixed capital employed in Chrysler (UK) was allowed to drift down from £53m to £46m. The entire stock of plant and machinery on Chrysler's British factory floors was shown in 1973 to have the incredibly low book value of under £19m. Since then this book value has continuously declined and is now in the region of £10m."

Possibly part of the explanation for this lies in one of the committee's other findings: that tools and machinery had been physically transferred to Chrysler's other subsidiaries, without any sort of replacement.

"Machine tools estimated to be worth £165,000 were shifted to Chrysler plants in South America and machines worth £700,000 were transferred from Coventry to Simca . . . We question whether the UK company actually received payment for this transaction and this is presumably related to the current low book value of Chrysler (UK)."

The other side of the asset stripping was in design. Since the Chrysler take-over, there had not been one single all-new Chrysler car made in the UK — in spite of assurances from the President of Chrysler International in 1970 that they would produce at least one new model a year. What have the 750 design staff at Whitley been doing all this time, asked the committee. Their answer was a list of designs for cars made outside the UK.

"The conclusion must be that the expertise of design and development staff at the Whitley plant has been exploited and abused by the Chrysler Corporation."

Finally, the committee drew on work by the Labour Research Department which showed that Chrysler (UK)'s statement of profits and losses gave a false picture of British performance. They suggest that artificially low export prices were charged to other Chrysler subsidiaries, particularly in Switzerland where taxes and profits are lower than in the UK.

To prevent this sort of anti-social behaviour by a multi-national corporation was, remember, exactly the object of the new industrial policies. Some Chrysler stewards were interested in, for example, planning agreements and industrial democracy. But the Chrysler crisis finally burst in December 1975 after any measures of control over private corporations had been taken out of the Industry Bill. Shop stewards and some of the office representatives had kept closely in touch with these developments partly through the Institute for Workers' Control. There was also a certain amount of scepticism about the reality of planning agreements and industrial democracy. This led the committee to make tougher demands.

John Sturrock — Report.

First, it demanded that if Chrysler UK was not prepared to provide job security, avoid redundancies and closure, then the government should meet workers' demands. They then spelt out in detail the sorts of short term changes, medium term investments and longer term alternative products which, under social ownership, would provide jobs and meet social needs.

In the immediate term, they stressed the importance of public investment being accountable to workers, shop floor organisation and the need for disclosure of all information relevant to collective bargaining and trade union activity. These sorts of demands, backed up by the explosive information of which we have just given a sample, caused consternation at a cabinet level as the Chrysler crisis deepened. The workers' report was becoming a focus for criticism of the government and the company. The government ignored it. But they could not unduly antagonise trade union leaders at that time, December 1975, when some of the partners in the trade union side of the social contract were beginning to lose their patience. A planning agreement, with all its radical interventionist sounding connotations, was the least they could do, especially when £169 million, government, or rather taxpayers' money was going to Chrysler in a combination of loans and grants. Moreover, Chrysler management were insisting that 8,000 jobs had to go. The stewards were sceptical, but in the end were prepared to give the planning agreement a chance.

This process, whereby the policies and images of the left were used by the government against the workers whose interests the left sought to represent, recurs again and again. We shall give it full treatment in another section, but this boomerang effect is worth noting at this stage, for Chrysler workers were perhaps hit the worst.

Vickers: prime candidate for a planning agreement

To some extent, this process was at work in the campaign to save the Vickers' Scotswood works on Tyneside, but that is a story for later. Now we need to look at the problems initially facing the workers at Vickers Scotswood; especially the nature of the government's past involvement with Vickers on Tyneside and the ways in which workers felt that, this time, there was a chance it might be different.

Vickers, like other major corporations, had received millions from the Labour government both in deferred taxation, in financial aid and in part compensation for the nationalisation of Vickers shipbuilding and aerospace interests.

None of this has gone into creating new jobs on Tyneside. Employment in the Tyneside plants had fallen in the last ten years from 12,000 to 5,000.

The Scotswood works at the end of the Scotswood Road had suffered the worst run-down of jobs. Since the war, it had been an odd jobbing factory making power presses (Scotswood has manufactured the equivalent of half the power presses in Britain), industrial plant, cranes, construction and earth moving equipment. All the products were licensed or subcontracted from other companies. Vickers had allowed its own design and research team to run down. So there was little attempt to develop new products or improve on existing ones. Investment generally had been low; buildings and machines were old and in urgent need of repair.

In spite of this general state of dilapidation, the plant had broken even until 1973. It even won the top award in Vickers' Export Year Competition in 1978. Between 1973 and 1977 it made a small profit. But for Vickers the profits were not high enough; a 30% return on capital was what they were aiming for. So Scotswood was being allowed to run down, gradually though, so that Vickers could squeeze the last profitable orders from the market. There was little doubt that without direct government intervention Scotswood would eventually close. Lord Robens, Chairman of Vickers, was quite explicit. For him, heavy engineering was 'finished as a trade in this country' and 'Scotswood is the remaining anomaly', after the rationalisations carried through in Vickers by himself and the Managing Director, Sir Peter Matthews.

The workers at Scotswood took a different view of things. They looked at the future of Scotswood from the point of view of the public, social benefits which heavy engineering at Scotswood would contribute. They would not accept a judgement based on the shareholders' profitability targets as the deciding criteria. For a start, they knew that the products they made and the

Wallsend, Tyneside.

alternatives they could make were vital to industrial production in Britain, as for any industrial country. There may have been a slump in the market for car presses recently, but the unique capacity which Scotswood could offer would be needed in the future. In the meantime, Vickers could introduce a shorter working week, or expand other products for which there was a clear need. For example, recycling equipment: shearers, boilers and pulverising plant in which local authorities had already shown an interest; equipment necessary for energy conservation; or the cranes they were already producing and for which there were steady orders. Why should 750 skilled engineers, boilermakers and design staff be thrown on to the dole, and cause an additional 500 or so jobs to be lost in the local area, when their skills and energies were so badly needed, asked the workforce.

They thought the government might share their view. They had heard, indirectly, that the government had been having talks with Vickers management on the possibility of government aid for Scotswood. Vickers had refused the offer. They wanted rid of Scotswood as part, some suspected, of a general move out of heavy engineering; which would be followed by the run-down of Elswick and other Tyneside works. But the interest shown by Leslie Huckfield at the Department of Industry in their case, and the memory of what had been promised in the original industrial policies led the Scotswood shop stewards to put most of their pressure on government. They hoped that the government would in turn exert pressure on Vickers. For a time they backed this faith in the government with industrial sanctions, a ban on the movement of work from the plant. However, in general they did not expect that direct pressure on Vickers would be necessary. Surely the government had some power to control the corporations, they felt.

69

> "Tony Benn and the left did support the Industry Bill — there must have been something in it for us"

commented Bill Jobling, one of the works committee, at Scotswood. As with other workers whose views are reported in this chapter, the response of the Scotswood workers to the threat of closure was significantly conditioned by the view that the government could be persuaded to respond to their demands. An important factor in this was a failure to recognise that the original industrial policies had been defeated, for all that the names remained the same.

Section 4:
The Co-operatives

In all three localities there were numerous occasions when workers faced the dole through being in a low priority plant of a multi-plant corporation. In most cases, workers in these types of companies had a vague hope that a Labour government would support the plants. But in two cases, at Kirby on Merseyside and Meriden in Coventry, the workers' self confidence, together with the encouragement they received from Tony Benn and Eric Heffer, produced a determination to run the companies themselves.

Kirkby: 'We could run it better ourselves'

One group of workers who were especially hopeful about the changed conditions in industry which a Labour government would bring about, were the workers in the IPD plant at Kirkby, an engineering factory employing at that time (after two large redundancies) about 900 men and women. In February 1974, they were facing the almost certain threat of closure from their third employer in the space of three years. Ever since 1970, workers at Kirkby had been a victim of the central managements of large multi-plant companies, to whom a low profit plant on Merseyside was a very low priority. Jack Spriggs, the AUEW convenor at the Kirkby plant (later known as KME), tells how he thought things would change with a Labour government:

> "I really believed the slogan 'back to work with Labour'. I thought there'd be more consideration for industry and for the regions. Not just through hand-outs — but through a generally more buoyant trading situation."

In March 1974, after an application by IPD for an Industry Act loan had been turned down by the Department of Industry, and after Spriggs and the T&GWU convenor, Dick Jenkins, had made direct contact with Tony Benn and Eric Heffer, the hopes of the Kirkby workers became more specific — Spriggs again:

> "With the ideas of workers' control and industrial democracy around at that time, especially through people like Tony Benn and Eric Heffer, we

gained enough confidence to put forward the idea of a co-operative. With all the chopping and changing of management, and of products, all the waste and lack of commitment'involved with this, we'd become convinced for some time we could run it better ourselves. But the fact that there were two other co-operatives on the drawing board (Meriden and the *Scottish Daily News*), made that feeling a real possibility."

As they worked on the proposals their demands and expectations developed:

"For the co-op to survive we needed to create a more planned situation. Without that, capitalism would clobber us. So we proposed that British Steel give us credit for a certain period. We proposed that we would have planned ordering from the British Leyland plants at Speke. The shop stewards there backed us on that one. Another thing would have been involvement with the NEB, at least with the original idea. That too would have given us a chance of survival and a chance to spread the idea of co-operatives."

Meriden: 'The idea began to catch hold of people'

At the Triumph Meriden factory near Coventry, the workers had been in occupation for five months by the time of the Labour government. The occupation started a few hours after Dennis Poore, their new employer, had announced his decision to close the factory. That was on September 14th, 1973. Poore was Chairman of Manganese Bronze Holdings, one of whose subsidiaries was Norton Villiers which, in the early '70s, was the one motorcycle company to be making a profit in a declining industry. Three months before Poore first tried to close Triumph Meriden factory he had, with the help of the Tory government, arranged a merger between Norton Villiers and BSA. As part of this deal, Manganese Bronze would buy up all BSA's non-motorcycle interests and combine Norton Villiers with Triumph to form a single motorcycle company. Poore claimed to be saving a proven natural asset when he accepted money from the Department of Industry to carry through the merger. But consequent events were to prove Philip Green, a Coventry officer of the T&GWU, closer to the mark, when he said:

"Mr Poore had to take Triumphs to get his hands on the more viable part of the BSA group when he bought it." (*Coventry Evening Telegraph* 14.9.73.)

Behind all Poore's public assurances that:

"No significant change in levels of employment is foreseen." (*CET* 8.6.73.)

It seems clear that Poore had never had any intention of keeping both the Triumph factories open (the other factory was at Small Heath, Birmingham). Workers at Meriden say the factory was being deliberately run down — from 1,400 units a week to a mere 500/600, in just a few months. Then came

Triumph Meriden Co-operative.

the announcement of the closure.

After some initial confusion, the workers acted decisively. They chained up the gates and began to plan an occupation. The idea of the co-operative was not at first seen as an extension of the occupation but, as one of the current worker directors put it:

> "Initially the threat of setting up a co-op was used as a bargaining lever to gain time. Poore needed the Triumph name but as the weeks of picketing and working-in stretched into months, workers saw the real possibilities and advantages of setting up a co-operative. The idea began to catch hold of people."

Les Huckfield MP and Jack Jones were brought in to try and help pressure the Tory government for support. Poore and Chattaway, at the Department of Trade and Industry, assumed they were in a good position to play the waiting game. Poore played the workforce along, giving the impression he would consider selling the premises. He thought the occupation would collapse given enough time. He admitted as much to the *Sunday Times* four years later (*Sunday Times* 4.6.78). But commitment to the job and the product, plus anger at Poore's behaviour and at the government's support for Poore, strengthened the determination of the workers to win. The occupation dug itself in for the winter. Despite severe financial hardships, most of the

73

workforce defiantly kept the picket line going. Some even had to sell their houses. Others were forced by their circumstances to find work elsewhere, but they pledged to return once the co-op was won.

The political mood of the Labour movement at the time, with the three day week and then the miners' strike sapping the authority of the Tory government, also contributed to this mood of determination. Neither Poore nor the government had calculated on such dogged resistance — a misjudgement of working class organisation and intransigence which, on February 28th, led to the downfall of the Heath government.

Then began the second phase of the co-op's struggle for recognition, for finance and for political support. With a Labour government elected to office on the basis of what looked like a radical industrial programme, the men and women on the picket line at Meriden thought the co-operative would soon be a reality. Within a fortnight of taking over at the Department of Industry, Benn met with the co-op's representatives and assured them of his department's support. He sent a government accountant to work with them on an application for financial assistance. At last, with 'their' government in power, things seemed as if they were moving in the right direction.

In conclusion

The problems facing these different groups of workers in the Midlands, on Tyneside and on Merseyside give some indication of the decline in manufacturing production for which top management, major shareholders and previous governments are clearly responsible.

Workers' organisations met the first mass redundancies caused by this decline in the late '60s and early '70s with militant industrial action. But, in spite of the limited success of workers at UCS, Fisher Bendix and elsewhere, a purely trade union response did not seem enough in the face of recurring industrial crises and deepening recession. It has been clear from our local inquiries that trade union activists were looking for a political solution. They were concerned to have some control over investment and production rather than always being at the receiving end without any effective power of veto.

On the whole, discussions of such political demands about the purpose and control of production have not had deep roots within British trade unions. Politics is seen as the responsibility of the Labour Party. The trade unions have tended to *react* to political ideas coming from within the Labour Party, to support them or reject them, not to *initiate* them. The development of the industrial policies of 1973/'74 was no exception. The trade unions supported these Party policies fairly automatically but did not discuss them deeply. However, once the Labour Party came to office, the promise of these new policies, with their emphasis on industrial democracy and workers initiatives, did, as we have seen, stimulate a more political type of trade unionism among some shop stewards.

We can see in these varied expectations and responses to Labour's industrial policies, that it was not just the NEC which had been doing some rethinking. Shop stewards and rank and file trade unionists were also reflecting on the experiences of the past. In one way or another they themselves drew up proposals and ideas which they hoped would make the promised extension of social ownership and control really work this time. Sometimes, as we shall see, they relied too much on the goodwill of parliamentary leaders, rather than building up their own political and industrial strength. At other times, debate about the new policies led indirectly to a political strengthening of industrial initiatives.

But this is jumping ahead. Why should workers *industrial strength* be necessary on these *political* issues? What was wrong with parliamentary methods? What were the practical and social consequences of the defeat of the original policies? What effect did the Labour government's final industrial policies have on the lives and communities of the localities we are writing from?

When Tony Benn was recommending these policies at the Party Conference in 1971, at a time when the campaign of the UCS workers and their presence in the conference hall was giving the proceedings a vigour and confidence quite untypical of Labour Party Conferences, he said, referring to the UCS stewards in the gallery:

> "It is not just a matter of the Party carrying the Conference, but both of us carrying the gallery and seeing that when they repose their confidence in us, we never, never let them down."

The gallery, whose expectations we have described in this chapter, *were* let down. The next chapter will describe just how far and why.

4.
...And realities

The general conclusion of this chapter is that jobs were lost, communities driven to despair and demoralisation, without any longer term benefits and without any say in the outcome by those directly affected. At the risk of driving the readers of this into further despair, much of this section will be about closures and redundancies and the decisions and institutions behind them. But it will not just be about this for, as one shop steward put it during the inquiry:

> "If all this destruction was to build something new, if all this sacrifice was to some better end, then it might be worth it, or at least it would be important to weigh things up. But it's been for nothing."

This raises the justification which the government gave and the trade union leadership largely accepted, for carrying out the rationalisations we shall soon describe. These rationalisations, social costs and all, were according to them a necessary part of the reorganising of British industry which would 'once again get us back on to the road to prosperity and full employment'. The same arguments now used to justify social cuts of a far greater magnitude are the arguments of Thatcher and Joseph.

We do not accept the logic behind this argument from either Labour leaders or a Tory government, but we thought it was important to inquire into what restructuring was being carried out by the government through the new Industry Act and the nationalisation of shipbuilding. Were these instruments of state intervention being used to restructure British industry? If so, what sort of restructuring was involved and who benefited?

We found that, although the government had confidently trounced the Labour left in response to the pressures of the City and big business, it was unable to carry through or even effectively begin the restructuring in capitalist terms which is necessary to restore competitive success to British industry. An important reason for this is that its political success against the left was not matched by a sufficient control over trade union militancy and organisation. For, while the long-run historical explanation of the weakness of British industry on the international market lies in a constant underinvestment in domestic production, the only solution acceptable to the most powerful industrial and financial interests is a massive reduction in the cost of labour.

A restriction in the supply of money and credit to force employers to reject

77

high wage claims is the present Tory strategy for lowering the costs of labour. Others, the leadership of the Labour Party included, prefer an incomes policy.

There is little doubt that if the goal of restructuring is to be competitive success, then some such onslaught on working class living standards and power is necessary. This makes it especially important and urgent that a socialist industrial strategy rejects competitive success as an overriding objective. Instead, we must reassert that the objective of a socialist industrial strategy is to match productive capacity and human energies and skills to social needs under democratic control. Such objectives are based on a criticism of the capitalist *market* – nationally and internationally as well as of capitalist *production.* In particular, it is based on an indictment of the market's failure to register social needs, because so many social needs are not backed by the resources necessary for purchasing or market power.

This chapter will primarily be descriptive of what has happened in our areas. But behind any description there are usually explanations. We have thought about and discussed these as we conducted the inquiry. In the following descriptions, we are trying to highlight not only the failure of government to invest sufficient funds to 'make up for' the investment failures of the past; we are also concerned to highlight the failure to restructure industry according to social need. This amounts to a failure to identify unmet social needs nationally and internationally which could be met by the 'redundant' capacity of British industry and then to put government resources behind these needs.

Section 1:
Nationalisation, Merseyside and Tyneside

The nationalisation of shipbuilding was no exception to this general failure. The nationalisation and extra investment in the yards was not matched by any attempt to identify and subsidise unmet shipping needs, for example in Third World countries, or to establish any planned ordering among British shipowners.

Nationalisation: too late?

As we saw in the last chapter, in the minds of the shipbuilding workers on Tyneside and Merseyside nationalisation meant the possibility of more secure jobs, more control over their working conditions, more planning in the relation between British shipowners and shipbuilders, and finally, more planning of alternative employment by sources of public investment in the areas where shipbuilding might decline. Nationalisation had long been the aim of the unions in shipbuilding; they wanted the nationalisation of shipping as well, for only then could there be any significant planning of work and employment in the yards. Both these demands had been the policies of the major unions concerned ever since the shipbuilders and owners had together murdered so many communities in the North East and Scotland during the 30s. But, as with most previous nationalisations, the hopes and aspirations of the labour movement have had to wait until the industry is in such crisis and ruin that private financiers are glad to see the back of it — so long as they are well compensated in order that they can invest and prosper elsewhere. If the industry is vital to the success of the rest of the economy, to the supply of raw materials, to the sale of industries and products, to the stability of the balance of payments, to defence interests, and so on, then, increasingly, Tory and Labour governments alike have been prepared to take over.

There are, of course, important differences in the approaches of the two governments to government takeovers. The present Tory government is encouraging as much as is profitable to be sold back to private owners. The Labour government was more responsive to union pressures for the whole of an industry to be government-owned. For example, in the case of ship-building, the owners of the profitable naval yards, Vickers, Vosper Thorney-croft and Cammell Lairds, formed a consortium in order to fight against nationalisation. With a Labour government they were not successful. Under a Tory government, on the other hand, this consortium would very likely have been allowed to remain in private hands while the loss-making merchant shipping was taken over. The important point, however, is that in general the demand for nationalisation of the shipyards was only carried out when it was in the interests of the shipowners to invest elsewhere with the com-pensation money, and when it was in the interests of private capital for the government to be in control.

There is, therefore, invariably a clash of interests and expectations. Workers have pressed for nationalisation, often on the assumption that this would mean some form of workers' control. Government, on the other hand, have been concerned with making industries commercially viable in as short a period of time as possible. The social costs are compensated for in the shape of redundancy money, but they are not taken into account in the decision-making. The functions and objectives of the new nationalised shipbuilding industry, spelt out in the legislation for nationalisation, make the overriding commercial priority quite clear.

The reorganisation of the industry put this into practice without much delay, certainly not enough delay to even discuss the sort of proposals for workers' control, described in Chapter three, put forward by the national-isation committee in Swan Hunters. The different companies and yards were divided into profit centres so that 'over-manning' could be quickly identified as the major inefficiency: within two years over 30,000 jobs had been des-troyed, including 7,000 in the North East. There were rumours of massive redundancy pay, but when the North Tyneside Trades Council carried out a systematic survey (with the help of the Tyneside Metropolitan Borough Council) they found that more than half the workers would receive under £1,000 – including everyone aged under 40, and that only four men in a hundred would get the much publicised £5,000. With unemployment at over 9% in Tyne and Wear, redundant shipyard workers have little chance of finding alternative jobs and little money on which to live in the meantime.

Section 2:
The National Enterprise Board

"No British institution has ever diverged quite as sharply as the NEB from the track which its designers tried to lay down", commented *Management Today* when it was summing up the experience of the NEB. We have seen how the legislative foundations for the NEB were rebuilt according to a different design from the original. In this section, we want to look, among other things, at the institution which was finally built on these shifting foundations.

The finances

The first important constraint limiting the new style NEB was its size. initially, the borrowing limit in the Industry Act was £700m, to cover its first five years. Then, in March '78, by which time most of the City's fears had been quietened, it was raised to the grand sum of £1,000m. Contrast this with the £15,000m received by private industry from the government over the same period! The NEB accounts for a mere 6% of this aid to private industry. The rest was given without even the minimal amount of accountability.

The sort of money available to the NEB could hardly buy two of the top 100 companies, let alone a 'major foothold in the profitable manufacturing industries', even if it had had the compulsory powers to do so. Certainly, with these meagre sums the NEB could not throw its weight around the stock exchange in the way that financiers feared.

The 'lame ducks'

The NEB's financial limits were in reality even worse than this. Its first acquisitions were the two major loss makers, Rolls Royce and British Leyland, which the government was only too pleased to take out of direct contact with the central political nerve centre (see Appendix 3). By 1978, these two companies had taken up nearly 94% of loans made by the NEB, which meant that only £50m had been spent on new acquisitions. It is important to note that British Leyland and Rolls Royce were not the only companies which could have been transferred to the NEB. Another Government controlled company, with more profitable prospects, was Kearney, Trecker and Marwin (KTM), the advanced machine tool company in Brighton. An ideal asset, you might have thought, which, with Alfred Herberts (also government owned), could provide a base for a socially planned machine tool industry, supposedly high on the government's list of priorities. But the government seemed more concerned to prove that the new style NEB had no desire to tread on the toes of private industry. So the government restored KTM to a suitable state for the sensitive hands of private enterprise. That meant writing off £5.2m of KTM's previous liabilities, giving and loaning another £2.9m in financial assistance and buying £900,000 of non-voting shares. The lucky private company, Vickers, only paid £803,000 for all this plus a £500,000 loan.

The profit targets

In its first two years, the only companies in which the NEB acquired a controlling share — apart from the transferred companies — were companies which had gone bankrupt or near bankrupt, but yet had profit potential. As the NEB guidelines put it, 'The NEB shall make acquisitions . . . only when they see the prospect of an adequate rate of return within a reasonable period'. And what was an adequate rate of return? Eric Varley, the Secretary of State for Industry, directed that an adequate rate was to be 15-20%* on capital employed for the whole of the board's activities by 1981. The only exceptions were to be British Leyland and Rolls Royce, for which an adequate return would be 10%. This overall target is very high when compared to the performance of most of British industry. The Bank of England shows that the average return moved very erratically from 19.0% in 1960 to 16.8% in 1976, never rising above 19.0% and sometimes falling as low as 13.5%.* Against this background, a target of 15-20% in a period of deepening recession does not leave much room for the NEB to carry out what the guidelines call its 'wider responsibilities', such as 'creating employment in areas of high unemployment' and 'promoting industrial democracy in undertakings which they (the NEB) control'. Both of these wider responsibilities, of course, might well interfere with the smooth and speedy climb to profitability.

So, the NEB's task with its newly acquired bankruptcies like the Fairey Group or, in a different way, with British Leyland, was to turn them into profit spinners. What did this mean for the workers in these two companies, by whom, after all, the profits must ultimately be produced? What happened to the wider responsibilities in these two companies?

---

*Pre-tax, measured on historic cost principles. If we took the measure in terms which took account of stock appreciation, the high target for the NEB would seem even more unrealistic in relation to the track record of private industry.

The Fairey Story — Part 2

The NEB took over Fairey on January 1st 1978. Apart from the Aviation Division, which had been the immediate cause of the bankruptcy, most of the other plants making hydraulic equipment were fairly profitable, Tress Engineering on Tyneside included. In 1975 and 1976 Tress had a rate of return near and then well over the 20% mark, though a small loss had been made in 1977.

But in terms of the central board's priorities Tress had always been out on a limb — 'the Siberia' of the group, according to the managers who faced the possibility of being sent there. Investment was low, machinery was old and little attempt was made to diversify, even though the valve market was subject to serious fluctuations. Local management and workers alike believed that far too much of the past profits had been siphoned off to head office. No wonder business was beginning to decline. As we saw in Chapter three the workers at Tress thought NEB control would change all this. They assumed that the NEB would change the priorities of the Fairey Board. They did not look at the fine print of the final guidelines for the NEB, which made it clear that NEB *control* did not mean *interference* in the day-to-day decisions of the company: day-to-day decisions like putting 300 men and women on the dole!

On June 1st, six months after the NEB takeover, Tress workers heard on the radio that Fairey had at last decided to get shot of its Tyneside company, and that the NEB was not going to stop it. The stewards were surprised because, as they say in the pamphlet they produced on 'The Fairey Story':

> "On March 8th [we had had] a meeting with Angus Murray, the new NEB-appointed chairman of the Fairey Board. He talked of expansion, of alternative products — different sorts of valves — which could help stabilise the company in the face of fluctuations in the petro-chemical industry. The clearest indication of his commitment was talk of rebuilding one of the factories. Overtime was worked regularly in some sections, the order book seemed steadier and extra work had led to eight new men being taken on."

The workers at Tress were to remain unconvinced and mystified as to why their factory should be closed. They were never told the arguments in detail. The closure had been the recommendation of a firm of consultants, P.E. Consultants, whose previous chairman was non other than Angus Murray, the very same Angus Murray who chaired the board of Fairey! No one on Tyneside was allowed to see the report, neither the convenor and shop stewards, the union district officials, the Chairman of the Tyne Wear Council, nor the Northern Group of MPs. The NEB seemed to have forgotten the second of its 'wider responsibilities' — industrial democracy. One might have thought that access to information is the first step towards industrial democracy. But, when the Secretary of the Newcastle Trades Council wrote directly to the NEB on the secrecy of the consultants' report, this is the reply he received:

> "You asked about the possibility of the consultants report being made available to you and your colleagues; since the reports were commissioned by the Fairey Board, not the NEB, this really is something for it to decide."

So much for the NEB's obligation to 'promote industrial democracy in the undertakings which they control'!

The effects of the closure were still being talked about on Tyneside two years afterwards. Although 'only' 300 people were involved, the closure of Tress has become a symbol of what is happening to Tyneside and the failure of the latest government remedy. The Policy Services Department of Newcastle City Council have produced a full report of the social costs of the redundancies at Tress. This is a summary of their survey:

1. One third of all the redundant workers from Tress were still without a job *over a year* after the closure. Some had, in effect, retired early, while the rest were registered as unemployed.

2. Almost half the workers had been unemployed for *at least six months* in the year after closure.

3. Older workers had been hardest hit — those over 50 were more likely to experience longer periods of unemployment.

4. *Every* skill level was affected — skilled workers had suffered as much as the unskilled.

5. Only one third of the workers now have a job in the engineering industry, and only a third have a job similar in skill level to the one they had had at Tress.

6. Only a fifth said they preferred their present job to their Tress job.

7. Over half found that looking for a job was worse — or a lot worse — than they had expected.

Since this Trades Council inquiry, for all its need to concentrate on institutions and politicians, is really about the human, subjective costs of industrial policies, it is worth quoting some of the Tress workers when they talked to the City Council researchers about the effects of being unemployed on them, their friends and their families:

"Not having any money's the main trouble. You lose your independence. I don't like having to depend on other people. It all makes you feel very small. You meet people and they ask what you're doing and you say you're unemployed, and you know what they are thinking. You can tell yourself that you don't care what they think but deep down it gets you. It always gets you. Sometimes people will say 'You're still not working? You're not trying man. I've got a job. There's plenty of jobs for those who want to work'.

"But I *am* trying. Sometimes, after I've been turned down for another job, I begin to think there aren't any jobs and that it's not me at fault but after you've been to a few interviews you get depressed and start to lose your confidence."

"Apart from the frustration and the boredom there's the worry. There's the heating and other bills, the future, the uncertainty, the wondering — things always on your mind. You can't stop thinking about them. The worry is always there — day and night. I can't sleep at night for worry."

"It's changed my attitudes to the unemployed. I used to think they were just skivers and was quite a lot against them, but now that I've experienced it, it's no joke man. Sometimes my mum and dad shout at me for not doing something I've had all day to do. And they're right. Some days I get up and it's all go: I get things done, but some days I'm just pissed off. I don't feel like doing anything. I just sit there, all day, thinking and worrying about what I'm going to do."

"Tress closing was a great shock. Last thing I ever thought could happen. It made me feel insecure for a time because there was always doubt if I could get another job and I had a family to support. It's made me realise engineering is a dicey business. Keep hearing another factory closed. Hundred here, hundred there out of work."

"I am short tempered. I have not had a proper night's sleep since the redundancy. My wife says I mope a lot. If only they would give us enough money to get by on things would not be so bad. I get very depressed. I can understand why people kill themselves, though I never would."

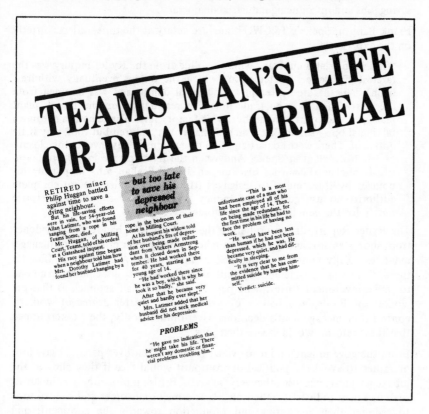

TEAMS MAN'S LIFE OR DEATH ORDEAL

RETIRED miner Philip Huggan battled against time to save a dying neighbour.

But his life-saving efforts were in vain, for 54-year-old Allan Latimer, who was found hanging from a rope in his Teams home, died.

Mr. Huggan, of Milling Court, Teams, told of his ordeal at a Gateshead inquest.

His race against time began when a neighbour told him how Mrs. Dorothy Latimer had found her husband hanging by a

– but too late to save his depressed neighbour

rope in the bedroom of their home in Milling Court.

At his inquest his widow told of her husband's fits of depression over being made redundant from Vickers Armstrong when it closed down in September. He had worked there for 40 years, starting at the young age of 14.

"He had worked there since he was a boy, which is why he took it so badly," she said.

After that he became very quiet and hardly ever slept."

Mrs. Latimer added that her husband did not seek medical advice for his depression.

PROBLEMS

"He gave no indication that he might take his life. There weren't any domestic or financial problems troubling him."

"This is a most unfortunate case of a man who had been employed all of his life since the age of 14. Then, on being made redundant, for the first time in his life he had to face the problem of having no work.

"He would have been less than human if he had not been depressed, which he was. He became very quiet, and had difficulty in sleeping.

"It is very clear to me from the evidence that he has committed suicide by hanging himself."

Verdict: suicide.

Liverpool

The murder of Speke

Some people *do* kill themselves as a result of the depression and loss of identity which comes from being out of work. The comparative studies of Professor Brenner of John Hopkins University, USA, have demonstrated this. He recently made a study of the relation between unemployment and mortality in Speke on Merseyside which further illustrated the close connection between the two.

The NEB was partly responsible for the high unemployment in Speke. For, the NEB ratified Michael Edwardes' decision to close BL Standard Triumph No.2 Plant. That meant another 3,500 on the dole. British Leyland had been taken over by the government in 1975 with a considerable fanfare about saving jobs and introducing industrial democracy.

Frank Banton, Speke's T&GWU branch secretary at the time, reflects bitterly on the experience:

"The industrial democracy which resulted from the Ryder Inquiry was the farcical Employee Participation (which the unions eventually withdrew from). This ill-fated attempt at industrial democracy was doomed from the start. There was no trade union representation on the Board; plant managers had overriding authority at factory level. Participation became a talking shop — something which management endured but took very little notice of. There were no participation discussions at any level re the closure of BL No.2 Plant at Speke. And when the fight to save jobs there intensified, Michael Edwardes blackmailed Jim Callaghan into supporting his policies by threatening to resign as BL chairman unless he got complete authority to use government money to run BL as a private enterprise purely for the benefit of the shareholders."

The Ryder Report, drawn up before the final collapse, had received evidence from shop stewards and appeared to take seriously their criticisms of management, especially concerning the lack of investment. As we saw in Chapter three, there was considerable optimism that NEB control would mean an end to under-investment (investment per BL worker is half as much as that per worker for Fords, Vauxhall or Chrysler), and a greater degree of workers' control over management's decisions. Over-optimistically, the workers hoped that these reforms would secure their jobs.

From the government's point of view, BL was taken over partly to save jobs or rather to avoid the political opposition it would face if they allowed the jobs to go; partly because other very powerful British motor supply companies, such as Lucas Industries, relied on BL as a major customer and needed time to redirect their marketing and production towards the continent; and finally, because there were sections of BL which were consistently profitable (BL trucks) or had profit potential. It was out of these profitable and potentially profitable fragments that the industry could be rebuilt. This was the priority of Sir Richard Dobson, appointed chairman of British Leyland in 1976. He made this clear in an interview in the *Times*:

"It was better for Leyland to have a businessman and a Tory at the head of it than to have a civil servant or even a committed socialist. My dream would be to see Leyland so profitable that its shares could again be distributed — perhaps under a different government, perhaps under a similar one — to the general public as a worthwhile investment." (*Times* 10th May, 1976.)

It is unlikely that British Leyland workers shared this dream or even knew about it, but there was a strong commitment to make the company succeed, especially from leading shop stewards. However, hard work could not overcome years of lack of investment in British Leyland and its predecessors, followed by intense competition and overcapacity in the industry generally: especially when the government was only prepared to give funds which matched those raised within the company. By 1977, the workforce (and therefore the wage bill) had been reduced by 50,000, yet still the funds could not be raised. The government was not prepared to relax its conditions.

Like any other business

The government was concerned to minimise the financial and market privileges which any NEB owned firm had over privately owned businesses. As we shall see again and again, the government and the NEB board did everything to ensure that NEB controlled firms were as subject to competitive pressures as any privately owned company. If they were not, the argument went, they would be upsetting the market and inviting retaliatory action from the City. The only feature distinguishing NEB controlled companies from those under private control was that they received loans on a longer term basis and with a rather longer term view of the required rate of return. The NEB was simply one sort of financial institution among others; it had its own particular features and priorities as did any other merchant bank.

The result of this in the case of British Leyland, as with Fairey, was that these stringent market constraints pushed the NEB's much acclaimed 'wider responsibilities' out of all consideration. On this basis, the NEB felt that what British Leyland needed was a chairman who had had experience of working under harsh competitive conditions and had increased company profit in spite of them. Michael Edwardes from Chloride was the man for the job. He made his intentions very clear:

"The Business Plan has already determined that by wastage and other means we must slim our labour force in order to reduce our overhead costs and improve our profitability. In addition, it is inevitable that we should consider whether to close an assembly plant and concentrate the production at another large site. It is essential to eliminate fixed overheads and this means the elimination of facilities. *And this becomes a question of deciding between plants.*" (Our emphasis.)

Speke was the first one to go. In many ways it was the test case. If a plant like Speke No.2, with a well-organised workforce and in a politically sensitive area like Merseyside, can be cracked, then further cuts are going to be very much easier.

No future for Canley

In the short run, it was the Canley plant which gained the TR7 work from Speke. But that in itself did not give the stewards at Canley much sense of security. They were pretty sure that Edwardes would have wanted to close Canley as well, but in the run-up to a general election two big closures in areas vital to Labour's electoral prospects were just not acceptable to the government. Without this political constraint, Edwardes would move against Canley, of that the Canley stewards had little doubt. The advent of the Tory government in May 1979 enabled the NEB to carry its rationalising role to its logical conclusion and, without any of the hesitations imposed by a Labour government, to slash away all the most costly units of British Leyland, in preparation, most likely, to sell the more independent ones to private investors. The desirability of returning healthy assets back to the share market is not, however, a principle unique to the Tories; it was built into the final guidelines and objectives with which the Labour government first established the NEB.

The NEB's regional responsibilities

The closure of Tress and of BL's Speke No.2 plant, in areas already suffering from industrial decline, was a high social cost to pay for restoring a company's profitability. Had the NEB completely overlooked its responsibilities towards creating employment in areas of high unemployment? No, not completely. It created two regional offices of the NEB, in the North East and the North West in order 'to ensure that the NEB can effectively discharge their employment responsibilities in areas of high unemployment'. What has been the record of these offices? Have the regional directors and boards found a way of making the NEB's social responsibilities consistent with its commercial constraints?

The results by spring 1978 did not give much reason for optimism. The North East office had committed only £1.6m of the £20m available. This had involved investments in five companies with a total of 540 employees. One of these — Hivent Ltd. in Washington New Town — suffered heavy trading losses and could not continue without a substantial injection of capital. The NEB, however, decided this could not be justified and the company went into liquidation. Registered unemployment at that time, in the area covered by the North East regional office, was about 120,000. The North West regional office, similarly, had little effect on the high levels of regional unemployment. One of the regional directors admitted as much when he told *Management Today* that the chief impact of the NEB on employment in the north west had been BL's closure at Speke.

All this seems to indicate very passive and tight-fisted regional boards. But they provided a useful pretence of special government action and concern. For example, this flurry of concern took place just a few days after the government had proved unable and unwilling to prevent Plessey Ltd. from closing two of its special grant aided factories in the North East and the North West (Plessey did not even feel obliged to inform the government of its intentions). The Prime Minister told the House of Commons that he was asking the NEB to investigate investment potential in the north east and north west. Investigations were carried out and reports produced, but the level of investment and of jobs in the area, the real tests of success, remained virtually unchanged.

This seems a long way from the regional role of the NEB spelt out in a 1976 White Paper:

> "The Government recognise the importance industry attaches to stability and certainty in financial incentives to stimulate industrial and commercial expansion in areas of high unemployment. *But the experience of the last 25 years shows that financial incentives are by themselves inadequate: the Government need a power of direct action and the National Enterprise Board will therefore have a responsibility on its behalf to create employment through commercially sound public enterprises and joint ventures with private enterprise in the areas of high unemployment . . ."* (Our emphasis.)

There is no evidence that the regional NEB created any employment whatsoever.

The IRC under a different name

The NEB was able to slim down British industry but not to expand it. The other task it tried to perform was to reorganise important sections of industry to compete more effectively on international markets. In this sense, it was taking over the role of the Industrial Reorganisation Corporation which, from the point of view of major industrialists — notably those who benefited from it — was perhaps the one achievement of the '66-'70 Labour government. How far was the NEB successful in their terms? How did the NEB attempt to carry out this restructuring role? What did restructuring mean for the people whose jobs were at the receiving end of the process?

A revealing example of the role intended for the NEB in encouraging the restructuring of crisis-ridden British industries is to be found in the power engineering industry. One important reason why we can find out so much from this example was that the workers organised themselves powerfully enough to impose, temporarily at least, *their* terms on the government's solution for the industry. At every point, as the Power Engineering Trade Union Committee resisted the manoeuvres of the government and of Weinstock, it uncovered more and more about the relations between government, the NEB and major industrialists.

The civil service had been arguing for mergers and a reduction in the capacity of the turbine and boiler manufacturing industry, ever since the reports drawn up during the days of IRC. The IRC had taken some steps in that direction, organising the mergers between three boilermakers — Clarke Chapman, International Combustion and John Thompson — and between the heavy electrical companies — Reyrolle Parsons and Bruce Peeble Industries. But as far as the civil service, the Labour government, and leading industrialists were concerned, the job had been left unfinished when the Tories dismantled the IRC. As we explained in the last chapter, the government believed that the process of rationalisation ought to be completed with a further merger in both boiler making and turbine manufacturing, the most controversial proposal being a GEC takeover of Parsons to rationalise the turbine industry. At first, as we saw, the Power Engineering Trade Union Committee saw NEB control as a protection against a GEC takeover. They were soon to be disillusioned.

The NEB backs Weinstock

On the 1st June 1977, The Secretary of State for Industry, Eric Varley, together with senior civil servants, met Arnold Weinstock, Kenneth Bond, Lord Nelson of GEC, and Sir James Woodeson and Mr D. McDonald from Reyrolle Parsons. At this meeting, Eric Varley made it clear that the Government, the NEB and the Department of Trade and Industry supported a GEC takeover of the turbine-generator industry. This was the only proposal they would be prepared to back. GEC had made it absolutely clear that they wanted complete control and would not accept any form of NEB involvement. Further, they were insisting that Parsons management carry out substantial rationalisation before GEC would be prepared to take it over. The following day, 2nd June 1977, Eric Varley met national CSEU officials and lay trade union representatives from GEC, C.A. Parsons, Clarke Chapman and Babcock and Wilcox, to persuade them to accept merger. At that meeting, Eric Varley again made clear the Government's position with regard to the merger. He confirmed that the Government wanted to see the turbine generator industry restructured with GEC control. The press release which the Department of Industry issued after this meeting was particularly blunt:

"The CPRS* had pointed out that the UK industry was small in comparison with its competitors and it was clear that there was not room for more than one turbine-generator manufacturer in the UK. The CEGB and the NEB regard this restructuring as essential and so, in principle, do the turbine-generator manufacturers.

After full consideration of the situation, the NEB advised the Government plainly that the right solution was to form a single company under the control of GEC. This *formal advice* (our emphasis) of the NEB was based on the relative strength of the two companies, both in financial terms and in the market place, and the need for a credible British Company to be able to deploy resources comparable to those of competing foreign manufacturers."

The 'formal advice' Varley referred to was not in fact a formal decision of the Board of the NEB, but was a letter sent to Eric Varley by Lord Ryder on 4th May.

Extracts from this letter had been made available to the CSEU Executive (one month after it was received), and make very interesting reading:

"There is insufficient business to support both C.A. Parsons/GEC's turbine-generator business . . . The key to the prosperity of the industry is securing sufficient exports so that, with a sensible long-term ordering policy by the home authorities, a viable single turbine-generator company might be kept going. The solution to this is obvious: *GEC should take over the turbine-generator business of Parsons,* GEC has the financial muscle to compete in world markets . . .

There is no doubt in our view that this is the right solution for the industry . . . and it would be wrong for the Government to place the order for Drax B unless restructuring on the lines indicated has been agreed.

The question then arises of the NEB involvement. As you know, the NEB has no wish to become involved if a solution can be found without us . . . We have made it clear to GEC that we could be able, provided an acceptable basis can be negotiated, to support the restructured turbine-generator company by taking an equity interest in it, or in any other way that GEC feels would be helpful to the long-term future of the business. GEC's attitude is that this would not be practicable because of the integration of GEC's turbine generator activities with its other activities . . . If no progress can be made over NEB involvement, the Government will clearly have to consider what other avenues are open. *The relevance of NEB involvement is now entirely concerned with the Parsons workforce.* Some other way of dealing with these anxieties should therefore be urgently explored. The

*Central Policy Review Staff – The 'Think Tank'.

rub of the problem seems to be that the Parsons workforce does not believe that, once the immediate redundancies have taken place, there will be any long-term security for them. *Surely, it would be possible to have some statement agreed between the Government and GEC safeguarding the long-term position which would be explained within the framework of the agreement and the Government would be able to monitor GEC's adherence to it."* (Our emphasis.)

The government and the NEB then went searching for a formula to placate the 'neurotic' anxieties of the Parsons workforce induced by GEC's history of redundancies. A leading trade union official on the board of the NEB had previously warned a member of the Parsons Trade Union Committee about manoeuvres going on in the NEB to obtain a GEC takeover. Various things had been suggested. One of these played on the hope which workers initially had in the NEB, to entice them into a deal with GEC. The idea was that the NEB should get involved and then at a later point arrange to sell off Parsons' interest to GEC. Leading members of AUEW-TASS also expressed grave worries about the back-room secret deal Eric Varley and the NEB were trying to arrange, especially since Eric Varley had received Lord Ryder's letter on May 4th, but only revealed the contents to the CSEU on June 2nd. In that time he had had two meetings with the CSEU Executive at which he had not even mentioned the letter.

"I wouldn't touch it with a barge pole now!"

These signs of backroom deals and manoeuvres began to cause worries amongst workers in the industry that the NEB might be used to persuade them to accept a merger. The fear was that the NEB would hold the ring for a few months or years and then withdraw, handing over control to GEC. According to Harry Blair (Secretary of the PEITUC and of Parsons Corporate Committee):

"We were always apprehensive about the NEB, we had only agreed to a 40%/40%/20% arrangement as a counterbalance to GEC taking over Parsons completely. Great pressure was put on us to restructure, and we believed that the NEB, holding 20% of a new merged company, would at least operate more in the workers' interests. But I wouldn't touch them with a barge pole now. At the finish we were fighting Weinstock, the NEB and Eric Varley and eventually the credibility of the NEB as it was constituted was practically nil with us."

John Sturrock — Report.

And against all the odds their fight was, for the time being, successful. Eric Varley, the then Secretary of State for Industry, was forced to shelve his plans for a restructured turbine industry. It was undoubtedly one of the most important political defeats of his career.

The power engineering workers' campaign was perhaps the first time workers had successfully challenged one of the most ruthless management teams in the country, a team supported by the NEB and by leading Cabinet Ministers. The story of this campaign and some explanation of its success will be an important part of the next Chapter.

Workers' needs, consumers' needs

The government's intervention in power engineering was an attempt to restructure the industry so that British owned companies could dominate the market. It failed because workers in power engineering, fellow trade unionists and the wider community, had other and increasingly contradictory priorities: priorities of secure employment, of preserving and developing the communities and regions in which people lived.

Moreover, the workers in power engineering were not just pushing their needs as producers or the needs of the communities around the production areas, at the expense of power consumers. Their demand for a planned ordering programme for power stations of the CEGB would have prevented the extremely costly and wasteful famine and glut ordering which had been typical of the CEGB in the past, and which had enabled power engineering companies to make massive profits at the expense of the consumer. Furthermore, the power engineering workers demanded diversification within the industry towards the production of equipment for combined heat and power stations. This sort of diversification would not only help secure the jobs in power engineering but also provide a cheaper source of heating for the community and reduce our dependance on nuclear power.

Restructuring for what?

In these ways, the resistance of the workers in power engineering exposed very clearly that the NEB's attempt to restructure industry was not a neutral, technical process, with unavoidable costs. *It was a particular sort of restructuring* based on following the dictates of the international market and building up monopolies which could dominate that market. The power engineering workers showed that this was not the only direction in which the industry could go. The power engineering industry and the CEGB could have been reorganised to meet both the social needs for secure employment and the need for cheap electricity. But that would have required workers' control and a government accountable to those workers and consumers.

Herberts and the restructuring of the machine tool industry

Similar possibilities for a restructuring which would benefit producers and consumers (including workers in other industries) existed within the machine tool industry in which, with Alfred Herberts, the NEB had a major stake. One of the main factors behind the relatively poor quality and/or high price of many products in the engineering and motor industries in Britain is the age and lack of productivity of a high proportion of the industries' machine tools. The NEB, controlling both a major machine tool company, Alfred Herberts, and major motor and engineering companies such as British Leyland and

Rolls Royce, was in an ideal position to restructure the industry in a way which would secure employment in machine tool production and improve the product quality and the job prospects of workers in the motor and engineering industry. We saw in Chapter three some of the ideas which workers in Alfred Herberts and Rolls Royce contributed towards this sort of objective. What happened to these proposals? What sort of restructuring took place?

'Banking, not industrial development'

When Benn was Minister of Industry, the workers' proposals were listened to. Joint union-management committees were set up and there was an atmosphere of co-operation. When, for instance, the Alfred Herberts management and their auditors Peat, Marwick and Mitchell presented a report to the Department of Industry suggesting a plan involving 1,400 redundancies as the best way of saving the company from immediate bankruptcy, Benn assured the stewards that this report was requested for form's sake and would be ignored. Everything would depend, according to Benn, on the tripartite discussions between government, management and the shop stewards. This tripartite committee produced a corporate plan involving a simplification of management structure, a modernisation of plant and equipment and a cut in product range. Management also wanted the closure of the Red Lane plant (involving 900 redundancies) but the stewards' commiteee resisted this.

Before any decision was made on this corporate plan, Benn had been removed from the Department of Industry. At this point, the whole process of joint discussions ground to a halt. The stewards' committee described the dramatic change, a change in atmosphere and procedure at least:

> "When Wilson removed Benn from the Department of Industry and put Varley in his place then the difference was immediate. You see, Benn had two principles which he stuck rigidly to: participation and accountability. These principles went out of the window. There was no effective participation. It was a myth from then on. If I remember rightly we were at a meeting with Leslie Murphy (Chairman of the NEB) after Benn's removal and Murphy said, 'Forget participation, go back to the factory and co-operate'. Benn would never have allowed that. I can't give Benn enough credit, especially for the way he received us. Varley would not meet us unless we went through the officials. For instance, there was a time we went to the House of Commons and went to the tea-room with three Coventry MPs. They had to go and vote. They managed to bring Varley back with them. Both the MP's and ourselves were disgusted at the way he emphasised that it could only be for a few minutes and he wasn't setting a precedent! It was as if he was doing us an exceptional favour."

It was not just style and procedure which changed. Once Benn had been removed, Herbert's management felt confident enough to move ahead with its rationalisation plans. In October they announced 550 compulsory redundancies at the Edgwick site and the imminent closure of their grinding business at Red Lane. A campaign by the workforce managed temporarily to save the Red Lane site but management announced a further 460 redundancies in their Coventry plants in late 1977 and another 250 in March 1978. A few months later, management closed the Herbert apprentice school, followed rapidly by the announcement of another 560 redundancies. In all, 2,400 jobs were lost at Alfred Herberts between October 1975 and July 1978, and few of the men concerned would have had much chance of equivalent employment elsewhere in Coventry.

While workers at Herberts received this treatment ex-Herberts directors fared rather better. Sir Richard Young, who had resigned in 1974, received £67,000. That was called 'compensation'. Raine, who had resigned in 1975 along with another senior executive, received in total £115,000.

Political camouflage

All the workers' expectations turned sour. At first, with all the talk in Labour Party policies about accountability, they expected the NEB would make the government *more* accountable than in, say, the nationalised industries. They thought the NEB might provide them with a powerful leverage and channel of communication with the government. But what struck them in practice, however, was the way the NEB *distanced* the government even further from shop floor representatives. Far from ensuring greater accountability of government, the NEB seemed to let the government off the hook. It prevented conflicts from becoming politicised; it warded off direct challenges to the government.

Yet the autonomy of the NEB was quickly forgotten when it suited Herberts management and the government, for example, over wage restraint. One steward commented bitterly:

> "When we went down to them (the NEB) over redundancies with our proposals, they said it was up to management to manage, they were not to be involved. But they're as involved as the Russians are in Afghanistan. Because, when it comes to pay increases, the company has letters from Murphy saying they must not exceed the 5%. Now, they're either involved or not involved. Let's have it one way or the other."

This non-involvement was one reason behind the NEB's response to the workers' suggestion for taking over the Herbert Ingersoll plant as a machine research and development centre. This proposal was quickly dismissed. The reason they gave was that their function was to act as a bank not as an industrial development agency. So much for the 'regeneration of British industry'.

In the meantime, they were spending money for non-industrial purposes "like there was no tomorrow", said one member of the committee. For example, the company recently bought a huge office block, for a new administrative headquarters, some two miles from the main Edgwick plant. In order to finance the furnishing of the new building, the company sold it for £1m profit to another company from which they now lease it. The stewards considered this to be a gross waste of public funds; particularly when this expenditure came after Leslie Murphy had said that there would be no more money for Herberts.

Herbert Machine Tool workers, Coventry.

Ron Doughty, the Herberts convenor throughout this period, made a lengthy statement on the whole experience of the NEB's involvement with Herberts, now nearing its end under the Tory axe. He said he felt the NEB could have provided the basis for effective worker participation. His explanation for the failure was first that:

> "The NEB's terms of reference were to run the company as a private concern and to make it viable. This I believe was the factor which provided the first stumbling block."

Second was the question of confidentiality:

> "This question came up with sickening regularity. We suspect that some members of the Herberts board would not have been able to stomach the idea of workers' participation. What made matters worse was that we knew that some decisions were lacking in judgement. We even put forward viable alternative proposals, only to have them ignored, and yet to know eventually that we were right and they were wrong."

Third, the NEB's terms of reference were too restrictive:

> "The NEB is simply a bank, utilising government money. It operates as a bank with interest terms etc. and, in Sir Leslie Murphy, even has a banker to run it; its terms of reference have to show a profit on investments. These terms of reference have proved restrictive in various ways; most of

97

all they have limited the parameters within which the NEB can effectively act."

The fourth major stumbling block was insufficient accountability of NEB members to either the Government or the trade union movement:

"This allowed for situations which, to be totally frank, could only be described as buck passing exercises. For example, in 1978 the Board of the company presented proposals to the Board of the NEB which catered among other things for a reduction of labour by 720. We were not consulted by the Board of the Company. Yet, the NEB Board sought to say they thought effective discussions had taken place. On seeking to get government departments to intercede, we were told that it is a matter for determination between the company, the NEB and ourselves – you should remember we had four national union officials sitting on the NEB Board. So we were left with only one alternative – to take the company on.

"In effect, we had a socialist government, a state owned company – a situation reminiscent of private enterprise under the Tories."

These, then, have been the experiences of the NEB for workers in our three areas. They have been uniformly negative experiences, especially relative to the expectations which workers in manufacturing industry had built up in the first few months of the government. Are these experiences typical? Is there a good word to be said for the NEB's contribution to employment?

Whitewash

Labour ministers certainly liked to create the impression of active job preservation and creation. When Jeff Rooker, MP for Perry Barr, Birmingham, asked whether "the Secretary of State is satisfied with the way the NEB is discharging its employment responsibilities", Mr Huckfield disingenuously replied, "Its subsidiaries already employ more than a quarter of a million people in the UK". (*Trade and Industry* – 16th July, 1976, p.155.) Most of that quarter of a million came from transferring government holdings from Victoria Street (Department of Industry) to Grosvenor Gardens (NEB), 191,000 jobs in BL and 62,000 in Rolls Royce. By comparison with the effects of the free market, these jobs were saved; but this is not the most important comparison. The idea of allowing BL, Rolls Royce, Alfred Herberts, ICL or Ferranti to collapse was not an option canvassed by anyone, not even by some of the more rabid free market Tories. The question then is, what is the record of job creation in addition to the jobs inherited? The answer to this shows that our experiences were typical of the overall pattern: 32,000 jobs have been lost at BL since 1975, 6,000 jobs at Rolls Royce, 2,400 at Alfred Herberts, and 350 at Tress, among others. Many of these jobs, as we saw in the local reports, have been lost in areas of high unemployment.

There is little evidence that the job *creating* function of the NEB, which Labour's 1975 Green Paper and the 1974 election manifesto proposed, led the NEB to create jobs anywhere, let alone to replace the jobs it destroyed. Only at Ferrantis, when Benn was still at the Department of Industry, were jobs genuinely saved.

Section 3:
Planning Agreements and
Government Aid

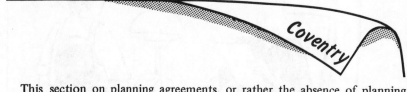

This section on planning agreements, or rather the absence of planning agreements, is mainly about two companies, Vickers and Lucas Industries, which in the original plans, would have been prime candidates for planning agreements. But first, let us look at the one planning agreement which did take place with the private sector: that with Chrysler.

We saw in the last chapter the context in which this agreement was introduced. Chrysler UK was in a deep financial crisis and was threatening almost total closure of its UK plants unless the government bailed them out. That meant £169m in government money — a combination of grants and loans. Management insisted that, even with this government aid, 8,000 jobs had to go. A planning agreement with all its connotations of making management accountable, and government taking a firm line, was a necessary cosmetic to preserve the credibility of the social contract.

The shop stewards and office representatives went along with the planning agreement reluctantly. In the past, they had rejected management's participation proposals because, "We didn't want to be sucked into a management role", commented one steward. Did they think the planning agreement would be any different? One of the TASS representatives from Coventry described their scepticism towards it:

"The stewards were in two minds, especially since, during the negotiations there were disputed points whenever it was the company's view which got into the final agreement."

At the delegate conference to ratify the planning agreement, a proposal just to note the planning agreement very nearly won.

The agreement was really between management and government. Trade union involvement was only consultative:

"It was a con. The two main parties of the establishment were imposing it on the workforce. It didn't take much intellect to see that. But we went along reluctantly thinking it might be an arena to use."

The TASS representatives felt that in general the experience of the planning agreement had confirmed people's worst fears. Few stewards had ever thought that trade unionists would have been able to use the agreement to influence

'Won't keep you a minute, Jackson—just like you to participate in the following decisions'

company or government planning. But some had hoped to use it to get information. That proved to be impossible. Even if useful information was given at the meetings:

> "There was very little report back because everyone was sworn to confidentiality. I must say that 99% of the arguments for commercial confidentiality are just hogwash. There is complete co-operation between the competing companies like Fords and ourselves on the introduction of a new model. But they use the argument so that we usually couldn't get to know, and certainly couldn't tell our members, of their plans for more than a year ahead."

'Confidentiality', then, was one limitation; another was the transnational basis of the company. This, if nothing else, made the planning agreement almost meaningless, as events leading up to the final deal with Peugot were to show. For, as another TASS representative said:

> "The planning agreement applied only to Britain, yet we were a European company with European control structures. Ultimately, we were controlled from Detroit. So a British planning agreement could not control the planning structures."

In what sense then was it a planning *agreement*, an agreement between two parties to plan together, even from the government's point view? What was the role of the civil service in the agreement? An office representative again:

"There was very little difference between the civil service and the company in the answers they gave. I don't know if that reflects a problem with any sort of changes which come from legislation, but that was certainly our experience.

The original design was heavily determined by the Civil Service. Their input was simply organisational. But management used it in a way they could control. The company killed it once they didn't need it. For instance, the planning agreement was going on at the same time as they were negotiating to sell the company. They told the Ministers about that a few days before the sale was complete."

So, in the end, the government's cosmetic washed off, leaving it looking very foolish.

In spite of the uselessness of the planning agreement, some stewards felt that planning agreement meetings served a useful purpose in strengthening their organisation and collective understanding. Many shop stewards would agree with the view of one of the office representatives who said:

"It did have some value because we used it as a forum to question management. If we'd let it happen the way they wanted, it wouldn't have been a two-way process. But we wouldn't let them get away with it. We used to go to meetings, have our discussion with the other shop stewards. And when we met management we were able to expose the lies in the planning process; we did this in front of stewards who might not otherwise have had enough information to fully realise what was going on."

John Sturrock – Report.

Chrysler workers, Coventry.

101

Some were less hopeful about this accidental spin off:

"For the company soon began to keep a strict control over the time-tabling of the meetings. It's fine that, to some extent, it helped to bring convenors into more regular contact with each other. It also meant better communication between staff and senior stewards."

What, then, was the balance sheet which they would draw? The representatives we talked to agreed with Jim Shutt, a TASS representative, when he identified the basic problem:

"The basic problem of the planning agreement principle is that you are in a planning arena talking about minor amendments to what is essentially management's corporate plan. You're not autonomous. You can't talk about things in terms of working class ideals or values.

It's a diversion from building company or industry wide structures out of our own shop floor and office organisations. That's bloody difficult. I don't want to pretend it's easy. But it is the alternative to these three-way structures."

Alternatives to competition

Most of the closures and redundancies looked at in this inquiry have been defended by management and government as unavoidable responses to market pressures. The products are not selling, fewer products must be made, or the present amount must be made more cheaply, or production must be moved abroad where labour is cheaper and/or productivity per worker is higher. This is the argument of management. It was rarely challenged by the Labour Government.

Many of the workers' initiatives which we described in an earlier section implicitly question the competitive priorities of government and management, at any rate where they conflict with employment needs.

Socially useful production

One such initiative – the alternative plan of the Lucas Aerospace workers – made this challenge both explicit and specific. It proposed that, in cases where competitive pressures led to the wastage of skills and resources, invest-ment, product and employment decisions should not be taken on the basis of the traditional market mechanisms and profit criteria. Instead, they argued that workers involved, in contact with other trade unionists, community groups and international workers' organisations, should identify unmet social needs – needs which are not backed by the resources necessary for satisfaction through the market – which their skills, and productive powers could meet.

One group of Lucas workers were in contact with a school for physically handicapped children, where many of the children suffered from spina bifida. The workers were shocked at the primitive apparatus which was the childrens only means of moving about. They designed and made a prototype of a 'hobcart', a self-propelling vehicle shaped to fit the child's back. If this was manufactured on a wide scale, those children's lives would be transformed. Other workers were especially concerned with the numbers of old people who died of hypothermia because they could not afford the high costs of heating. So they designed and made a prototype heat pump, working on the reverse principle of a refrigerator and able to provide a cheap, economical form of heating. Other Lucas workers were interested in transport systems, especially in forms of transport which would be useful for the mountainous terrain of many Third World countries and rural areas in Europe. They designed and made a vehicle which could go from rail tracks to roads with the pull of a few levers. These are just three examples of the sort of products which made up the Lucas Aerospace workers' plan. They illustrate the principle of socially useful production. As we shall see, the problems of getting the company to change its priorities are overwhelming, but even though the Lucas workers had little *positive* success with their company, they were able to defend the jobs the company wanted to destroy.

Part of this defence was based on traditional industrial sanctions. The alternative plan provided the arguments which gave the members confidence to exert these sanctions. In the next chapter, we describe in more detail the relationship between the combine committee's plan for socially useful production and the industrial strength of the workforce. We also discuss the significance and the problems of the idea for workers' plans for other workers faced with the threat of redundancies. What was the response of the government to this initiative? Did the Lucas workers receive the political backing they required?

John Sturrock – Report.

Lucas Aerospace Combine Committee launch their alternative plan.

The government's response: pass the buck

It was late 1976 when the combine committee first approached the Department of Industry to support their plan and to put pressure on Lucas management. Although the combine committee had won support in the Labour Party — the 1976 Labour Programme referred to it approvingly — the committee did not approach the government until the company had refused to negotiate over the plan. Even then, the shop stewards were sceptical about whether they would get a positive response from government, and many combine committee delegates were wary of getting sucked into an endless and futile process of parliamentary lobbying. Their doubts were confirmed by industry minister Gerald Kaufman's reply to their first approach:

"I had been firmly of the view that the proper place for the examination of your ideas must be, at least initially, within Lucas Aerospace. I understand that appropriate discussions are taking place within the normal machinery."

This reply came *after* the company had refused to negotiate on the plan. Management had tried to divert the combine committee with suggestions of informal site-by-site discussions. The shop stewards had firmly rejected this approach. They insisted on negotiations, and negotiations over the plan as a whole. This was made clear to Kaufman. After his reply, the combine committee made it clear for a second time. And again they got the reply:

"For some time the company and its employees have been examining a number of suggestions in your plan within the normal consultative machinery."

Maybe that is what the company wanted but it was not what was actually happening. Huckfield, also at the Department of Industry, laboured under the same comforting illusions. It was a very convenient way of avoiding any government responsibility. He said in a letter to Christopher Price, MP:

"My understanding is that the more promising ideas put forward in the corporate plan are in fact already being discussed within the works council structure that has been set up in various Lucas Aerospace divisions. If there is a feeling that some of the suggestions are not getting a fair hearing, then the work force would have a strong case which they could take up through their established union organisations directly with management."

His last comment hinted at the next direction in which the buck was to be passed: to the Confederation of Shipbuilding and Engineering Unions. The problem must be solved through 'the proper channels' was the argument. Somehow elected shop stewards from all the sites were improper. They were just 'lay' representatives, literally 'unordained'. The CSEU was the proper channel.

The relationship between the Labour Government and workers' organisations

The content of the relationship between a Labour government and the

104

other organisations of the labour movement, is a vital determinant of what pressures shape government policy. So it is worth stopping for a moment to ask why the government was prepared to talk to the CSEU national officials, whose responsibilities cover the whole of engineering, but not to the Lucas Aerospace shop stewards, who have detailed knowledge of the situation and the aerospace industry generally and who have the industrial strength to challenge management's policies.

The CSEU was established primarily to co-ordinate and conduct central national negotiations with the engineering and shipbuilding employers' federations on minimum wage rates, and basic hours and conditions of work. Negotiations on other matters, extra payments, redundancies, additional conditions, took place at a plant level, involving the shop stewards and occasionally local officials. However, as the major corporations have begun to carry out rationalisations on a national scale, and as central government has become increasingly involved in this process, there has been a strong trend towards negotiations at a national company level. Where the negotiations are multi-union and within the Engineering Employers' Federation (EEF), the CSEU national executive have retained a negotiating monopoly.

The CSEU have held on to this monopoly, partly by refusing to recognise combine committees and partly by seeking to prohibit shop stewards from meeting government ministers. When Tony Benn was at the Department of Industry, he encouraged stewards to come directly to see him. The CSEU executive was not too pleased. It asked him to go through 'the proper channels' in future — themselves, and it sent out a memo to all CSEU district committees reminding them that all contact with government ministers should be through the CSEU executive. This usually suited the government ministers (other than Benn): workers directly affected by the redundancies are usually much more insistent and demanding, while the national officials 'understand the problems'!

This is how it proved at Lucas Aerospace when the Victor works in Liverpool, along with the Bradford works were threatened with closure. The final agreement between management, government and the CSEU national officials gave the company £8m in exchange for a general commitment — not an absolute condition — to retain 500 of the 1,100 jobs which they initially wanted to destroy. £8m in exchange for destroying 650 jobs in Merseyside and Bradford, and for showing a non-commital interest in one or two of the workers' alternative products! Not a bad deal for Lucas management! This was a deal which the combine committee refused to accept.

Close relations

The combine committee want to know how it was that Lucas did so well out of a Labour government. At one of the delegate conferences which were eventually called by the CSEU, they demanded an inquiry into the Department of Industry. Two very important exchanges of personnel between Lucas and the Department of Industry especially aroused their suspicions.

i. John Williams was seconded for two years from his post of Deputy Chairman of Lucas Aerospace to be Sir Lesley Murply's right-hand man at the NEB, with special responsibility for British Leyland. Williams moved to the NEB on April 3rd, 1978 (*The Times*, 3.2.78).

ii. Sir Antony Part, formerly Permanent Secretary, Department of Industry, is now on the Board of Directors of Lucas Industries. Sir Antony left the Department of Industry in June 1976, and took up his directorship at Lucas in October 1976.

The Lucas stewards, in their own report on the relations between Lucas and the company, placed responsibility for the biased dealings of the Government on the Department of Industry and 'particularly Sir Antony Part'. They go on to document their grounds for this and to ask a few questions:

> "Sir Antony has himself described the power and scale of operations of this vast Department which he controlled (*Financial Times*, June 25, 1971). With 7 Ministers, 2 Second Permanent Secretaries and 17 Deputy Secretaries he inevitably set the tone of its operations through his control of information channelled upwards to Ministers, and instructions passed down to the Department as a whole.
>
> He was thus formally responsible for the almost daily contacts between his Department and leading British manufacturing companies — at both regional and national level — and the decisions reached in the award and administration of grants, premiums and other awards of public funds made to industry. At the personal level he averaged 'about four business lunches a week' (*The Director*, Jan. 1975), many of these with industrial chief executives. Sir Antony has himself stated (in the article referred to above) that 'as a former intelligence officer in the Army' he attached first importance to communication. He therefore organised a Top Management Group which met under his chairmanship once a week and which planned and reviewed all aspects of the Department's work. He was thus fully involved in the major decisions of his Department, such as the grant of £3.5 million to Lucas in 1971. Sir Antony also had close contacts with the media, and it has recently been revealed by Brian Sedgemore, MP (in the House of Commons, 16 Jan. 1979), that in his opposition to state intervention in industry he had consulted with the press to damage his Minister, Mr Anthony Benn. In view of his key role at the interface between government and industry, it is not surprising that Sir Antony's services should be in demand. It was therefore understandable that he should take a directorship with Lucas whose Chairman, Bernard Scott, is as hostile to state interference as he is. (See, for example, interview with Roland Gribben, *Daily Telegraph*, 19 July 1976.)
>
> We consider it quite wrong that Sir Antony Part's unrivalled knowledge of the inner workings of the Department of Industry and of its previous transactions with Lucas should have been at the disposal of the Lucas board throughout the period when the present reorganisation proposals were discussed with his former Department."

The workers who will be most affected by the proposed closures have had no such special assistance from past or present officials of the Department of Industry.

106

They then quote *The Director* (Jan. 1975) which said of Sir Antony Part's desire to take up a second career in commerce or industry:

> "Unfortunately there are complications here, owing to the civil service rules about retired top bureaucrats going into firms with which they have had official dealings . . . it doesn't look as if there'll be many firms which won't fall into that category for Sir Antony Part."

The stewards then go on to ask:

> "Who authorised Sir Antony to join one of the Department of Industry's most important 'clients' within three months of retirement and what were the grounds for ignoring such a clear conflict of interests?"

Their questions were never answered. But the shop stewards learnt the general answer through their direct experiences. As a result, they are not likely to expect much from a Labour government unless its relations with the workers' shop floor organisations on the one hand, and employers on the other radically change.

A powerful bargaining weapon

To those Lucas stewards, who did believe initially that the government might help, the most revealing and damning experience was the way ministers, civil servants, management and officials alike ignored the report which they, the stewards, had spent three months preparing. If the government had been in any way concerned to get the best possible deal for the workforce, then this report, the product of full interviews and investigations at all the sites, would have proved a powerful weapon.

The report of the shop stewards (manual and staff from all sites) exposed the misleading, simple-minded arguments which management thought would sound convincing enough to the workforce and the politicians. A central argument was that Lucas Aerospace faced shrinking markets, the implication being that the problem is out of management's control. The logical conclusion from this would be that trade union pressure would only exacerbate the problem, and ultimately cause the company's collapse. When the committee investigated the 'shrinking markets', with the help of trade union members in Lucas' marketing and costing departments, they found a very different picture. For all the talk of a general recession, aerospace was and still is going through a major boom. The report documents this. Moreover, it documents many of the major orders which Lucas has turned away, and for which it has refused to tender. (There was the massive order from Boeing, for instance, for G220 gas turbines.) To meet this order Lucas would have had to invest in new machinery and take on new workers. Even with its easy access to government money, Lucas *decided* not to take the risk. In addition to this, there were other orders which again Lucas management *decided* not to tender for because, to do so would contravene important trading agreements with Plesseys, Dowty and GEC. It is not so much that markets have uncontrollaby, of their own accord, shrunk. It is rather that management have decided on a particular strategy to meet their long term profit targets, and have tailored their markets to suit.

Alternative products

The shop stewards were not only concerned to expose the weaknesses of management's arguments. That might provide a basis for resisting management's proposals temporarily, but the committee's brief was to identify a long term future and jobs which would not be saved at the cost of jobs in another plant, company or country. In other words, they were fighting to save and create jobs on their own terms. The title of the report, 'Turning Industrial Decline into Expansion – a Trade Union Initiative', conveys something of the positive, confident spirit with which it was drawn up. So, too, does the committee's work on possible alternatives for Bradford and Liverpool. In relation to Liverpool, for example, they began by arguing that an immediate solution would be to cut down the amount of sub-contracting which was sent outside the company. They showed in detail, with all the information on sub-contracting which they had gathered from the sites, that there was easily enough work to provide all the Liverpool labour force with jobs. But this would not be a real saving of jobs; Lucas workers would keep their jobs, but, most likely, at the cost of jobs elsewhere. And even for the Lucas workers it would not have provided much security. The report therefore goes on to suggest products which could give the Liverpool works a secure future, and could even require the creation of new jobs: products such as the G220, which Lucas had recently refused to accept orders for, fuel control systems, coal-fuelled gas turbines, and the full scale production of the heat pump, for which there was already a prototype at Burnley. For each of these products, there were wider social arguments as well as the case for job creation. The two turbines were especially economical in their fuel consumption and the heat pump provided a particularly cheap form of domestic heating. These products would take some time to become established at Liverpool; in the meantime, Liverpool could produce kidney machines, for which the works were easily adaptable and for which there was a clear social need. In connection with all these products, the Lucas stewards made contact with workers producing similar products in other companies, to work on a more co-ordinated strategy – a sort of trade union planning.

Given all the arguments which entirely undercut management's justifications, given the detailed elaboration of alternatives, and with a group of shop stewards representing all the sites and able, with the combine committee, to take the arguments back to the membership, how could any competent negotiators lose? But, as we have seen again and again, government ministers had no intention of winning victories over Lucas and other big corporations.

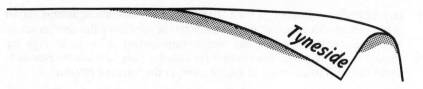

Scotswood: a case for government action

The government's general posture was made most clear during the events that led up to the closure of one of Vickers' Tyneside plants at Scotswood. The problems at the Scotswood heavy engineering plant were typical of those which, according to many government and party spokesmen, are at the root of industrial decline in Britain: research and design was a low priority, the design team having been allowed to fall by nearly 90% since 1960. Most of the products were made under licence from European or American companies, using their designs; investment had been low, machines and buildings were very old. For instance, some of the cranes were 60 years old, and many of the machines were pre-war. Not only this, but Vickers' reluctance to invest in Scotswood lost the plant some valuable orders: an order was about to be made for £250,000 a year of stone crushing equipment by Rexnord, but Vickers did not buy a new large vertical borer (which had been included in the budget for the initial contract) to machine the larger parts. As a result, Rexnord only made orders worth £100,000 a year. Finally, even the machines they did buy did not receive the planned maintenance. There was only an understaffed central breakdown service. As a result, machines sometimes lay idle for several weeks.

'In the National Economic Interest'

Yet, in spite of this gradual run down, Scotswood had more than broken even over the last twenty years, earning a profit during the difficult years 1973-'76, and winning the Vickers export award in 1977. This latter success underlines its contribution to wider government economic objectives; from the balance of payments point of view, both short term and long term, the closure of Scotswood was a loss. It manufactured half the power presses used in the British car industry, which in future will be imported. On the export side, it had more orders for portainer cranes than it could cope with. But these wider considerations of economic policy, let alone consideration for the social needs of West Newcastle, did not enter into Vickers calculations: heavy engineering was just not profitable enough to warrant further investment. The shop stewards discovered that Vickers was aiming for a 30% return on its investment. There was no way Scotswood could meet that. On Vickers' calculations, one of the last remains of heavy engineering on the banks of the Tyne would have to give way to more warehouse and property development.

A lot of talk and no action

Here was a classic case, then, for government intervention, even within the very orthodox objectives of the Callaghan government: strengthening export industries, blocking further import penetration, rebuilding Britain's industrial base, maintaining commercially viable employment in areas of high unemployment. Moreover, the minister for industry does have reserve powers to direct the NEB to intervene in special cases, in the 'national interest'.

This, then, is the sorry saga of the government's attempt to save Scotswood. For eighteen months or so before the closure announcement, the government and, for a time, the NEB, had been having talks with Vickers. The government offered every conceivable grant to persuade them to keep the factory open. As Les Huckfield commented, after the closure announcement:

> "In my experience at the Department, Vickers have had the best offer ever made to a private company. In my opinion, they themselves would have had to find very little new money for Scotswood."

There was even an offer from the NEB to take a major share in a new company.

All this was news to the shop stewards. No one reported the discussions to them. Once they had heard of the talks on the grapevine, they had to prise out the information from the local MP, Bob Brown, who had known of the talks and the possible closure for over three months!

You would have thought that after nearly a year's discussions with Vickers, exploring every way of saving the plant, the government would have tried stronger pressure. There was no shortage of bargaining levers: negotiations over Vickers compensation money for the shipbuilding and aerospace interests were not yet completed; Vickers was heavily dependent on government contracts and on financial aid. If the government was not going to use these levers, its ministers might at least have been franker with the Save Scotswood Campaign about the limited pressure it was prepared to impose on Vickers. Instead, the charade went on. First, a meeting between Huckfield and Robens; Huckfield called the meeting 'reasonable', he even thought that Robens was reconsidering the closure. Then a meeting of campaign representatives, Department of Industry officials and ministers; this was rather more revealing: the campaign committee saw that the ministers were not even prepared to admit they *had* reserve powers, let alone express a willingness to use them. But still the campaign representatives were given the impression that the government would exert *some* control over Vickers.

Peter Tolchard, the convenor at Scotswood and chairman of the campaign committee, summed up his expectations:

> "Right until the last minute I really thought that they could help us, so did most of the works committee. Les Huckfield seemed very much on our side. And Robens was insulting the government, we thought that would polarise things. When the tripartite meeting was arranged our hopes were confirmed. We thought things would get moving from there."

The promises made at a tripartite meeting with Hendon (Chairman of Vickers Engineering), Huckfield, union district officials and the campaign committee, did seem like a partial victory: a delay of several months and an investigation

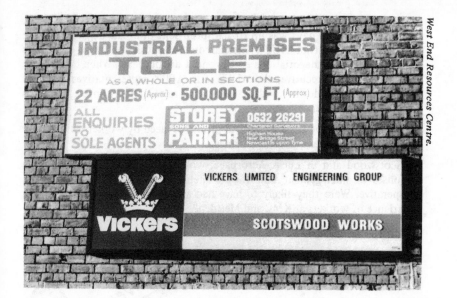

into ways of modernising the plant through a joint committee. The works committee lifted its very effective sanctions against all movement of work on the strength of it. Just as Hendon hoped, it seems. For once the workers had stopped hitting the company in this way, once they had dropped their own material source of bargaining strength, the promises vanished into thin air.

The convenor and local officials found it impossible to get negotiations going. Management insisted on discussing redundancy terms and a phased redundancy programme. The workers staged a last minute occupation. But they felt let down by the government and demoralised. The occupation was lifted, the closure went ahead. They were right to feel let down. The government had been a party to the tripartite meeting; was it not then in a position to keep Robens and Hendon to their promises? The fact that a general election was announced soon after the tripartite meeting weakened the government's position. But it could have blocked Vickers' plans for a few more weeks. That would in turn have strengthened the campaign on Tyneside.

The role of the Government throughout the campaign reveals a pathetic cowardice in the face of powerful industrialists like ex-Labour minister turned industrial baron Lord Robens. He knew they would not touch Vickers. The force that could touch Robens, the shop floor organisation in Scotswood and in other Vickers plants had, in the meantime, been led up the garden path by the very same ministers who, when it came to the crunch, would not even insist that the closure be delayed.

When the campaign asked the CSEU for support it did not get much joy either. The campaign committee proposed a delegate meeting of Vickers' workers from different plants to discuss what could be done to save Scotswood. The proposal did not come before the CSEU executive until a week or so before the 90 days was up (it had been sent in at the beginning of the campaign). The district AUEW official did not push the issue, as he was reluctant to let the negotiations go beyond a district level. When it did come up at the CSEU executive, the AUEW and APEX representatives said that they were already dealing with it. Under the rules of the Confed., that was the end of the matter.

These, then, were the experiences and problems faced by workers in privately owned but government aided companies.

At Scotswood and in Lucas Aerospace, workers were so frustrated by the responses of management that they sometimes raised the possibility of a co-operative. Were they likely to have had any more success? What was the experience of workers at KME and Meriden?

Section 4:
The Co-operatives

Sabotage

In Chapter three we saw the determination of the workers involved to make a go of the KME and Meriden co-operatives, though in neither case did they start off with fantastic optimism. They received encouragement from ministers in the Department of Industry.

However, civil servants at the Department of Industry seemed determined that these co-operatives should not survive. For a start, the co-ops were knowingly underfunded. KME eventually, and only after long arguments, political rows, media hostility, and a vote in parliament, received £3.9m, though the workers had originally proposed a figure of £6.5m.

> "By creating this figure the civil service had put a time and date on the collapse of the new venture,"

is Jack Sprigg's view. For the Civil Service knew that:

> "we needed to spend £200,000 per month on that one item of raw material, as well as wages and other costs, such as rent paid quarterly in advance (£60,000), rates (£160,000 per annum) payable in advance, and that we had to pay for the purchase of the assets from the Receiver (£1.8 million)."

The treatment they gave to Meriden was no better as we shall see later. Would major private corporations have received this sort of treatment?

Remember the £8m given to Lucas Aerospace in Liverpool, in spite of its moving production abroad and hoping to put 650 men on the dole.

Remember the loan, aid and debt write-offs which Vickers received through Kearney, Trecker and Marwin. And yet they say the civil service is neutral! Underfunding was not the only problem created for KME by the civil service. Civil servants drew up what Jack Spriggs described as:

"a carefully-planned scheme to make the rules of the co-operative such that its life, as earlier stated, would be determined from the beginning. They made rules, which the Cabinet accepted, that the co-operative would be a limited liability company under the Companies Act, that we could not borrow from any source, that we could not go into debt other than what is considered commercial under the Companies Act Section 332. They would not allow us to merge or bring about any association with any other organisation which could prove of benefit to us, and the final stipulation was that the Government would declare in the House of Commons that the Grant was once-and-for all, never to be repeated in any shape or form.

All this, in fact, left us with more restrictions than any other company within the public or private sector."

The workers' representatives at KME did eventually manage to get one of these restrictions relaxed: they pressurised the government to allow them to negotiate further finance from whatever source they wished. The civil servants only gave in because, Spriggs says:

"They were convinced that we could not raise finance anywhere outside of Government. We were told this."

But the civil servants proved even more conservative than the bankers and accountants:

"They were totally wrong and in fact we persuaded our own bankers, National Westminster, after a thorough survey of the Company's activities by Peat, Marwick and Mitchell, to grant an overdraft facility up to £320,000, later increased to £600,000."

This overdraft facility, plus the fact that, again after long argument, KME received the Temporary Employment Subsidy, kept the co-operative going two years more than the civil service anticipated. But it was not enough to ensure its survival.

There is a revealing footnote to the experience of the workers at KME which reinforces the points made earlier about the NEB. The shop stewards at KME felt that the co-operative could be integrated into the NEB. This, they thought, would enable them to be part of a more planned sector of the economy which would consciously nurture experiments in workers' control. They made contact with Arthur Ward, Director of the North West Regional NEB, who had been a civil servant at the Department of Industry during the earlier days of the co-operative and, like most of his colleagues, had been completely opposed to the co-operative in the first place. Jack Spriggs continues the story:

"Mr Ward, on a number of occasions, openly admitted his opposition and had told us that if Government forced the issue of the NEB with regards to KME, then all of the Board would resign en bloc. This threat never altered the cause, as far as we were concerned, but as events turned out Eric Varley and Alan Williams were not prepared to risk the resignation of the NEB, and it was because of the risk of hostility that we never entered within the NEB criteria. I feel this was gross political opposition to a future that would have been secured, not only for the co-operative, but for certain aspects of the NEB locally on Merseyside."

Meriden

The chances of survival for the Meridan Motor Cycle Co-operative were also undermined by civil servants putting up every conceivable obstacle and strengthening anybody remotely hostile to the project. At Meriden, the civil service had, in Denis Poore, encouragement from within the industry. He deliberately encouraged the hostility of the NVT workers at Small Heath towards the co-operative, and used this as a bargaining lever to get an extortionate price for the Meriden premises and to ensure that the machines manufactured at Meriden still belonged to him. The Parliamentary Committee of Public Accounts published figures in 1974 which corroborate the former point. They show that Poore received *twice* the officially estimated value of the premises.

While Poore was driving a ruthless bargain with the Meriden workers, the civil service were exerting pressure on the Meriden workers from another point. They were fighting hard to stop funds going to the co-operative. This was more than a silent bureaucratic blocking process. According to Benn (*Sunday Times*, 4.6.78) the battle was:

> "fought with a fierceness and passion the like of which I have never come across in ministerial life."

All the big guns fired down on the co-operative. The Industrial Development Advisory Board (which vets all major applications for funds and on which sit industrialists, bankers, and trade union leaders) rejected Meriden's application more or less outright. The Department of Industry, the Cabinet and the Prime Ministers Offices each referred the issue to the Central Policy Review Staff, which gave a critical and pessimistic report. Finally, the Treasury, the most powerful office of all in Whitehall when it comes to providing funds, opposed the plan.

The Meriden workers battled on. Their determination had its effects on a number of trade union and labour leaders. Jack Jones was the most important. The workers' campaign made their co-operative a major political issue. Jack

114

Jones and others took up their case with Wilson and Harold Lever. Jones used his bargaining position with Wilson in a way which was not to occur again on a major issue of industrial policy. Jones' intervention was decisive. In July 1974, £4.95m was voted to Meriden: £4.2m in loans, plus a £740,000 grant. But the money did not last long. Immediately, the co-operative was required to pay out £3.9m to NVT for the premises, plant and work in progress. The government's accountancy services cost £200,000. This left Meriden with £850,000 in hand, and a debt of over £4m. Benn had to warn the Meriden workers that, should the co-operative fail, no more money would be available. So no one was really celebrating the announcement.

Good news did come in December 1974, though, when the NVT workers at Small Heath gave their support to the co-operative, after they had received a commitment from Benn about the future of their own employment. This was followed by millions of pounds worth of credit for NVT's marketing operations, including the co-operative. By March 1975, after a second winter without money, the co-operative's future seemed secure enough to disband the picket — after eighteen gruelling months. Only 150 of the original 1,150 workforce remained, though others were keen to return once they saw that the co-operative had a chance.

But it also had many things going against it. Like KME, they suffered from being ridiculously underfunded. Also like KME, they suffered from what the present worker directors call 'government interference not intervention':

> "Interference meant that the civil service were continually making life difficult; continually scrutinising the books and making impossible demands on us. We even had to get the approval of a minister before we could work Saturday overtime!"

In addition, they faced the problem that Dennis Poore retained control over the vital sales outlets for Meriden bikes. The government had no powers — had it had the will — to get control for the co-operative. Finally, as a result of the legacy of previous management, they depended on just one production model, using a single motor. Their source of strength was their skill and their tradition of collective organisation; a present worker director explained:

> "We proved that through our own democratic endeavours we could keep the company alive. We'd done a job at Meriden that only the unions with their history of collective working could have done. We broke new ground, particularly in the area of working relationships and in control and determination of work."

It was this, plus the precarious but enthusiastic support of the ministers at the Department of Industry, which saw them through to getting production properly under way by June 1975.

But, soon after Benn was removed from the Department of Industry, one of Varley's first moves was to make it clear that the motorcycle industry would not receive any more money and to withdraw £4m from NVT in export credits. Within months NVT collapsed, putting the co-operative's survival in serious jeopardy once again.

The next stage of the story is too long and involved for this inquiry, but the apparently bizzare involvement of Arnold Weinstock is worth noting.

After the collapse of NVT, the most common explanation of Meriden's problems was, oddly enough, 'weak management'. Geoffrey Robinson, a Coventry MP and ex-manager of Jaguars, had been advising the co-op on management problems and agreed with this view. On this basis, he contacted Harold Lever and persuaded him that with a 'fresh approach' to management and marketing, Meriden could be made to work. Harold Lever found this fresh approach in his friend Arnold Weinstock who offered managerial and technical advice as well as financial aid. This made Varley more sympathetic to the whole project and he agreed to inject a further £2,500,000 into Meriden so that it could buy NVT's marketing operations. Many people were puzzled by Weinstock's involvement. The idea of co-operatives in selected parts of British Industry was being suggested in the columns of the *Times* and in some management circles as the only way of avoiding industrial confrontation. Through co-operatives, workers would learn the realities of business. This might have been a factor in GEC involvement: to set an experimental example. At any rate, the climate was favourable to such an initiative from a major corporation. Perhaps the more immediate factor was GEC's need of government support over the power engineering industry, as we saw earlier. Dennis Skinner went straight to the embarrassing point when he asked in the Commons on Feb 8th 1977:

> "Could it be that the Weinstock involvement in the Meriden plant is a sprat to catch a mackerel?"

In the event, the mackerel got away but the sprat certainly had little life in it, as a co-operative, once the 'fresh approach' — the old approach — to management was introduced. Production continued, but a sign of the changes which had taken place came in September 1977 when Dennis Johnson, the former Senior Shop Steward, a stalwart of the picket and later the co-op's chairman resigned:

> "To me" he said, "the idea of employing full-time executives at around £10,000 a year plus a car plus expenses is in total contradiction to what we were aiming for at Meriden."

In conclusion

The NEB and Planning Agreements

"I wouldn't touch it with a barge pole". Harry Blair's comment on the NEB after the experience of its intervention in the power engineering industry sums up the attitude that many workers now have to the NEB.

They felt they were sold something which turned out to be quite the opposite.

The question this raises is whether, once the White Paper and the Industry Bill had been shifted so drastically from the original proposals, Benn and Heffer should have continued to defend and push the Bill through?

This is one of the questions we will discuss in more detail in the next section, when we describe what little resistance did take place. The question is important because a similar process takes place under every Labour government, leaving socialists and trade unionists on the ground demoralised and confused. It may well happen again. What happens is that the programme agreed at party conference gets defeated or completely transformed in government, but the words, symbols and rhetoric of the government's new policies come from the original programme. So people are not clear until too late that the defeat took place or about the issues involved. As a result, they are weakened in fighting its effects.

A reformed NEB?

It may be that the original proposals themselves contained the seeds of this process, which brings us to the second question raised by the experiences reflected in this report. How far could the NEB be reformed? Should we be fighting for a return to the original NEB?

In our analysis so far, we have argued that a problem with the original analysis was that, although in some respects it appeared to pose a real threat to the vested interests of private capital, at the same time, one of its objectives — competitive success for British industry — required an *alliance* with private corporations, or at least some of them. There are clearly conditions under which such competitive success is compatable with the social objectives of the original policies: full employment and some form of industrial democracy. But was this possible in the '70s and could it be possible in the '80s?

To answer this, we should look first at the conditions in Italy under which a state holding company, plus the equivalent of planning agreements, *did* go a considerable way for a short period towards providing employment in areas of dire social need. As we saw in Chapter one, this Italian experience was an important model for the original policies.

There were three vital features of this early post-war period in Italy which made possible such a socially as well as commercially successful restructuring.

First, most markets for manufactured goods were expanding rapidly as people made good the losses of the war. Second, private financiers and employers were in an extremely weak position both politically and materially following the experience and the defeat of fascism; in many cases they were almost relieved to be subordinate partners in the government's reconstruction of the war ravaged economy. Third, there was a powerful sense of national unity between the labour movement and sections of the middle classes to carry through such a centrally planned reconstruction.

While many of the problems faced by working class people in Britain today are similar to those faced by workers in Italy in the late '40s — regions with high unemployment and social decay, a decrepit industrial base and chronic underinvestment — *the conditions under which these problems have to be solved are entirely different.* For a start, far from markets booming, the capitalist economy internationally is going through not just a minor cyclical downturn but a deep recession from which there is little immediate prospect of recovery. Up to 1973, the volume of trade grew at an average rate of about 8% a year. *It is now some 15% below that trend.* Secondly, as many of the proponents of the alternative economic strategy have themselves shown, the shareholders (or rather shareholding institutions) and top managements of the major corporations are politically very powerful and feel themselves to be financially strong — if it were not for the obstinate strength of shop floor organisation. These corporations may well be in grateful receipt of large dollops of government money, but they are not in so weak a bargaining position vis-a-vis government that they would accept government control over their corporate plans as a condition for this aid. There are numerous more attractive investment opportunities within their global reach. Thirdly, far from their being, as in Italy, any strong impetus towards a national alliance for government-directed reindustrialisation, there is a strong and confident section of the employing and middle classes who feel that the private corporations are the main source of economic dynamism, if only shop floor trade unionism can be tamed.

In sum, while in early post-war Italy a strong socially oriented interventionist programme for government control over investment coincided with the interests of a weak capitalist class faced with booming markets, in Britain such a programme runs in direct conflict with an immensely powerful class of corporate management and financiers competing in a stagnant international economy.

The bargaining power of the corporations today vis-a-vis government, a power strengthened by the pressure of the recession, was the main reason why, in virtually all the cases covered by our inquiry, the social objectives and 'wider responsibilities' contained in the Industry Bill and the NEB guidelines lost out to the requirements of competitive success.

It is true that these social objectives were not pursued with any great conviction by the cabinet and the ministers in charge. The intention to carry through the original spirit of the policies was not there. (This cannot be put down to the minority position of the government in parliament from 1976-79. For, in 1974 and 1975, when the defeats took place, the government had a narrow overall majority. And in any case, many of the problems we have described, such as those of Lucas Aerospace, Vickers, Meriden and KME, did not require legislation.)

We would argue, anyway, that compulsory planning agreements and a larger NEB would not have been enough in the face of the economic conditions and power relationships we have just described. We shall spell this out in our concluding chapter, but a delegate from the Liverpool Trades Council summed up the problem when he said:

> "What the whole experience of the NEB and planning agreements has confirmed for me is that you cannot plan what you do not control and you cannot control what you do not own. That's why the government's buying of shares in selective companies, rather than the socialisation of whole industries, can never lead to general workers' control."

So in the opinion of our four trades councils the NEB is nowhere near an adequate policy. But what are the alternatives? What are the lessons of the other forms of social ownership discussed in this section?

Nationalisation and government financed co-operatives

Workers in the newly nationalised shipyards and in the two co-operatives met a similar fate to workers in the NEB controlled companies: no control over the major decisions concerning their future, such control being blocked by the civil service, the government and/or the pressures of collapsing markets; no consideration of the social costs of job loss, other than in terms of financial compensation; and no questioning of the purpose of the product or to whom it is sold (a point raised very strongly by workers in Rolls Royce, until recently an NEB controlled company).

A drift running through most of the discussions during this inquiry was the feeling that even a left wing Labour government would not have the power to impose genuine social control over investment and production. Unless, that is, such a government was based on a degree of industrial and community readiness and capacity to establish workers' control, such as has never been seen in Britain or, indeed, in any major capitalist power. How to create this power, how to overcome the apathy and sense of powerlessness which exists in so many workplaces and communities, was the most common starting point from which people evaluated the policies for the future, and from which they viewed the issue of reforming the Labour Party. For, whatever the outcome of the struggles within the Labour Party, whether the left do succeed in gaining a stronger position or whether it becomes necessary for socialists to consider creating a different kind of political organisation, it is the growth of this wider industrial and social power which will make socialism possible.

5.
Opposition

Part 1: Silence

"A campaign for wider public understanding and public support" was what Tony Benn called for as the industrial policies came under attack. The Labour Party-TUC Liaison Committee nodded in agreement. But no campaign ever materialised from this or any other body of the Labour Party or the TUC.

The TUC and the Social Contract

At no time were the TUC in the mood for such a campaign. Jack Jones said as much very frankly during our inquiry:

> "To be honest with you, I don't think there was enough understanding of planning agreements and the NEB. We had not sold the ideas to the membership. The TUC Economic Review, where these policies were spelt out, might be intelligible to you but it's not understood or read by most of the members – this is not a criticism of those who wrote the review."

As the cutting edge of the policies was blunted, the TUC stood by, complaining occasionally but not exerting any pressure. So as far as the TUC were concerned it was no time to rock the boat: parts of the social contract which they thought more important were being acted on. As Jones put it in an interview during our inquiry:

> "Other things were being done at the time, the Employment Protection Act, social policies like better pensions and food subsidies. These were important to us. We could not say 'we're not playing', just because of the industrial policies. Anyway, there was not the emphasis in the TUC that there perhaps should have been on the industrial policies. The removal of compulsory powers and so on were not seen as major breaches of policy. Moreover, we were not prepared to do anything which might threaten the Labour government. We were almost more concerned to keep the Labour government in power than was the Labour government itself."

Towards the middle of 1975, around the time of the Common Market referendum, there was also an intensifying atmosphere of financial crisis, which further strengthened the pressures against rocking the boat. The sale of sterling was going on at a massive rate, not so much by those nameless bogeymen the 'gnomes of Zurich' but, as the *Financial Times* said in mid-June, by 'big corporations, including UK corporations'. The main effect of this was to build up pressure on the TUC and back up the argument for them to accept some form of wage restraint, and hold back on the social contract's more radical policies. An additional effect was to ensure that Wilson acted quickly to get rid of Benn, in the interests of business confidence. But, more generally, it combined with the Labour left's defeat in the referendum to create a mood of uncertainty among activists within the trade unions.

Rearguard resistance

Against this overwhelming pressure towards unity, preserving the Labour government, being grateful for anything you could get, a small group of back-bench MPs did put up a rearguard resistance. Throughout the committee stage of the Industry Bill, these MPs attempted, as we saw in Chapter two, to put back into the Industry Bill the Labour Party's original programme: power to enable the NEB to acquire companies even if the existing shareholders were unwilling to sell, a larger budget for the NEB, obligatory planning agreements and stronger disclosure of information clauses. One of the MPs concerned was Audrey Wise who described how:

> "We were always being warned against bringing the government down. But this was a completely phoney argument. The government was quite safe because the Tories were cuddling up to our front bench on these issues. It was the Labour front bench against us back benchers. And that went for the early period as well as under Varley."

So these amendments could never get anywhere. And they had little meaning to workers outside the four walls of the standing committee room, however hard the MPs tried:

> "We did bring the committee to an end once by walking out so that it was without a quorum. We did our best to introduce an element of drama", said Audrey Wise, though, as she admitted,

> We failed to take the message outwards. That's partly because there aren't the channels of communication. The press aren't going to tell workers of the efforts which are made on their behalf in Parliament, and we don't have any media of our own. We don't have the right sort of organisation either, bringing together industrial and political issues at a grass roots level. That's why factory branches are going to be so important."

Trade Unionists on the Board: accountable to whom?

Another reason why shop floor trade unionists found it difficult to discover what was going on was that the trade union leaders who sat on the NEB were under no obligation to report back to their members. As Jack Jones told us:

> "They (the trade unionists on the board) might talk to David Lea and the Economics Department (of the TUC) but that's about as far as it would go. And that would be informal."

Formally, the trade unionists on the NEB at national and at regional level were not representatives. They were not elected. They were appointed by the Secretary of State for Industry, who would consult the TUC or individual trade union leaders informally, in the same way as he would consult the CBI before appointing industrialists to the Board.

Yet these individual trade union leaders, Harry Urwin, Hugh Scanlon, David Basnett, and Jack Lyons were only on the Board *because they were trade union leaders.* * To many trade union members, however, it seemed as if these

*Though they never met prior to NEB meetings to agree on trade union interests.

men *were* trade union representatives. Shop stewards in NEB owned firms assumed that these trade union leaders would in some sense represent their interests, that they would, at least, contact trade union members in NEB factories about the Board decisions affecting them. Shop stewards at Tress, Alfred Herberts and British Leyland, Speke all tried to make this contact themselves. A shop steward from Alfred Herberts described the response:

> "We just got letters of acknowledgement saying Scanlon or whoever was away but would deal with the matter as soon as possible. We heard nothing more."

Neither was there any accountability at a regional level. Take the North East for example: one demand of the Save Scotswood Campaign was for NEB investment in Scotswood. The director of the Northern Region NEB, Mr Connolly, had made it clear that the NEB were not interested in investing in Scotswood. The only trade unionists on the Regional Board was David Williams from the G&MWU, again appointed by the Department of Industry without any elections and with no obligation to report back to the regional trade union movement. The Scotswood campaign was not even able to make direct contact with him. They were told that this would be 'putting on undue pressure'.

So in terms of information or support, trade unionists in the NEB meant nothing. But their presence on the Board was another factor which contributed to the false impressions which trade unionists had of the NEB.

The Grand Illusion

What effect, if any, did the lack of communication about the defeat taking place in the House of Commons have on workers in the localities? In most cases, the left wing build-up of the government's industrial policies in the early days, when Benn was at the Department of Industry, created a positive impression in the minds of many trade unionists which was not contradicted until the reality of the industrial policies hit them directly, when it was usually too late. At Tress Engineering, at British Leyland, Speke, at Alfred Herberts, at Chryslers, at Vickers (and only just avoided at Parsons), the workers' illusions about the radical nature of the new industrial policies were played on by management. This was not necessarily a conscious ploy by management, but workers' representatives were significantly disarmed by being unaware of the true nature of the policies until too late.

Turning defeat into 'a step forward'

However, it was not simply lack of communication which left these false impressions. It was also the content of Labour Party statements and the resolutions passed at party conferences which reinforced these illusions by welcoming the diluted industrial policy as if no really serious defeat had taken place. According to this view, all that was needed were some improvements. For example, the resolution carried in 1975, moved by David Basnett of the G&MWU, welcomed:

> "the introduction of legislation to set up a National Enterprise Board and a Scottish and Welsh Development Agency, and a system of planning agreements with industry and the trade unions."

It then went on to reassert a weak version of the earlier party programmes, proposing that:

> "The planning agreement system should be supported by a policy of indirect sanction, including making selective financial aid, selective price relaxations . . ."

The NEC's statement to the 1975 Labour Party conference "Labour and Industry: The Next Steps", similarly gave the impression that the Industry Bill was a good beginning. There was no hint that it might be a very different animal from the policies originally intended. After it had spelt out the policies in the Industry Bill, as amended in the committees, policies over which Eric Heffer nearly resigned, the statement went on to say:

> "These are important achievements. But we believe that they can mark only the beginning of Labour's drive to carry through its programme. The Government must now begin in earnest to involve itself in the kind of economic and industrial planning originally envisaged in Labour's Programme. It will need to support this planning with new statutory powers, and with a powerful, efficient and profitable public sector in manufacturing. And it will need to launch a massive new investment drive, supported by new initiatives in the fields of manpower and of finance for investment."

You would think reading this that the problem with those drafting and amending the Industry Bill was that they had simply not yet gone far enough. The foundation stones already had been laid; the house just needed to be built. *There is no hint that Labour's initial programme had been positively and aggressively defeated.*

Media images

The press reinforced the impression that the policies had not changed. This partly reflected the CBI's determined press campaign to eliminate any clause which enabled the state or the unions to interfere with management's right to manage business as they wished. Throughout the period when the Bill was in its Committee stages, the *Mail*, the *Express*, the *Sun* and the *Telegraph* continued to refer to the Industry Bill as "Benn's Red Revolution" and the "hard-line Socialist measures in Mr Benn's controversial Industry Bill". The *Daily Mirror* told its readers that the Industry Bill was "designed to shift the balance of power towards the workers" and that "it is seen by both Labour and Tories as a major advance of socialism". In this sort of atmosphere, it is not surprising that shop stewards and convenors at Tress, Vickers and Chrysler looked to the NEB for protection against the ravages of private industry, only to find themselves devoured all the more effectively. Rather like the experience of Red Riding Hood, the fearsome instruments of the corporate state seemed to be wearing socialism's clothes.

Socialist Worker.

No focus for action

This, then, brings us to the content of the policies themselves. The last point indicated a lack of sharpness in distinguishing socialist industrial policies from forms of state intervention which merely carry out the wishes of private employers more ruthlessly than private employers would have the power to do themselves. This explains why the defeat of the policies was so easily blurred. Another aspect of the policies which explains the lack of pressure against this defeat is their abstract and general character.

Benn himself at the inquiry's national tribunal pointed to this problem from the point of view of mobilising industrial pressure:

"The NEB was only an instrument, we never named the companies, whether we should have done was a subject of controversy. If you don't name a company you can't mobilise. You can't mobilise workers from un-named companies to support a general policy. With the NEB, you can only mobilise workers in a case like Alfred Herberts when, before the employers admitted the company was in trouble, George Park (the local MP) brought a delegation of shop stewards to see me; they were mobilised to use the instruments of the industrial policy because they knew the company was going bust. The principles behind the NEB mean that it is primarily a reactive, responsive instrument. That's an important problem to think about further."

He went on to contrast the NEB with the direct nationalisation of shipbuilding and aerospace:

126

"In that case, a tripartite committee of the Labour Party, the TUC and the CSEU worked out proposals, took it through the Confed. conference, the Labour Party conference and the TUC, and talked to shop stewards about it. In this way, people could be mobilised around specific proposals in advance. Where you are specific you can mobilise people in the industry; where your policies are general in character you'll only mobilise in the lame ducks."

The clearest illustration of the difficulties faced in mobilising around the general principles of the NEB and planning agreements, is the demise of the Tyne Shop Stewards Conference. On Tyneside, such an unofficial local organisation did a lot to educate and inform shop stewards about the general principles behind the Party's policies and their relevance to workers on Tyneside. The discussions which it organised probably led workers to be more demanding of the NEB and government ministers when their companies were in trouble. It also helped to get several shop stewards combine committees off the ground. It put out some general propaganda against the changes in the original industrial policies, but it was not able to organise any local resistance to these changes. It did not survive the sacking of Benn from the Department of Industry.

What if the companies had been named?

Would a naming of companies to be taken over by the NEB have led to a comparable building up of expectations leading to action? It would be unlikely in many cases, especially in the less traditional industries, where workers have come to expect very little from nationalisation. The delegates to the Lucas Aerospace Combine Committee expressed this when they discussed how they should respond to the new opportunities presented by the Labour government. Many of them reported back on the difficulty of winning shop floor support for nationalisation, after the experience of the already nationalised industries. This led to the Combine Committee deciding that, before they could win support for social ownership and workers' control, they needed to campaign over the sort of plans which showed what social ownership would be *for*. This would make social ownership less abstract and it would expose the social irresponsibility of a management whose responsibility is to the shareholders and to the requirements of private profit. Moreover, the fight for such plans in response to redundancies would build up the strength of organisations that in the future would be the basis for workers' control.

Part 2:
Resistance

It is worth looking at the campaign of the Lucas Aerospace shop stewards in some detail; similarly with the campaign of the workers in power engineering which we referred to briefly in Chapter four. For, while socialists in parliament were unable to carry through legislation that would control the powerful corporations, these industrially based organisations did manage, for the time being, to block the rationalisations and redundancies which the corporations were intending. They did, at least temporarily, win the argument for social rather than commercial criteria to determine investment and operating decisions. How did they do it? What do their experiences, their successes and their reflections on their mistakes tell the rest of us about how the power can be built up to carry out policies based on social need?

Power Engineering: the campaign for Drax B

At Parsons, the campaign began in March 1976 when the managing director told the unions of his plans for redundancies. He told them that orders were drying up and the recession was deepening. 400 jobs would go in 1976 and 900 in 1977.

Workers at Parsons had already had experience of fighting redundancies because of the cyclical market pressures on the industry. They had won an important victory in 1971, stopping 950 redundancies. The key to their success then was a joint committee of representatives of all the unions in the plant, staff and hourly paid – 'the Corporate Committee', as it was called. Over-confident perhaps, as a result of their success, they had allowed the corporate committee to disintegrate. But they had learnt from their mistake, which the March announcement only confirmed: "If we only learnt one lesson, it should be that we will never disband again; we will never rely on the Company to pull us through", commented one member of the Committee. So the different unions came together to re-constitute the corporate committee and discuss a policy and strategy to cope with the situation.

The main problem was to identify an alternative to the redundancies, a focus for trade union and political pressure. The obvious general need was for a steady ordering programme from the CEGB, and an end to the famine and feast cycles which we described in Chapter two; more help for exports was important too. But something more immediate was needed. The extension of the Drax Power Station in Selby was planned for the early 1980s; that order could be brought forward as a first move towards a steady ordering programme.

The problem of lack of orders and the threat of redundancies was not just a problem facing the Parsons workers. Workers at Babcock and Wilcox and at Reyrolle Parsons had the same threat hanging immediately over their heads. At Clarke Chapmans the threat was not so immediate, but it was there nonetheless. So, from the Parsons Corporate Committee the campaign moved outwards to create the 27 man committee – nine from Parsons, nine from Clarke Chapmans, nine from Reyrolle Parsons. The Tyne and Wear District Confed. gave this committee official recognition – a virtually unprecedented step. The CSEU does not normally recognise shop stewards committees beyond the plant level. At the same time, the committee made contact with workers at Babcock and Wilcox in Renfrew and at the various GEC plants throughout the country.

An important impetus to get organised on an industry wide basis was the fact that the Government was now actively seeking a "solution" to problems of the power industry. In July, the Government referred the whole matter to the CPRS "on an urgent basis". The future of the power industry was fast becoming a national political issue. Unless the workers got themselves organised on a national political level, the future of the industry could equally rapidly be taken out of what little control they had. Plant based, locality based organisation was not enough; neither were traditional trade union sanctions, they did not give the workers sufficient leverage over the powers that made the decisions: in this case, the government. The Parsons Corporate Committee, along with the 27 man committee, took the first step in a more national and political direction with a lobby of the TUC annual conference. Representatives from other plants from other areas were there too – though not from all the GEC plants – and a very well organised lobby took place.

At the TUC lobby, the representatives from the different plants decided to arrange a meeting in Carlisle for shop stewards and office representatives throughout the industry, in order to create an industry wide organisation. This was held on September 22nd. The main task at that time seemed to be to develop a trade union policy, to put it to the CPRS, and to start winning support for it among MPs, the Labour Party, union executives, related unions like the NUM and to build up an understanding of it and support for it on the shop floor. The policy agreed at the first meetings focused on the demand for a steady home ordering programme starting with the bringing forward of Drax. This was the demand which trade union representatives stressed when they met the CPRS. Once the CRPS report was published, with its proposals for restructuring, the shop stewards put forward their own conditions for restructuring. These were: that no one company must have a majority share-holding and that the balance should be held by the NEB. There should be no redundancies. The long term aim must be the social ownership of the industry.

For the first five months, senior shop stewards from GEC attended the Power Engineering Industry Trade Union Committee (the name of the organisation set up at the Carlisle meeting) but, as soon as the main issue became opposition to GEC takeover and the distribution of Drax mainly to Parsons and Babcock and Wilcox, the majority of the GEC delegation stopped attending. This was not a matter of the committee's policy becoming too narrow and basing itself only on the interest of workers at Parsons and Babcock and Wilcox. On the contrary, the committee's policy on the distri-bution of orders was based very firmly on the *employment needs* of *all* the different workforces. The needs were most urgent at Parsons and Babcock and Wilcox; detailed redundancy figures had been given in both instances. Delegates from Clarke Chapman's and a minority from GEC accepted that Parsons and Babcock and Wilcox should get the bulk of the Drax B order. Further distribution of the order should be made according to the employ-ment situation within each company. PEITUCs policy, then, was not narrow;

the problem was that the GEC '16' (as the committee of GEC senior shop stewards was called) had been convinced by GEC management that what was good for Arnold Weinstock was good for GEC workers. Instead of becoming involved in formulating a policy to meet the needs of workers throughout the industry, they supported resolutions like the following one which was passed at GEC plants after the takeover bid had failed.

1. A. GEC believe that they are the best equipped to run the turbine generator industry.
   B. It would appear from recent press reports that the Government share this view.
   C. The trade union members employed by GEC are also of this view.
2. GEC trade union members are prepared to co-operate in the establishment of the single technology providing that it is not done to the detriment of their security of employment.
3. GEC employees are not prepared to see their employment prospects put in jeopardy by preferential treatment being given to Parsons by the advance ordering and placing of DRAX.

(Passed by the GEC Turbine Generators Joint Trade Union Combine Committee, 28th April 1977.)

So, not only was PEITUC up against the most politically influential of British industrialists, a Cabinet committed to cutting public expenditure including public ordering programmes, and an NEB committed to rationalising British industry, but also most of the representatives of at least one quarter of the workers in the industry were supporting the other side. It is not surprising, then, that when the CPRS report came out in late 1976 the industrial commentators predicted the worst:

> ". . . the most likely outcome seems to be a forced marriage between GEC and Parsons, no forward ordering programmes and many redundancies."

The marriage between GEC and Parsons came literally within a day of being forced through; and the CEGB came very near to blocking any forward ordering programme. If the power relations between major industrialists, the Civil Service and the Cabinet had been able to shape the decision making processes in the normal way, these predictions would no doubt have proved accurate. But they took no account of a less predictable but potentially decisive power: the power of those who, more often than not, are simply on the receiving end of the decisions. By mid 1977 the industrial press were having to admit this power. Articles on the power industry refer to the government's positions which:

> "appear to have been abandoned in the face of opposition from the unions at Parsons" (*Financial Times* 19.5.77.);

to Varley's:

> "underestimation of the determination of trade unions to have their say in matters of industrial reorganisation";

to what was seen as the basic problem:

> "how to persuade unions and employees at Parsons to accept a merger

with GEC on terms which would give GEC majority control."

By July 19th, the Drax B order had been made to C.A. Parsons and Babcock and Wilcox with no restructuring conditions. At one point during the campaign, Tony Benn, speaking on the restructuring, stressed that because the companies were privately owned:

"The powers do not lie with us to impose a solution."

That may be true of parliament on its own, but the workers in the industry created a power which eventually produced a solution entirely against the will of one of the most powerful private managements in the country.

How did the workers in power engineering create that power?

We have referred briefly to the foundations of their organisation: close union co-operation at plant level; regular bulletins; section meetings and mass meetings for the membership; unity across plants regionally and nationally, based on a clear uncompromising policy for workers throughout the industry. But they recognised that to be successful in a tough political campaign this rank and file level organisation was not enough. They had to make sure the official leadership would support the policies they had developed at their shop floor level.

The TASS representatives at Parsons are very clear about the role of officials:

"We do things ourselves as far as possible. But once we knew we had a political campaign on our hands we did everything to keep the officials involved."

'Everything' literally was everything, from pressing successfully for the Confederation to call delegate conferences (at that time this sort of Conference was very unusual) to interrupting the executive's breakfast at the Royal Station Hotel to present their case and, finally, to lobbying Moss Evans in the toilet at York! In all this, they had the strong advantage of having the full backing of their district CSEU. National Confed. officials might have given a groan when they caught sight *yet again* of the power engineering workers, but the constant pressure paid off.

When the campaign began, only a tiny minority of the CSEU executive supported the case for Drax B against a GEC takeover. Others tended to accept the government view and some were influenced by the divisions within the GEC workforce. The first success was a CSEU delegate conference in December. Entry to this was mainly restricted to delegates chosen through the union executive, but the Parsons' representatives had credentials from the sympathetic Tyne and Wear District Confederation, so they got in to present the case for Drax B. The arguments were well documented by a report on the power engineering industry, prepared for AUEW-TASS by the Newcastle based Trade Union Studies and Information Unit and by a document from the Tyne and Wear District Confederation. The general case presented in these documents became CSEU policy. But the pressure had to be constantly kept up to harden the waverers. For, members of the CSEU executive were under considerable pressure from Varley on the other side. Newspaper reports give some hint of the fact that the CSEU's support could not be taken granted:

> "In spite of the uncompromising line of the Confederation yesterday, some union leaders think that the industry needs to be reorganised, and that some redundancies are virtually inevitable." (*Financial Times* 1976.)

or

> "the unions are beginning to accept that they will be overruled on this demand (NEB control). . . . The government is therefore trying to persuade the national representatives of the unions that substantial redundancies are inevitable, irrespective of the part played by the NEB. Mr Varley has had some success in persuading them that the over capacity cannot be entirely filled in the short term, however the industry is organised." (*Financial Times* Feb. 19th, 1977.)

John Sturrock – Report.

But whenever Varley spoke to the Confederation, the executive would know that outside there would be a delegation of their members from the power engineering industry, who would hold them to their initial commitment.*

*Since then, an important breakthrough in terms of lay representation on Confed. subcommittees has been made in relation to power engineering. There are now three representatives of PEITUC on the CSEU power engineering committee; one from N.G. Parsons, one from Babcock and Wilcox and one from GEC.

At the same time as the power engineering workers put continuous pressure on national trade union leaders, they kept up a constant campaign to win support from MPs and ministers. This campaign was two-pronged. On the one hand, building up local and regional support on a mass scale for the demands which would save Parsons and Babcock and Wilcox. On the other hand, through persistent lobbying, constantly reminding the MPs and ministers that this popular support was there and would not go away until Drax B had been brought forward. In these two ways, and by the strength of their arguments, the power engineering workers turned the pressure for Drax B and the strength of opposition to Weinstock into a major political constraint on the Labour Government's room for manoeuvre.

The parliamentary lobbying was on a massive scale; it was not just the usual matter of lobbying one or two MPs and having an interview with a minister. The first lobby was on the 20th October, 1976. It was organised through the northern group of MPs. Sixty-two MPs, and fourteen ministers gathered in the Grand Committee room of the House of Commons to hear the case presented by over seventy shop stewards. But the shop stewards were not the only people presenting a case to the ministers. As the *Financial Times* reports:

> "Over Christmas, the civil servants held a series of meetings among themselves, which resulted in complete agreement, even from the Treasury Ministry, that the ordering of new power stations to help the industry should be conditional on agreement on mergers."

The case presented by the civil service was the one which the Cabinet preferred.

> "On January 12th the Cabinet approved the main recommendations, and talks with the industry started in earnest." (*Financial Times.*)

While these "talks with industry" went on throughout January and February, two more lobbies were organised, one by the Newcastle City Council and one by C.A. Parsons Corporate Committee. On one of these lobbies, some of the Parsons delegates got a good indication of the sort of opinions which were prevailing in Cabinet circles when they went to see Bill Rogers. Rogers' main theme was to point out how unjustified was their opposition to Weinstock. His argument was that Weinstock was an excellent businessman, and had proved himself time and time again. The Parsons workforce expected this sort of thing from Tory ministers, but they had not heard a Labour minister being quite so blatant, so they came in hard. One of them described what he said to Rogers:

> "Has anybody in the government, any committee in the Cabinet, ever worked out the cost of sixty-odd thousand redundancies", I said, "how long these people stay on the dole, what upheavals there are and nervous breakdowns, extra hospital treatment, and so on? Has any Cabinet committee gone into this, worked out the total cost and then said, 'Weinstock is a good businessman'? Because, unless the other side of the coin is turned over, and you do those kind of sums, you can't say that Weinstock is a good businessman, just because he happens to make a profit."

But, as we saw earlier, it was Weinstock's ability to make profits for GEC which convinced the NEB and the Department of Industry. If Weinstock would not accept NEB's involvement then, as far as they were concerned, GEC takeover was the only solution. Reyrolle Parsons' group management also would have accepted that solution had it not been for the derisory offer which GEC made for the company and if it had not been for the intransigent opposition of the Parsons' workforce.

The decisive meeting between the Chief Executive of Reyrolle Parsons (MacDonald), the managing director of Parsons (Bob Hawley) and the Parsons' corporate committee took place on April 21st. MacDonald had just returned from the House of Commons. He opened by saying there were now only two options: Parsons going it alone without the guarantee of Drax or Parsons being controlled by GEC and Drax being given to the new, restructured company. A member of the corporate committee continues the story:

"He kept emphasising that it would be extraordinarily difficult to go it alone. It came up again and again. Employment prospects would be grave if we go it alone, he kept saying.

His argument was that Parsons would like to go to GEC and have talks on safeguards with regard to employment for the future at Heaton. We should see what options are available from GEC without commitment. That was his play.

That was when the corporate committee said that under no circumstances do we go down to see Weinstock, even without commitment, to see what options are open. For, as soon as the Government see that there are any talks between the Parsons' workforce and the GEC management, then the pressure goes off them to place Drax."

MacDonald considered it out of the question that the Government could be pressured to go against the wishes of the CEGB and of so powerful an industrialist as Weinstock, and place Drax B without the type of restructuring they wanted. In a sense, that was true from the Parsons management's point of view; they were in a weak position; their power was minimal. The corporate committee though, felt they, the workforce, together with the wider labour movement on Tyneside, and with the support of power engineering workers elsewhere, *did* have the power to force the Government to bring forward Drax on their terms. So, one of the committee continued:

"We really set to and blasted them on behalf of the corporate committee. We repeated that never, under any circumstances, will we go down to GEC. And then we said, we will launch, as the corporate committee, the biggest political campaign that the North East has seen for a long time.

MacDonald and Hawley were very nervous at this. 'Are you sure you know what you are doing', was MacDonald's response. The talks for the merger had all been set up. They would have begun on Monday. MacDonald had to leave the meeting and ring a civil servant called Bullock, to tell them the merger was off."

Another reason why Hawley was so nervous became clear at the end of the meeting, after the civil servant had been told that the merger was off. Hawley told the corporate committee that the work situation at Parsons was even worse than expected. Consequently, there would have to be 1,600 redundancies by 1978.

It was after this meeting that the campaign took off and became a genuinely mass campaign. First, the argument for a strong campaign had to be won among the workers at Parsons. So, throughout the following week, meetings took place in every section and every office. All this led up to a mass meeting of different unions. The feeling was strong. Every meeting decided to back up the Drax campaign, to fight on for the order, to reject all approaches from the GEC, and to press for social ownership, or, second best, for control by the NEB.

Once support within the factory was secure, the next thing was to get a wider political initiative off the ground. After all, this was a political campaign, not primarily against the Parsons' management. By this time they were not a major factor in the campaign, so long as they put no obstacles in the way of the corporate committee. The first opportunity for such a political initative came when Callaghan brought President Carter to the North East. The corporate committee decided to organise a demonstration, much to the dismay of Callaghan himself and some of the Northern MPs, who would have preferred the "Parsons lads" to stick to lobbies, and warned the corporate committee against the demonstration.

One of the reasons this demonstration was so important was that it began to lift the feelings of pessimism and fatalism of people in Tyneside about what seemed the inevitable decline of the area. One of the corporate committee described the support they got and their plans to build on it, in the *Workers' Chronicle,* the Newcastle Trades Council newspaper:

> "People spoke to us all along the way. There is no doubt that there is enormous sympathy in the area for our fight back. Our main problem is to maintain the campaign, and it has been agreed at meetings of representatives throughout the factory that another march will be held. This time wives, husbands, children and friends will take part. The local trade union movement will also be invited to play a major part, and other workers from factories throughout the area will be invited to join us in a *massive* demonstration, rejecting the high unemployment in the area."

So, while some members of the corporate committee, along with others from PEITUC, were keeping up the lobbying pressure, the others stayed on Tyneside to organise one of the biggest demonstrations which the area had seen for years. Other workers were fighting redundancies at the same time, like the workers at Vickers Scotswood and in the shipyards. The demonstration was a focus for them all. The slogan common to them all was "Don't let the North East Die". Contingents from different factories and different parts of the city converged on the Civic Centre to unite to save the area by strengthening the pressure for Drax B.

As the pressure built up on Tyneside, Varley and the Department of Industry were making a desperate last attempt to win over the CSEU executive to the government's restructuring proposals. But, by 18th July, the Cabinet had decided that proposals for a GEC-Parsons merger had hit an immovable obstacle. That same obstacle, the campaign in the power engineering industry and on Tyneside, was also the force that made it necessary to give Drax B primarily to Parsons. If Drax was not ordered from Parsons, and management carried out its threat of 1,600 redundancies — as it would — the government would be clearly seen to be responsible. The campaign had made sure of that. The political risks of such a responsibility would be too great. Already, Northern Labour MPs were restless over the government's devolution proposals; allowing Parsons — the largest employer on Tyneside — to collapse would be the final straw. Moreover, the strength of working class support for the campaign could, in the event of the government's refusal to order Drax B, spark off an occupation which would have brought the spectre of UCS much nearer home. So, on 19th July, Tony Benn announced, to Tory cries of "what a surrender", that Drax B would be ordered mainly from Parsons without any further conditions.

Lucas Aerospace: blocking management's plans

The campaign of the Lucas Aerospace workers illustrates some of the same relations between industrial and political organisations as the campaign of the Parsons corporate committee. As in the power engineering industry, the impetus and the direction of the campaign came mainly from strong, industrially based organisations. This was not just a matter of these organisations having 'the muscle'; it was also that they had developed their own policies for the future of the industry. In the case of power engineering, it was ordering, investment and restructuring policies within the existing product range — though workers in power engineering, too, are considering demands for diversification according to social need.* In the case of Lucas Aerospace, the workers' plan — as we saw in Chapters two and four — involved a challenge to the purpose of the company's production decisions and to the priorities of government expenditure.

In both cases, the fact that workers' industrial organisations had positive policies for the future of the industry and the markets they produced for, meant that these organisations took on a political role. They campaigned over issues which have traditionally been the exclusive concern of governments and employers.

The way that political and industrial action went together varied in the two campaigns, because the immediate source of the threat to jobs in the two cases was different. In the case of Lucas Aerospace, management announced redundancies of 1,000 in 1977, and 2,000 in 1978, not because of lack of orders, but because of a rationalisation programme closely connected with new technology and a switch to more overseas production. Workers at Lucas Aerospace had anticipated these rationalisations. The increasing investment in capital intensive plant and the trends towards moving production abroad

---

*Mainly for combined heat and power systems.

has led the combine committee to develop stronger tactics for fighting redundancies.

For this to have become possible, the joint combine committee had previously won credibility and support among the plant membership through successful united action on wages, pensions, health and safety, and some of the previous small scale redundancy threats in 1971. In most plants there was a strong relationship between the combine committee and the plant organisation; as a result, combine committee recommendations really meant something. The committee normally acted as a catalyst and as a support for plant action, and tried to avoid the danger of becoming a substitute for plant strength. From the start, the combine committee emphasised the need for unity of staff and hourly paid; though a section of hourly paid workers had been persuaded by the company's offer of negotiation rights to stick to a separate hourly paid 'combine'.

Not only were the Lucas Aerospace workers prepared organisationally, but they already had their own policies and arguments in the form of the alternative corporate plan which had been drawn up in 1975 and 1976. Terry Moran, an AUEW shop steward at Burnley, where 300 redundancies were threatened as part of the 1977 rationalisation, commented on the importance of the workers' plan in the fight against redundancies:

> "It made our job as shop stewards trying to save those jobs much easier when people could see that there *should* be a future in their jobs; and, very important, a future which they felt would be worth having a fight over. Heat pumps was the main demand at Burnley. My members knew from their own experience of how old people suffer in the winter, that heat pumps were needed, as a form of low cost heating. With this sort of campaign we had none of the usual bother, men running after the big redundancy carrot. We saved all the jobs."

An important reason why they saved jobs — in Birmingham and Liverpool, as well as Burnley — was that the plan helped to create the will to fight. In the atmosphere created by the drawing up of the plan, which had been done at a plant level as well as within the combine committee, it was much easier to win support for industrial sactions for an overtime ban, for selective blacking, and for the threat of more to come.

In March 1978, management tried again. This time, 2,000 redundancies were threatened, with factory closures in Liverpool, Bradford and Coventry. Management had learned some lessons: they had drawn the government and the CSEU into discussion of the redundancy plan before they announced it publicly or to the shop stewards. This tactic did succeed in putting the combine committee in a weaker position than over the earlier redundancies. The reason why the combine's position was weakened by the involvement of the CSEU has to do with the inappropriateness of the existing trade union structures for challenging company and government decisions over investment and products. Once the company had involved the government and the CSEU, negotiations over the redundancies were in the hands of the CSEU executive.

But the CSEU has no provisions for recognising shop stewards' combine committees. As a result, it had no contact with the Lucas stewards or any discussion of their alternative plan before 1978, even though several constituent unions of the CSEU had given it their support.

This feature of national trade union organisation is one reason for its inability to anticipate industrial problems and draw up and campaign for solutions in advance. The very constitution and structure of the CSEU, for instance, makes it a purely *reactive* body, brought in to negotiate when there is a problem, without any of the necessary resources to work out independent policies. Not only is it itself limited in this way, but its constitution means that it discourages, rather than supports other, 'unofficial', multi-union attempts to anticipate management and prepare alternative policies well in advance.

The Lucas Aerospace Combine Committee, however, did manage to break through these constitutional restrictions, as did the power engineering workers, and make their plan the basis of a strong bargaining position. But, looking back, they feel this weakened the combine committee itself. So, although they have managed so far to hold back all but 100 of the redundancies, their organisation has suffered in the process.

This seems contradictory. Normally, an organisation is strengthened by victories. What was the process which led to this contradictory outcome? Once the CSEU was in control of negotiations, the problem for the combine committee was how to introduce some element of direct accountability of national officials to the workers in Lucas Aerospace. In the CSEU constitution, the only way in which the executive is accountable to the membership is indirectly, via the separate procedures of each union. That is not much comfort to workers facing redundancies which would have been carried out long before they could go through the Confed. procedures to criticise and change the direction of negotiations. So, the combine committee pressured the executive to call regular conferences of delegates from every Lucas Aerospace plant and union. At the first of these, the Confed. national officials proposed a tripartite meeting with the government and Lucas Aerospace management. The delegates, many of whom were involved in the combine committee, responded by insisting on lay representation at these tripartite negotiations. They went further, and passed a resolution to set up a fourteen man committee to prepare a report on the company's proposals, and to draw up alternatives which would retain all the jobs in the existing geographical locations and create further jobs in areas of high unemployment.

This committee, whose report we described in Chapter four, drew from the initial alternative corporate plan, as well as from three months investigation into the company, to produce a strong bargaining position. At the same time, industrial sanctions were imposed to maintain the status quo.

While all this was going on, Lucas management were pretty confident that this time their rationalisations would go according to plan. They made this quite clear in an interview in *The Engineer*:

> "A Lucas spokesman told *The Engineer* that nothing dramatic was expected [from the fourteen man committee]. He claimed that Lucas' plan to close the factories had not been affected, and that the whole working party just represented the next step in the negotiating procedure . . . This was confirmed by the Department of Industry."

These predictions turned out to be very naive. For a start, the committee dug out a lot more information about the company than ever plant shop stewards' committees could get their own. Management was grilled and interrogated until the committee were satisfied. A member of the committee gives a flavour of these investigations and of the confidence which the shop stewards gained through carrying it out:

> "When we got to a site, we'd sit down with the local trade union representatives. We'd ask them the problems they had, and what questions they'd asked management about the rationalisations. We found local representatives often got fobbed off. We had information from the other sites, so it was easier to see when we were being conned.
>
> Then, always with a senior plant union representative, we would see local management. Management would often start off, as is their wont, assuming they were in charge – they set the rules. For example, at one site they began the meeting by saying, 'Well, are you all here? Are there any apologies?' The co-ordinator of the committee said very cuttingly, 'We don't ask for apologies from your side or determine who comes from your side. Similarly, you have no control over who we bring. Sit down and behave yourselves'. Another time, management expected to be able to adjourn and prepare the answers as soon as we'd asked the questions. But we soon put a stop to that.
>
> The whole experience was quite new for all of us. For nearly six weeks we were investigating and going round the country full time. What I learnt during those six weeks makes my 26 years on the site seem like nothing."

If the gaining of information was a major challenge to the normal hierarchy within the factory, the way it was written up was a challenge to an aspect of the wider social hierarchy: the committee was a CSEU committee, but the CSEU had none of the resources necessary for fourteen plant representatives to write up a lengthy report. Nor, for that matter, had many of the member unions. That would have meant room enough for fourteen stewards to write and discuss over a period of two weeks, good library facilities, back-up research, and good typing and xeroxing facilities. What was needed was the sort of facilities normally only available at academic institutions for the use of academics alone.

In 1978, the combine committee had succeeded in 'liberating' some academic resources for the use of shop floor trade unionists like themselves. They had gained the support of the Engineering Department of North East London Poly', and, with a grant from a charitable trust, they set up the Centre for Alternative Industrial and Technological Systems, a resource and research centre, based in the Poly' with access to all its resources, but for the use of trade unionists. It was here that the fourteen man committee spent a fortnight of intense work and discussion, drawing up the report. One of the members from Liverpool expressed a fairly typical assessment of the experience:

"At first, I did not feel that I could write up reports and things like that. During the first two days I felt I could go on for ever. My confidence had really been lifted. And we worked as a very good team. Without the mix of technical and manual workers I don't think we'd have done anything like as good."

The production of the report further strengthened the determination of plant committees to continue to black the movement of work. It strengthened the determination of the general workers in Liverpool, who were the ones most likely to suffer from the rationalisation.

This determination proved vital. For, as we saw in Chapter four, the final deal negotiated by the CSEU national officers meant 600 redundancies in Liverpool. The CSEU delegate conference following the negotiations was critical of the agreement and insisted on no redundancies. But this conference had no constitutional power to bind the officers. So the delegates had to rely on their own strength to carry through the resolution. And the strength of the combine committee. So far, the confidence generated by the report and the industrial campaign which went with it, has proved sufficient to hold back most of the redundancies. The upturn in aerospace markets has, for the time being, made this fairly easy. But 100 jobs have gone in Coventry and in Shipley. Combine committee delegates feel that these, especially the research centre at Shipley, would not have been allowed to go if the combine committee had kept up its independent organisation and pressure during the work of the fourteen man committee.

However, the combine committee's industrial strength, linked to alternative policies based on social need, did achieve something. It did, like the power engineering shop stewards' committee, save hundreds of jobs at a time when management and government elsewhere had faced little sustained resistance.

The methods of organisation and the policies of both these campaigns are important to bear in mind when, in the conclusions, we discuss what policies and ways of organising are necessary to challenge and finally destroy the power of corporations like GEC and Lucas.

Conclusions:
Learning the Lessons?

Part 1. At Congress House and Walworth Road

The story of the last Labour government's industrial policies has revealed a lot about how the political system reacts when policies which pose a threat to the prerogatives of powerful sections of private capital get near to becoming legislation. The fact that radical industrial policies got as far as they did — or appeared to — was partly due to the absence of any policy initiative from the centre or right spur of the Labour Party in the early '70s. The centre/right leadership of the Labour Party had temporarily lost the initiative after the debacle of the 1964-'70 government, when their much vaunted plans for economic expansion were subordinated to the conservatism of the Treasury and the rationalisation schemes of industrialists like Arnold Weinstock. A further reason for the rapid headway made by the left's industrial policies at party conferences and on the NEC in the early '70s was the growth in trade union power — however precarious — which had been building up over the previous fifteen years. The defeat of Labour's 'In Place of Strife' and the Tories' Industrial Relations Act; the militant picketing of the miners' strike in 1972, and in 1974 when the strike turned out to be a successful challenge to the Heath government: together these led to a new political confidence within the left of the Labour Party. They were also warning signs to top management, civil servants and leading politicians — both Tory and Labour — of a challenge to their power.

The emergence of a political programme which seemed to challenge the free control over investment which employers have always taken for granted, combined with growing strength and rising expectations on the shop floor, led powerful industrialists and civil servants to make sure that this political programme got no further than Benn's "polemical, indeed manacing draft White Paper".*

*Quote from Harold Wilson's autobiography.

141

The left was defeated easily, partly because it was in such a small minority in the Cabinet, partly because that minority did not openly fight and partly because the parliamentary left was not prepared politically and industrially for the opposition it was to face.

Central questions

The following questions arise from our inquiry into the consequences of that defeat and the powers and vested interests which brought it about.

Can we separate completely the *content* of the Labour Party industrial policies of 1973 and '74 from the *failure to implement* them in 1975-'79. That is, does our inquiry indicate that the 1973 and '74 party policies were fundamentally correct, with minor improvements to be made here and there? Does it indicate that what is needed is changes in the constitution of the Labour Party and possibly the civil service that will, in the words of one left MP, "tie the buggers down this time" and prevent yet another betrayal by a Labour government?

Or were the policies flawed in ways that made them vulnerable to defeat; ways that led those who advocated them to under-estimate and to be unprepared for the opposition they faced?

Change the structures not the policies?

At the time of the inquiry the prevailing emphasis on the left of the Labour Party was that they had got the policies fundamentally right. The emphasis was therefore on getting the party and parliamentary structures 'right' in order to make sure that, next time, the policies would be carried out. According to this view the problem was mainly that the original policies were not carried out. The lack of trade union resistance to the defeat of the policies is, on this assumption, blamed mainly on insufficient debate and education within the trade unions, not on an inadequacy in the politices themselves. At the national tribunal for this inquiry, the Presidents of the four trades councils put the following question to the MPs:

> "After the experience of the last Labour government would you support the original industrial policies as future policy for the Labour Movement?"

Stuart Holland's reply summed up the dominant response on the Labour left:

> "Yes I would. I understand the bitter disappointment with how the NEB and planning agreements have in fact been operated in areas like the North East, Merseyside and the Midlands but, nevertheless, although we might not have been completely spot on in what we were arguing, there was a certain coherence in what we were arguing."

The Labour Party NEC have since reaffirmed the industrial policies

142

contained in the 1973 Party Programme. An NEC statement, *Jobs, Peace and Freedom,* passed at a special party conference in 1979 contained the following section on industry and the economy:

> ". . . we re-assert our belief, based on experience of recent Labour Governments, in the crucial importance of extending public ownership and planning the economy. We shall establish the machinery and take the powers we need to translate our plans into action. Planning agreements must guide the activities of the huge companies which dominate the economy and be backed by the statutory powers — especially discretionary powers over prices — set out in Labour's Programme."

More recently still, in its 'Draft' Labour Manifesto 1980, the NEC has continued to reaffirm its faith in the original policies, strengthened by greater state powers and financial resources. But since then the debate on Labour's future industrial and economic policies has been widened to take into account some of the failures which this inquiry has highlighted and also criticisms, especially from socialist feminists who believe that the policies are too narrow in their objectives.

Within this debate our inquiry leads us to disagree with some of the basic assumptions behind those aspects of present Labour Party policy which reaffirm the original '73 and '74 policies. We suggest the need for a more fundamental rethink than is at present going on within the labour movement. This does not mean, though, that we reject the industrial policies of 1973 and '74 — now extended into a full economic strategy known as the Alternative Economic Strategy (AES) — as being totally without value.

We intend therefore that our criticisms of and questions about the industrial policies of the Alternative Economic Strategy should build on the radical elements of the 1973-'74 policies rather than sweep them totally aside.

First, we will identify those aspects of the AES and the assumptions behind it which we believe make it open to a similar fate to that which befell the 1973 policies. Then, in Part 2 of these conclusions, we will suggest a different starting point for developing an alternative economic strategy and illustrate some of the initiatives which are already creating an alternative economics in struggles which can now be waged against management and government.

A real conflict

What were the features of the 1973 policies which made them vulnerable and disarmed their supporters; and do these features reappear in the Labour Party's policies for the 1980s?

The most obvious weakness was a *gross over-optimism* about the power

143

of a Labour government in the midst of a recession to negotiate agreements with transnational corporations. Under these agreements it was assumed that the corporations' investment policies could be made to conform with policies of full employment and industrial democracy. In other cases, it was thought that these policy objectives could be met by purchasing a majority shareholding in leading profitable corporations.

Related to this was an *underestimation,* in the economic circumstances of the '70s, of the conflict between even the minimal social objectives of full employment and an extension of workers' rights over company information on the one hand, and the objectives of private corporations on the other. The objectives of private corporations were, of course, corporate growth and an improved market position relative to competitors rather than real expansion of production and employment. This conflict was blurred by the use of expressions like the "regeneration of British industry" — an ambiguous phrase if ever there was one! The Labour and trade union left interpreted this phrase to mean regenerating and expanding manufacturing capacity in Britain, while corporate management and private financiers interpreted it as meaning strengthening the market position of British-owned companies.

These two interpretations have quite different implications. Most major British-owned companies have become successful through establishing overseas manufacturing bases — mainly by takeover. In some instances they have made overseas investment an overriding priority because of the relatively low rate of return on investment in Britain. Moreover, investment is usually highly capital intensive.

Yet the consensus within the party in the build-up to the '74 election was greeted with too much relief for any such difficulties to surface. The consequences of this was that by the time Harold Wilson and Michael Foot had rewritten Tony Benn's White Paper in 1975, giving it the consensus title 'The Regeneration of British industry', few in the labour movement were clear enough about the points of difference to complain.

The impact of the recession

In the late '60s and early '70s, before it was widely accepted that the recession was here to stay, this optimism and ambiguity may have had rather more purchase on reality. In conditions of economic boom or anticipated boom the gap between what firms regarded as optimal economic behaviour and what a party committed to full employment and industrial democracy regard as optimal economic behaviour might well seem negotiable. Now, however, particularly in Britain, the gap is huge. Moreover, the gap between the employment objectives of the Labour Party and the corporate growth and profit requirements of the major manufacturing companies is the result of far deeper processes than a simple cyclical downturn in demand — as we shall see below.

144

Changes in investment patterns

Even if world trade does slowly pick up — and this is by no means certain — there are no signs that employment levels will improve proportionately. Both academic studies and the experience of workers in the most competitive corporations indicate that the traditional assumption that employment levels rise during periods of high investment no longer holds. Recent studies of manufacturing industry in Britain show that investment has become so capital intensive and therefore the rate of output per worker has increased so much that it would require over 6 per cent growth in overall industrial output under our present economic system even to *maintain* employment levels within manufacturing.* At present, few forecasters anticipate anything much beyond a 1 per cent rate of growth, so it is very misleading to assume that if trade picks up so, inevitably, will employment.

Workers' experience of competitive success

Workers in some of the more competitive and 'successful' companies — the companies least hit by the recession — bear witness to this process. For example, GEC is a company which in terms of value of its shares, profits and even the overall output is one of the most successful of British-owned companies. If the competitive success of the company were to benefit the workers as well as the management then one would expect good job prospects in its more successful divisions like the telecommunications factories in Coventry. But in fact the reverse is the case.

GEC Ltd currently employs 157,000 people in the UK and is one of the largest companies in Britain by turnover. According to a press report in 1981, GEC "has beaten the recession" and is "sailing through with flying colours" (*Guardian* 3.7.81). Turnover in 1980-'81 totalled £4,129m — an all-time record. Profits were up 15 per cent on the previous year and were more than four times greater than ten years before. Over the same ten-year period, however, GEC eliminated an incredible 83,000 jobs, or about 40 per cent of its total workforce worldwide. About a third of last year's record £476m profits were derived from GEC's telecommunications operations, based mainly in Coventry.

Between 1975 and 1981, almost 9,000 telecommunication jobs disappeared from GEC, whilst output, sales and profits all soared. In the light of this kind of experience, it now makes little sense to the trade unions at GEC's Coventry plants to talk about the need for keeping the company competitive and profitable. The only growth they can predict

*See John Clarke *'Growth and Productivity'*, Science Policy Research Unit, Sussex University.

with any certainty is in the rate of further job losses as GEC speeds up its introduction of automated and computer-controlled design, production engineering, clerical and manufacturing processes. The trade unionists with whom we have talked in Coventry estimate that there will have been a staggering 96 per cent reduction in the numbers needed to produce the latest generation of electronic telephone exchange equipment — System X — which GEC is developing apace. And the impact of investments in such systems on employment in British Telecom exchanges themselves is likely to be no less devastating.

The importance of these studies and workers' own experience is that they indicate trends quite opposite to those assumed by the economic models underlying Labour Party and TUC policy.

TUC policy statements on future spending in the telecommunications industry illustrate the problem all too well. For example, in a recent publication entitled 'The Reconstruction of Britain', the TUC argues that a future Labour government will have to spend hundreds of millions to support British Telecom's much-needed investment programme:

> ". . . to expand and bring the telecommunications network up to date. For instance, 70 per cent of telephone exchange connections still go through old-fashioned 'Strowger' exchanges and this needs to be replaced by 'System X' exchanges . . . the main effect will be to protect existing jobs in BT (British Telecom) and in its supplying industries".

The assumption of 'growth with modernisation' underpinning this rosy view of the future disguises the fact that such growth refers only to increases in the amount of *capital employed* and *profits expected* — not to numbers employed or levels of wages. It is already clear from the experience of workers in telecoms and other 'growth' sectors, that investments in computer-based and automated systems are being made in order to increase managerial control and cut the costs of labour — not to safeguard employment.

Labour Party policy making — along with that of the Tory and Liberal parties — has tended to assume that growth rates of labour productivity are fairly easily matched by overall increases in output and therefore in employment. Versions of this assumption, with only minor elaborations, are the basis of the Treasury medium-term model (which the TUC now uses to spell out the implications of its policies) and those of other major forecasting units. The studies and experience which we have reported show that these assumptions lead to over-optimistic predictions about the future based on *past* trends in the relationship between investment and output on the one hand and employment on the other.

Rationalisation rather than expansion

One explanation for this change in the relationship between labour

146

productivity, employment and overall output in manufacturing industry lies in changes which have taken place in the pattern of investment common to the Western world. These changes affect British manufacturing industry particularly severely. Recent studies by the Organisation for Economic Co-operation and Development (OECD) show that there has been an increase in the relative proportion of *rationalisation* investment at the expense of *expansionary* investment. By rationalisation investment they mean investment which has the predominant effect of increasing productivity and reducing labour requirements. For example, by introducing Computer Aided Design to meet the same output targets, companies can replace design workers. Expansionary investment is investment which increases output and generates employment, for example, by introducing computer-aided design machinery to *expand* output and maintain the number of designers.

A further indication of this change in investment patterns lies in what has been happening to manufacturing employment per unit of investment over the last 50 years. For instance, OECD studies show that throughout Western economies during the 1930s the ratio of manufacturing employment to each unit of investment increased over time. However, since 1950 there has been a *steady decline* in the ratio, and after 1966 it became negative. That is, increases in output have not been matched by increases in employment. The main factor behind these investment trends is the pressure of competition between manufacturing corporations. This competition has become so intense internationally that to succeed the corporations have to rationalise. Growth today is more often achieved through takeover and is followed by rationalisation investment in high technology machinery and plant which replaces labour.

And so we get the apparently contradictory phenomenon that those corporations which are the most successful, competitive and expanding — like GEC and ICI — are actually cutting rather than increasing the numbers of workers they employ.

The above section may have seemed rather technical but its implications are very political. For it means that, in foreseeable economic conditions, policies which place a priority on full employment and an extension of workers' rights *will directly conflict* with the main drive of the corporations' own investment strategies.

Two problems flow from this:

First, while we need radically new policies on investment, technology, public purchasing and foreign trade which can provide fulfilling employment for all, these policies must inevitably challenge the pressures and constraints of the capitalist market. Do the Labour Party's industrial policies contain such an alternative strategy for the *content* of investment, purchasing and technological decisions, as distinct from alternative *institutions and mechanisms* such as the NEB and planning agreements? One weakness of the industrial policies of 1973-74 was that their objectives were formulated at only a very general level: 'full employment' and 'industrial democracy'. The institutional mechanisms they proposed were spelt out in detail, but the content of the plans to be implemented through these mechanisms was not. Are there any signs that the Labour Party and the trade unions are remedying this failure?

Second, where will a Labour Government find the power needed to back objectives that run counter to the investment strategies of the private corporations? Are the Labour Party's industrial policies adequate to mobilise that power?

Restructuring in the interests of labour

By criticising the Labour Party for under-estimating the conflict between their objectives and those of the major industrial corporations and financial institutions, we do not want to give the impression that we have got a ready-made escape route from the capitalist market. However, we would argue that neither the Labour Party's 1973 policies nor its 1981/82 policies recognise that *there are different ways of being competitive*. TUC and Labour Party documents tend to assume we have no option but to compete according to the standards set by West German and Japanese companies. They assume that we have to compete in the same markets occupied by these companies. They also tend to assume that competitive success means the competitive success of private corporations in their present form, including those conglomerates which bring together hotels and newspapers, or tanks and office equipment under one management. The assumption seems to be that, armed with planning agreements, the National Enterprise Board and a new Department of Planning, a Labour government can ensure that these companies can be competitive in a conventional way *and* at the same time socially responsible.

No to competition on capitalist terms

There is insufficient emphasis given in Labour's thinking to policies for restructuring industry in the interest of labour rather than capital. For instance, in the car industry, capital will restructure by closing down unprofitable plants and investing in new methods of production in order to compete with Japanese, West German or Third World products. Management's interests will be dictated by whatever is needed to raise the rate of profit for that particular motor corporation. They will not be thinking about transport systems more generally, other than to devise ways of weaning the public away from public transport and towards buying new cars. A more adequate alternative strategy from labour's point of view is not one of subsidising decline but rather of identifying new products; for example cheap, light, town cars with hybrid and non-polluting engines; cars with a long life backed by a more extensive network of repair workshops. Potentially new consumption patterns could be identified, and products manufactured in ways that do no replicate the alienation of the assembly line.

This might involve breaking up the structure of existing car companies. It might mean a municipal enterprise in different towns producing town cars, while inter-city public transport could be expanded to include new systems like the Lucas workers' road-rail vehicle. All this would not only save but create jobs. The new investment would not necessarily be especially capital intensive, probably the opposite. Yet it would be efficient and competitive in the sense of providing things or services that people want to use at a price they or the institution that carries out the purchasing is willing to pay.

We can take another example from the power engineering industry where capital, led in Britain by GEC, is already restructuring the industry in its own interests. This does not simply involve reorganising production and destroying jobs; it also involves restructuring the consumption side, that is the power-generating industry and energy-supplying services. For several reasons well documented elsewhere* nuclear power is the form of energy which most suits the strategies of the multinational corporations in this industry. In particular, it is the most capital intensive of all energy sources and provides a market that favours the largest corporations over their competitors. So the form which capitalist competition takes within this industry is for tenders for nuclear power stations throughout the world. An alternative for labour which has to be considered is the development of renewable, safer and more democratically controllable forms of energy such as wind and solar power, or more efficient forms of energy supply and conservation which can be sold to governments or local/regional authorities which have rejected nuclear power. This alternative strategy may be no less 'efficient' than the first, though the criteria for efficiency are different. Moreover, these criteria can find financial backing, through the purchasing power of governments and local authorities who believe in them, with the support of the people who ultimately use and consume the energy. Our point here is not that nuclear power must be abandoned. The Joint Trades Councils have not yet discussed this issue thoroughly and have not therefore reached an agreed position on it. Our argument is that the possibility of developing alternative sources of energy must not be obstructed by the powerful vested interests of capital in the nuclear lobby.

In the next section, which shows how labour itself is already laying the groundwork for the kind of restructuring we have in mind, we will give

*Martin Spence 'Nuclear Capital', *Capital and Class* No.15.

149

some further illustrations. One reason why it is more appropriate to develop the idea of restructuring for labour in the section discussing workers' own plans and initiatives is that this involves restructuring both production and consumption. The proposals for this restructuring have to be drawn up by workers themselves both in their position as producers and as users and consumers.

TUC and Labour Party industrial policy dissected

Such a thorough-going strategy of restructuring for labour will come into direct conflict with the strategies of the corporations. But it is more likely to convince people who were disillusioned by the experience of Labour governments in the '70s. It is more likely to gain popular support and galvanise popular power than a strategy which claims to share the corporations' competitive objectives whilst at the same time seeking to control and redirect their methods. The institutions and mechanisms proposed in the 1973 policies, however, were shaped to implement the latter strategy.

Previous chapters have shown that this strategy contained the seeds of its own defeat. But is there anything to be salvaged or built on as far as those institutions and mechanisms are concerned? Could they provide or mobilise the power needed to back the kind of industrial restructuring for labour just outlined? The latest proposals of the TUC and the Labour Party again put forward the institutions of the 1973 policies, in particular the National Enterprise Board and, in a watered down form, planning agreements. Are they wise to do so? Do they develop them in a way which overcomes the flaws revealed by our inquiry?

Perhaps the most detailed proposals on Labour's industrial policy are those of the TUC-Labour Party Liaison Committee on industrial democracy and planning. The full title of these proposals is 'Economic Planning and Industrial Democracy: The Framework for Full Employment'. Michael Foot has described it as "in some respects the most important report we have produced since the last election". And here Foot is probably not being purely rhetorical.

Though it has not hit the headlines in the same way as the controversial Labour Party NEC, The TUC-Labour Party Liaison Committee is perhaps the most powerful body in the labour movement as far as policy making is concerned. It has existed on and off in different forms ever since the trauma of 1931, and has acted to patch up the rifts which occasionally threatened to cause the two 'wings' of the labour movement to fly in different directions.

As far as the institutions of planning are concerned, the background arguments of the TUC-Labour Party Liaison Committee's report do try

150

to learn from the failure of planning agreements and the Industrial Strategy of the last Labour government (as well as George Brown's ill-fated 'National Plan'). But we would argue that the Liaison Committee's final proposals do not represent a significant improvement on the 1973 policies.

The following is a summary of the main proposals of the Committee's report on 'Economic Planning and Industrial Democracy':

— A new *Department of Economic and Industrial Planning* to act as a central focus for planning in the machinery of government. This Department will initiate a "national economic assessment" covering the broad allocation of resources, and negotiate "agreed development plans" with companies.

— An independent *National Planning Council* to channel and develop the trade union role in planning at sector and national levels. This body will be "stronger" than the National Economic Development Council, which it will supersede.

— New *statutory rights for workers* to information, consultation and representation in the enterprise and in wider planning. Workers themselves will decide how and when to use these rights through their joint union committees, backed by new facilities and rights to time off.

— New *regional planning bodies* to give planning a regional focus and encourage and co-ordinate local initiatives. Trade unions and local authorities will have a representative voice on these bodies.

The report assumes that a National Enterprise Board will be an important part of a future Labour government's industrial strategy.

We will discuss these proposals against the background of our assessment of the two main features of the last Labour government's industrial policies: (A) Planning and Planning Agreements; (B) The National Enterprise Board.

(A) Planning and Planning Agreements

The main problems with planning agreements were as follows:

1. In their final form in the Industry Bill of 1975, planning agreements were not backed by powers to require companies to negotiate over government and trade union plans. Neither was there any willingness on the part of the cabinet to make use of the financial, purchasing and ultimately nationalisation sanctions available to the government as bargaining weapons.

2. Even in the original 1973-'74 proposals, the vital role that would have to be played by the trade unions — with government support — was not fully recognised. In order for the proposals to have any chance of major impact, the trade unions would have had to be actively involved in drawing up alternative plans. The importance of new forms of shop stewards' organisation — like combines — was not thought through; neither were the implications of such organisations for the Labour Party's rather passive relationship to the trade union establishment. The 1974-'79 Labour government itself reinforced

151

existing inadequacies in established trade union structures, thereby blocking the growth of the multi-union shop stewards committees which could have given planning agreements a cutting edge. For instance, members of the elected shop stewards combine committee at Lucas Aerospace were refused access to government ministers on the grounds that they had not been through the CSEU — the official multi-union body in engineering — even though they had the support of individual union conferences. This helped to delay negotiations and industrial action and gave management the advantage.

3. The arguments for planning agreements were not based on detailed plans for particular sectors, and certainly not on any clear strategy of restructuring for labour. In a sense it was a reactive strategy as far as corporate plans were concerned. The theory was that the company would come to the government with its latest corporate plan and that the government, with the unions, would insist on certain additional targets being met: e.g. greater job creation, more exports, more innovation. There was no conception that the government and the unions would have their own plans to which management would be forced to respond. Eventually the government launched its Industrial Strategy — worked out on a tripartite basis through NEDC — but it had little or no impact on company decision-making. And anyway, by then, the planning agreements idea was in practice dead.

4. Related to this lack of detailed plans and priorities for labour was a lack of a broader mechanism for sector, regional and national planning that would integrate company-level plans.

Do the Liaison Committee proposals overcome these problems? As far as points 1 and 2 are concerned, those covering the power and cutting edge of planning agreements, the Liaison Committee falls between two stools. On the one hand, it does not propose strong powers with which the existing state could intervene, if necessary against the will of the private sector. Its proposals on government/company agreements do not, for instance, give the government the power to *require* companies to enter into agreements as did the 1973 proposals. On the other hand, it does not significantly strengthen the power of workplace representatives to influence planning decisions. These representatives are given more rights, but the question of organisation — the *means* of making use of these rights on a companywide basis — is evaded.

The limits of statutory power

Our view, developed in discussions during the inquiry, is that statutory powers to influence the investment plans of the major corporations are not enough. A socialist government resting only on the power of the ballot box does not start off with control over the main centres of wealth and economic power. In particular, it has little control over the most profitable sections of the economy, the major manufacturing corporations and finance houses. Worse than this: increasingly governments have come to *depend* on these institutions far more than the institutions depend on government.

Parliament alone therefore does not have the material power to take real control of this wealth-producing capacity, however many formal planning agreements and declarations are signed by private companies. Parliament does not, on its own, have the power to monitor and control their implementation.

The example of Chrysler in 1977-'78 illustrates the strong bargaining position of the multinational corporations. Chrysler could ignore the government's planning agreement not so much because of accommodating ministers, though such ministers were clearly a help, but because of Chrysler and Peugot's global investment options and the bargaining power this gave them *vis-a-vis* the British government. The only way in which a socialist government could have a countervailing power would be through an active alliance with those who have a day-to-day knowledge of production and who have the material power to veto management decisions and draw up alternatives.

Only such an alliance can effectively replace the alliance which we have found to be built into the existing state: that between top civil servants and the financial and industrial power elite.

The Liaison Committee is far too complacent about the attitudes and interests of the present Department of Industry civil servants. At one point it says:

> "The DoI's strength lies in *its detailed knowledge of industry acquired through its sponsoring divisions,* but it is arguable that this very closeness to industry often prevents it taking a strategic view about the national priorities" (our emphasis).

The problem is not so much the civil servants' inability to take a strategic view (though this might occasionally be the case) but the fact that *all the detailed knowledge comes through management channels.* The civil servants' strategic view therefore reflects management's point of view.

Side-stepping industrial power

A trade union input into planning has more radical implications. First, multi-plant, multi-union combine committees are essential for any successful trade union negotiation over corporate plans. And even this is skirted around in the report. The background documents put forward a strong case for multi-union shop stewards combine committees within the major corporations. In the final proposals, however, the problem is left unsolved. Instead of saying clearly that new forms of shop-floor organisation are essential to the success of planning in the interests of labour, the report talks, at some length, of new legal rights for trade unionists. Now, many of these rights are necessary and important, but talk of 'rights' still begs the question of trade union organisation and of how these rights can most effectively be exercised. This issue would seem

153

to be taboo in the delicate division of responsibilities between the Labour Party and the trade unions. The spread of multi-union shop stewards committees across corporations and then sectors would be the ideal basis for the trade union input into a socialist planning process. It would be most effective at drawing together the ideas, insights and skills of the workers concerned, and it would be potentially the most powerful back-up for legislation. But, and this is a very big 'but', as far as several of the trade union leaders sitting on the Liaison Committee are concerned, such organisations would cut across, and be seen as a possible threat to established structures.

An equilibrium or a transition?

A further question we would raise about the Labour Party and TUC's proposals for planning agreements or 'development contracts' is whether they are envisaged as the basis of a more 'socially responsible' partnership between the private sector and the state, or whether they are seen as preparing the way for a real transition to a socialised economy.

In some versions of the AES there is a tendency to assume that an equilibrium is possible between the government and the corporations on the basis of negotiated agreements. Here, the proposals are still heavily influenced by the continental experience, and that of France in particular. In the 1960s the French government used a system similar to planning agreements to keep the private companies in line with its employment, export and anti-inflationary policies. But this was during a period of expansion. In Britain in the 1980s, with over 4 million unemployed, a world recession and industrial capacity down by 25 per cent in ten years, planning mechanisms would have to be used for more radical purposes. It is not a matter of encouraging companies to bring forward their investment plans or to locate a new plant in Liverpool rather than London, nor is it a question of subsidising a declining industry on condition that management retains jobs. Planning agreements would stand or fall as one means of implementing the kind of restructuring for labour described earlier. Government and union plans based on this kind of industrial strategy would, more often that not, meet with determined resistance. The government, therefore, would always need to prepare the way, with the aid of the unions throughout an industry, to acquire companies under some form of social or co-operative ownership. Planning agreements should be seen not as a way of consolidating a stable tripartite relationship between government, management and the unions, but as a transition to socialisation of the company under workers' control.

Beyond the company

We turn now to the TUC-Labour Party proposals concerning planning beyond the company: the proposals for a new Ministry of Planning and

154

an expansion of NEDO into a National Planning Council. There are two main problems here. The first concerns the connection between national and regional planning and the plans drawn up by workers in particular corporations. There is no detailed discussion of how the two processes would connect and what might be the tensions and conflicts between them. For example, serious conflicts could occur if trade union inputs into the wider planning system were not based upon the multi-union combine committees which give workers' plans their force. Without this kind of input, union contributions to planning beyond the enterprise would, as in the case of NEDO and most other quangos, be through a mixture of full-time officials or high ranking lay officials from individual unions or from the TUC. Without the direct links that a structure based on the combine committees would provide, there will be no way that the ideas arising from workplace plans can adequately inform the national planning process.

Consider the Lucas Aerospace or Chrysler workers' plans described earlier in this inquiry. Their proposals included equipment and components for transport services in the case of Chrysler and, in the case of Lucas Aerospace, for medical equipment, energy conservation, non-polluting car engines, and the exploitation of the ocean bed.

If plans like these were followed through, they would have economic implications far beyond the particular companies in which they were drawn up. For instance they would require an assessment of need and possible markets in all the areas suggested by stewards; this would involve consultation between workers and existing and potential users. They would involve planning discussions with other shop stewards in the aerospace and motor industries and in other sectors covered by the plans.

In the long run, such plans might imply the break-up of conglomerates like Lucas and Chrysler and the integration of each productive unit into the new industry for which the plan proposes they produce. After all, from a worker's point of view, there is little logical connection between the different activities that some conglomerates bring together.

This inquiry bears testimony to the fact that when workers do gain the confidence to plan their own collective future they come up with schemes whose economic implications go far beyond the company they work for. Nearly every group of stewards who gave evidence in the course of this inquiry was involved in drawing up plans, independently of management, both for their company and for their industry.

It is important to understand that *workers' plans* are a lot more than *company plans*. In other words, workers' plans cannot be adequately drawn up or negotiated simply within the framework of a planning agreement for a single company. Such plans point to the need for structures of democratic planning to cut across companies and sectors but, at the same time, to be based on the multi-union workplace organisations which alone are capable of drawing up plans at the base.

Representatives of individual unions and the TUC who are scattered about various national planning bodies do not provide the most effective or democratic way of synthesising local and workplace plans for a number of other reasons. For instance, conflicts over plans between shop stewards committees in different companies and different sectors can best be resolved through direct association between these committees or their immediate representatives. Such direct association makes it possible to hammer out policies which are of mutual benefit; for there can be a growth of mutual understanding and a dynamic which leads to new policies.

This is less likely through meetings between national and regional full-time officials responsible for many different negotiations. Moreover, although full-time trade officials are in theory able to transcend the sectional interests of different groups of workers in one industry, this tends to be true only in the context of traditional trade union bargaining. That is, they can take account of wage rates in other regions or sections of the industry; or they can warn against action by one group of workers which might put another group out of work. However, they are not usually in a position to harness and synthesise the ideas and knowledge of workers throughout the industry as the basis of positive industrial policies. Again, that is best done through a system of planning built up directly from multi-union workplace organisations on the one hand and consumer/user organisations representing a locality or special interest on the other. Full-time officials can help to service this process but *they cannot be the main channel through which it takes place.*

There is a further consideration that workers' plans will need to be fought for, and here a planning system with a direct line of accountability and communication back to the workplace and locality is essential. Industrial and community strength could be mobilised far more successfully through such a system when workers' plans face resistance. Moreover, there would be less chance of the pressure for such action being diverted and diffused than with a system in which workers' input was channelled through the officials of separate unions.

Beyond production

There is a further weakness in the Labour Party-TUC proposals for wider planning structures. They take no account of the consumption or need side of workers' plans. They say very little about public purchasing and how decisions about it are to be taken.

Although the Liaison Committee documents talk a lot about policies for production, albeit in rather general terms, they say nothing about consumption. It is as if consumption is 'out there', something that cannot, perhaps should not, be influenced by planning.

Let us briefly explore why this is a serious weakness. A policy document from the headquarters of Ford, or any of the major corporations, would contain a lot about consumption patterns. These would not be simply passive responses to market research, they would be plans for actively intervening in and shaping consumption. To shape consumption patterns does not mean to impose forms of consumption on people in a crude way, regardless of their will; rather it means to channel people's felt desires and needs towards one type of consumption rather than another. For example, the secret of Ford's success in the '30s, '40s and '50s was not only that it introduced the assembly line into production but also that it helped to devalue the image of public transport, to reduce the resources allocated to public transport and to make ever faster, short life cars more desirable.

During the '50s and '60s capitalists were sure of the direction of consumption in many spheres. They were in large part responsible for it — that was part of their success. Part of their crisis now is that levels and forms of consumption characteristic of the boom years have begun to change. The market for cars and other consumer durables has begun to approach saturation point in advanced capitalist countries. A decline in real income as a result of inflation has meant more expenditure on secondhand products and on repair and maintenance. As a result of this and other changes, capitalism in the advanced countries has, to a certain extent, lost its sense of direction. If you asked a European capitalist in 1950 "What will people be buying in twenty years time?" they would have replied without hesitation "cars, fridges, TVs and washing machines". If you ask a capitalist the same question today the answer is more likely to be "Who knows?" or "You tell me". This uncertainty is a very important part of the present crisis. Indeed, it is possible to see the crisis as a kind of limbo, a period of searching during which capitalists are looking round for new patterns of development.

So far, they have not found any they can be sure of. In one sense, of course, capitalist innovation is always a gamble — it always involves uncertainty and an element of risk. What is different about consumption forecasting in the 1980s, however, is just how unsure capitalists appear to be about future patterns.

This uncertainty is betrayed, for example, by Western capitalists' reluctance to invest in much more than electronic gadgetry. And even here — in an economic age of space invaders — the rate of capital accumulation is so fast, technological change so rapid, and competition so intense, that only the largest corporations can survive the rat-race to quick profits.

One of the new markets they seem to be gearing up for is in services like education and health. Indeed, the impetus behind the privatisation of such services stems from, and is proof of, a deepening conservatism in corporate investment strategies.

So far, then, there is no clear and well defined pattern of future development to which capitalists and the state are willing to commit themselves. This is not to say that there is no vision of the patterns they would *like* to create. They have not given up thinking or planning strategically. They have rather been forced to reduce risks by, amongst other things, intensifying competition in already established markets.

Privatisation — that is the move by private capital into well established and easily exploited patterns of *social* demand — is of considerable political importance. It does not just illustrate a particularly spineless and unimaginative form of investment — there is not much risk of 'failure' in these markets. It represents a serious threat to areas of *public provision for social need* which, for all their many serious faults, at least offer arenas within which labour, community and, increasingly, women's organisations can fight for improvements and for more democratic control over social provision than either the market or electoral politics can provide. The growth of womens' campaigns around health care, nursery provision and against commodities harmful to women, the strength of the anti-nuclear movement and groups organising for more socially efficient forms of energy, the plethora of campaigns for better, cheaper transport all testify to this.

We need forms of popular planning which give expression and encouragement to these attempts to resist the consumption strategies of the corporations. We use the word 'popular' because it allows for people's involvement in planning as users and consumers as well as workers. In the next section we shall be discussing these campaigns around consumer and user needs in more detail and exploring the kind of alliances that are being and could be built between users' and producers' organisations. Our basic argument will be that a system of popular planning is the only way in which the interests of *labour* — that is, of people without either the power of wealth or the power of bureaucratic position — can govern economic decision making.

We started this section by asking whether or not the latest proposals coming from the TUC and the Labour Party would overcome the inadequacies our inquiry identified both in the industrial planning policies of the last Labour Government and in the original Labour Party proposals. Our answer to this question is: No. The latest proposals, however useful the background analysis, are in some ways *weaker* than the original 1973-'74 Labour Party proposals. The strengths of the original proposals — definite powers to require companies to enter planning agreements and at least some recognition of the need for new forms of trade union organisation to back them up — have been dropped in favour of non-committal statements about statutory powers to back up what are now weakly called 'development contracts' (rather than 'planning agreements'), and talk of extending workers 'rights' without any proposals for the kind of organisations which could best make use of these rights. Not much sign here of lessons being learned!

What are the lessons to be learned from what happened to the other crucial part of the industrial policies of 1973 — the National Enterprise Board? Are there any signs that the leading committees of the Labour Party and the TUC are learning them?

(B) The National Enterprise Board

The National Enterprise Board was and still is the lynch pin of the industrial side of the Alternative Economic Strategy. The idea was, and still is, that the NEB will acquire one or two leading private companies in each important industrial sector and set an example as far as job creation, industrial democracy and innovation are concerned. The planning agreement system would then provide a back-up and a means of ensuring that other companies followed the example. Is there anything worth holding on to in the idea of the NEB and planning agreements? Or did they in effect contain the seeds of their own defeat?

On the basis of our inquiry the factors which explain why the NEB acted as it did can be summarised as follows:

1. When the NEB was finally established in 1975 it had been deprived of the power to require, by law, that an intransigent company sell its shares to the NEB.

2. The objectives of the NEB were too general and ambiguous to ensure the implementation of the manifesto. The priority given to job creation, particularly in areas of high unemployment, existed on paper, but in other paragraphs it was hedged about or cancelled out by commercial requirements.

3. The rate of return required by the Labour Government from the NEB was far too high: 15-20 per cent. It was high even by commercial standards at the time. The consequence of this was that whenever employment priorities conflicted with commercial ones, it was the commercial priorities which were overriding.

4. Trade unionists on the NEB Board were there as individuals. There were no serious attempts to make them accountable to the trade union movement or to ensure that they resisted the pressures of the City on the NEB.

5. The Department of Industry had no detailed strategy for how the NEB was to create jobs in a period of recession. The Government's industrial strategy, such as it was, was NEDO's responsibility. The NEB was asked merely to 'take account' of it.

6. The Department of Industry had very few direct means by which it could influence the NEB — even if it had wanted to.

7. The NEB exerted very little control over the managerial policies of the companies it acquired, beyond some initial changes in management.

8. The NEB never attempted to use its acquisitions to achieve planning between companies within a sector, e.g. machine tools, or across a sector, e.g. machine tools and the motor industry. Nor did the NEB use its holdings to set an example of job creation and industrial democracy within any sector.

9. The NEB budget was reduced massively from the original £1,000m *per annum* to £1,000m over the first *five years,* with which it could not buy more than two major companies. This should be contrasted with the £15,000m received by private industry over the same period.

10. Trade unionists in the companies taken over or in contact with the NEB were never told by sympathetic Labour politicians of the limitations and weaknesses of the NEB until it was too late. As a result, expectations were too high and the degree of independent organisation and initiative too low.

Could these failings be overcome to create the kind of pace-setting, socially responsible public enterprises for which the NEB was originally intended? Our analysis of investment trends, in an earlier section, indicates that under present circumstances the employment policies promoted by such an NEB would conflict with the direction in which capitalist corporations are going. The original idea of the NEB underestimated this. Some of its early supporters saw it as a kind of nationalisation by stealth and assumed that it would meet with less opposition than direct takeovers by the state. This might have been so had a moderate Labour government embarked on an NEB type strategy in the '50s instead of nationalisation. But, as we have seen in this inquiry, an NEB with a significantly different approach to investment from that of a merchant bank would be treated as anathema. So long as Benn was at the Department of Industry and the radical version of the NEB was on the agenda, then the City and private corporate management treated it *as if it was* nationalisation. Was there and is there any reason why an NEB should be able to outflank or overcome that opposition more effectively than some more direct form of political takeover?

Out of the frying pan into the fire

The theory was that a state holding company independent of Whitehall, with trade union representation on the Board, would be a way of evading the conservative grip of the Civil Service. There may be some truth in this, but the problem then becomes how to avoid public

160

investments coming under the even harsher, albeit more dynamic, grip of the big corporations and City financiers. In other words, just as the politicians can lose control in the face of opposition from the Civil Service, so the independence necessary to avoid the Civil Service makes the NEB prey to the powerful pressures of private capital. This is a matter of out of the frying pan into the fire.

A determined left-wing government with a good majority might be able to counter these dangers to some extent. It would need a group of politically appointed officers at the Department of Industry overseeing the NEB's guidelines and overall strategy. It would require trade unionists and other socialists elected to the Board and made accountable. However, apart from the problems of achieving such a government, which we will come to later, there is the more fundamental problem which no amount of manoeuvring within the state machinery will overcome: that is, the very nature of the state machinery itself.

It is part of the conclusions of this inquiry that the structures of the present type of state are so biased towards the private corporations that working-class people cannot rely on a socialist government being able to use this state to destroy the powers of these corporations. As soon as a socialist government moved to control them, the powers of the corporations are such that they would be used to destroy or undermine whatever socialist intent existed within the government; unless, that is, such a socialist government rested on a source of political power outside the existing state.

Our conclusion, then, is that working-class people have to build up their own forms of political power based on their material power as producers, as the people on whom the distribution of goods and services depends and, in the home, as the people who reproduce and service the present and future labour force. We are not so naïve as to think that organising around workers' plans can substitute for a socialist state. Rather we would argue for extending workers' ability to draw up and fight for their own plans as one way in which, with the support of socialist political parties, we can create a new, more democratic way of co-ordinating the economy, a new kind of state.

Not by economics alone

The implication of this is that industrial policies cannot be judged simply or even primarily in terms of economic criteria; that is, in terms of what economic consequences would result if the policies were implemented in the way intended. Rather industrial policies have to be judged also in terms of whether they help to strengthen the power and capacity for control of workers' organisations. For without that power

161

and capacity, the most internally coherent industrial policies are pipe dreams. In the following section we will discuss what can be done now, under a Tory government, to strengthen and build this power.

Part 2. Learning the Lessons in the Localities

Popular planning for social need

In this section we hope to illustrate a new approach to economics, which we have begun to develop in our own localities. It is an approach which starts from social needs and from the question: "How do we organise production to provide people with things like cheap and efficient heating, care for our children and useful, fulfilling jobs in safe and healthy working conditions?" This kind of question has to be discussed and answered by the people affected in every locality and workplace. The mechanisms for the kind of economic planning we have in mind do not yet exist but the basis for them is in every tenants' campaign over heating costs, every trade unions' fight against unemployment, every childcare campaign and every workplace health and safety committee. In the following sections we will illustrate some of the initiatives and ideas developed by such organisations towards a new economics of social need. We will set these against the background of the wasted resources and unmet needs that exist within the old, capitalist economics.

Starting from childcare

"How should we organise the economy in order best to care for and support our children?" Not a question asked very much, if at all, in conventional economic policy making nor, until recently, in Labour debates about economic strategy. But the idea of making this kind of question the starting point for economic policy illustrates our theme of production for social need most vividly. It is not simply that it is a different starting point from "How do we restore the profit margins of British industry?", or even "How do we regenerate British industry to restore full employment?" It implies a reversal of all the most central economic relationships which make up the taken for granted framework of policy making. First, it brings to the *centre* of policy making an issue which is normaly *subordinate* to the objective of the profitability, competitive success and growth of the commercial sectors of the economy. 'Social Services' take care of childcare partly in order to ensure an adequate supply of the right kind of labour and partly to resolve problems and needs not met through the individual family. To

162

say the needs of childcare should in part determine the way the economy is run is to see investment in childcare provision as a mainstream economic activity which measurements of economic success should include.

This would in turn require a new approach to economic calculations, or at least an expansion of the 'social accounting' and investment appraisal techniques which are used increasingly in arguments against factory closures and redundancies. This approach moves economic calculations away from the balance sheet of individual companies and towards an assessment of the costs and benefits of a particular economic activity to the economy and society as a whole. Social accounting provides a way of recognising the total social cost of unemployment. Once we see economic decisions from the point of view of childcare, a far wider range of considerations come into play. These include the value of extending the social contribution of women's creative and productive capacities, and the value to both adults and children of collective, co-operative child care.

Second, the reverberations of making childcare an economic objective would shake the whole structure of working time. For, as has been pointed out frequently, men's relation to working time reflects their absence from the work of childcare and other domestic responsibilities. The whole notion of a full-time working week for some, usually men, depends on there being others, usually women, who carry out the childcare unpaid. Two out of five female employees work less than 30 hours a week, compared with one in twenty men. Ninety per cent of women who work less than 30 hours are married and two-thirds have children. Sixty-five per cent of men work 44-48 basic hours a week. And almost twice as many men as women work overtime. If childcare was a social priority, then economics — as the means of allocating resources to meet given ends — would have to find a way of fulfilling this priority. If it was recognised that childcare should be shared equally between men and women, the statistics above would become intolerable: just as intolerable as the statistics on absenteeism and bad timekeeping are to the management of the present economic system.

In many unpublicised ways, women *are* asserting different values and *men* are pleased to follow. For example, at Ford Halewood in June 1982 the women in the trimshop took strike action, initially against the advice of the male shop stewards, so that they could finish work at 2.30pm on Fridays. At first they just took Fridays off and then, when the company remained unmoved, they went on strike for a week and forced the mighty Ford company to let them have the extra hour off so that they could meet the children from school and get ready for the weekend. Admittedly, the Ford women's action assumed that the children and the household were their responsibility, but it also asserted that children's needs and personal life were worth striking over. It has jolted some of the men to take their claim for a shorter working week a bit more seriously.

Women are also taking initiatives to get collective care under community control taken seriously as an economic activity. Women in Lambeth have persuaded Lambeth's Employment Committee to include childcare as an area of job creation and economic expansion. It required some direct action, with children invading the committee meeting, but now childcare in Lambeth is no longer simply the responsibility of the Social Services Department. The women concerned are moving on to a wider front to convince the GLC's Greater London Enterprise Board to fund a network of co-operative childcare centres. Local employers would then be pressed by the unions to pay for places in these centres for their employees' children. It will need a strong alliance between the women's movement, the trade unions and socialists in local and national government to carry it through on a national scale. However, such a project could provide an exciting illustration of what might be possible.

This points to a general feature of an economic strategy that starts from social needs: victories like that of the Ford women, exemplary projects like that of the Lambeth women, can be achieved *now*. We do not have to wait for government action to get beyond just talk of an alternative to Thatcherism.

Jobs from warmth

Initiatives over energy problems — heating costs, the need for renewable and safe sources of energy, unemployment in the power, engineering and construction industries — illustrate the same point. Numerous campaigns have developed in the last few years: some based on tenants' groups, some based in the trade unions, others encompassing a wide range of groups. All, in effect, are pressing and bargaining for energy policies which will meet the heating and employment needs of users and producers in the energy sector. We will give a brief outline of their work, to indicate the kind of national and international problems which this new approach to economics is trying to tackle as far as energy is concerned.

Large numbers of homes are under-heated in urban areas of Britain. People fall ill and sometimes die as a result. In fact, the World Health Organisation recently noted that Britain has amongst the highest incidences of illness and death resulting from bad heating. One estimate put the number of pensioners at risk from hypothermia during a British winter at 700,000; and the substantial rise in infant mortality during winter is caused by the same inadequate heating. Dampness and mildew is another related problem. Local housing reports from all over the country have vividly documented the premature deterioration of

164

furnishings and fittings as well as high rates of illness which result.

These heating problems cannot be put down to the price of oil or coal alone. First, there is a considerable waste of existing resources — especially of the human skills which could be employed to carry out major insulation programmes. Local authority Direct Labour Organisations should and could be used to do this work. Tenants and DLO workers themselves should determine together the kind of insulation material to be applied. Shop stewards from DLOs in several regions, the North East in particular, are attempting to form a DLO shop stewards combine committee to co-ordinate a campaign for the expansion of the DLO. One of the urgent tasks of such an expanded DLO would be a thorough-going insulation programme.

A different approach to energy economics would also mobilise against the waste heat that currently warms the sky above power stations. There is now strong pressure from trade unions, local authorities and tenants' groups to introduce combined heat and power schemes which would use this waste as an extremely cheap and efficient form of heating. These schemes would not only provide cheaper heat for consumers, but also many jobs in mining, pipe manufacture, engineering, construction, insulation and instrumentation. In Tyneside, several of the AEUW-TASS shop stewards at NEI Parsons, building on the ideas developed towards the end of the Drax campaign, have played a leading part in a local and national drive for combined heat and power. "Jobs from Warmth" is the campaign's slogan. The employment emphasis has attracted a broad range of unions in the North East. The NUM, UCATT and NUPE, for instance, have all affiliated to the campaign. It is designed to benefit users and consumers as well as workers; and tenants' groups, campaigns against high heating costs and dampness, and the local anti-nuclear campaign all see "Jobs from Warmth" as an important part of their activities. The Trade Union Studies and Information Unit (TUSIU) in Newcastle provides a base for the campaign and a full-time worker who used to be the press officer for the Parsons Corporate Committee.

Another element in the solution to the problem of energy prices is the development of renewable sources of energy. Wind, wave, solar and tidal energy systems have developed rapidly over the last decade despite minimal funding. In the UK, the total research and development budget for all 'renewables' was £11m in 1980-'81, as opposed to £170m for nuclear research and development. We can see the importance of massively expanding the 'renewables' development programme most clearly if we view the problem of energy needs from an international perspective. On present trends, the advanced countries, East and West, will be consuming 85-90 per cent of the world's energy and over 90 per cent of the world's oil by 1990, yet they will form only about 25 per cent of the world's population. Thus, each person in the advanced countries will, on average, be consuming about 25 times as much oil and other forms of energy as the average person in the Third World. If there were unlimited supplies of energy readily available this would not matter, but there are not.

Over the medium term, supplies of energy from non-renewable sources are limited and expensive to produce. The more the advanced countries consume, without developing renewable sources, the more expensive and difficult it becomes for the Third World to get energy, and the cost to their economies is in many cases catastrophic. Any alternative strategy in Britain and other industrialised countries should make energy saving a major priority. This is potentially a very fruitful field for working class initiative, as many of the savings do not rely on the 'high' technology of a few specialists but on the intelligent use of information readily available to a fairly wide range of workers.

A workers' plan for better transport

In transport too, workers and users are taking initiatives to organise transport to meet their needs. Here also people are seeking to reverse the economic relationships — which are also power relationships — that lie behind existing transport decisions. Present transport policy and spending is heavily biased toward the richer sections of society. It strongly favours the car user and the better off and discriminates against old age pensioners, children and women. Mick Hammer, an expert on transport policy, comments:

> "It is a common fallacy among transport planners to assume that the ownership of a car — and 57 per cent of households have a car — caters for all a family's transport needs. Research carried out by the Policy Studies Institute has demonstrated that this view is wrong. Teenagers in particular, but also other members of the household, do have a need for independent movement. Moreover, use of the car tends to be controlled by the male . . ."

Public spending ought to be positively biased towards those who need support most — those without regular access to a car. There are also strong environmental, health and economic arguments for subsidising public transport rather than expanding and improving the motorway system. Yet in 1978-'79 three-quarters of the capital budget of the government's transport spending was devoted to road building. This road investment is almost exclusively concerned with long journeys, yet only one journey in ten is over ten miles.

Several Labour controlled County Authorities, notably South Yorkshire, Greater London, the West Midlands and Merseyside, have attempted to reverse this trend by introducing very much cheaper fares on the buses and tubes. These attempts have received clear popular support, despite the government's onslaught, which sabotaged the policy in London and the West Midlands. In the areas where cheap fares have been introduced the use of public transport has increased dramatically. During the six months of cheaper fares in London, Ken Livingstone, Leader of the Greater London Council, reports that:

> "When the fares were cut for the first time ever in London Transport's history, the drift of passengers from public transport to private cars was reversed. Previously the number of passengers using London Transport had been going down by about 2 per cent a year. With the cheaper fares, passenger use overall went up by 12 per cent".

In the West Midlands, the first few months of the cheap fares scheme led to a new alliance between Labour councillors and trade union activists among the engineers and drivers employed by the West Midlands Passenger Transport Executive. This alliance did not prove strong enough to stand up to government pressure, but it did achieve some victories and raised the possibility of transport workers and users together drawing up plans for transport to meet the needs of the majority of West Midlands people. Jack Gould, an EETPU shop steward in the West Midlands PTE and a delegate to Coventry Trades Council, wrote the following notes on this experience. We print them in full because they give a vivid idea of the kind of thinking going on amongst active trade unionists involved in PTEs, where the politicians have initiated policies to meet social needs. Jack wrote it before these same politicians had backed off the cheap fares policy in the face of the Law Lords judgement.

> "The Labour controlled West Midlands County Council (WMCC) have conducted a cheap fares scheme through its Passenger Transport Executive (WMPTE) only to suspect that the directors of the PTE were not whole heartedly behind it. At the same time the employees of the PTE, both engineering (approximately 2,500) and drivers (approximately 5,000) fully supported the cheap fares scheme. When the PTE attempted to send out 400 vehicles to be serviced by private garages, the engineering workers prepared for strike action, but at the same time called on the WMCC to intervene.

> "The Labour councillors on the WMCC Transportation Committe, without waiting for a committee meeting, ordered the PTE to back down, which it did. The response among the engineers has been a sharp boost in morale, not just at twinning the issue but also because a new form of struggle has opened up which offers a greater possiblity of success in the present circumstances than just militancy. The Labour county councillors, on the other hand, have realised that they have allies in their coming struggle with central government, and have responded by seeking close contacts with the shop floor activists and shop stewards, and also by transforming the WMPTE advisory committees, formerly public talking shops with no teeth, into sub-committees of the WMCC Transport Action Committee. In other words, a process has taken place to by-pass the bureaucracy and link the workers in politics with politics in workers."

Taking advantage of this in Coventry, the Trades Council has gained the agreement of drivers' and engineers' representatives to begin a study of the industry and together with the local Trade Union Resource Centre — Coventry Workshop — to develop alternative plans for transport.

The initial response has been very encouraging particularly as the intention is seen as also involving the public by setting up a Transport Users Association. Also the development of the vehicles themselves is to be considered, an item of interest to the drivers' representatives, particularly as the Road/Rail Bus is one of the Lucas alternative projects to be developed at the local Polytechnic. The basic policy statement being worked out reads like this:

> "The development of a systematic public transport system requires the establishment of a planned socialist economy. Integrated transport must be developed as part of such a plan, which must be based on the needs of society as a whole.

> " 'Private enterprise' undermines economic planning and ties public transport to the requirements of big business and commerce, run only for profit and in direct competition with private transport. It is necessary for a socialist economy that *all* forms of transport be brought under public ownership including the car industry, shipping, airlines, coach companies, freight operations, together with oil and road construction firms.

> "This is to allow planning to take place and systems to be developed to provide the fastest and most efficient service. There is no reason why public transport cannot be free and run for the benefit of the society as whole. Under the present system transport is in chaos. It is starved of investment, owes hundreds of millions in interest and capital to the banks and, apart from a few short term experiments, had raised its prices beyond the means of ordinary travellers.

> "Buses in towns have to compete with cars, which means that cities are clogged with traffic, leading to accidents, strain, and the destruction of the environment through noise and exhaust pollution.

> "Services are cut, prices raised, leading to a decline in passengers, redundancies for transport staff and immobilisation of large sections of the population.

> "It is vital therefore that public transport workers join with public transport users, to take responsibility for their industry, not only in defending existing services but also in developing alternative plans to the bureaucratic chaos which threatens the jobs and services of the industry".

This last statement was agreed by Coventry Trades Council and by the craft negotiating committee of the West Midlands PTE. On Tyneside too, trade unionists working for the Tyne and Wear PTE have put forward plans for an integrated transport system providing cheap journeys throughout the area. As yet there is no co-ordination between the activists, both workers and users, involved in campaigning for a transport economics based on social need, but contact is growing and we hope this book will help.

Jobs from peace

Producing arms or losing jobs presents workers in the armaments industry with a false choice. Money and resources currently spent on defence could be redirected to new markets and new jobs. The plant and skill used in military production can be converted to civilian use. And civilian production, if it is directed to supplying the elastic demand of currently unmet social needs, means *more* jobs.

The Vickers Shop Stewards Combine Committee, for example, have emphasised persistently over the last decade that if what remains of Vickers on Tyneside is to survive new products must be developed. Those they have highlighted include car presses, brewing, mining, agricultural and offshore machinery, a host of general engineering products and, most promisingly, two types of energy equipment — heat pumps and recycling equipment. Heat pumps work like refrigerators in reverse, taking heat from the environment and returning it in a more efficient form. Vickers could make condensers and evaporators for the heat pump.

At Vickers Scotswood in Tyneside, before it was shut in 1979, a range of recycling products — such as scrap baling, scrap shearing, waste paper baling and domestic refuse baling equipment — was manufactured under licence from an American company. When Vickers proposed to close the works, the 750 workers undertook an investigation which showed that, even under existing market conditions, sufficient demand existed to make this a viable range of products. Two orders had already been received for domestic waste balers from local authorities. What was lacking was adequate design and development work, and co-operation with local authorities who could either market the processed 'waste' to buyers or use it themselves to generate heat at specially designed plant. As at Byker in Newcastle, Vickers management refused to co-operate and closed the works.

Similarly, Vickers Elswick, also on Tyneside, formerly manufactured the Seerdrum pulverising plant which separates metals from domestic refuse and turns the remainder into fertiliser. A further development of the pulveriser could separate and recycle metals for use in specialised metal-working industries. Plastics recycling equipment could also prove a viable alternative product for the Elswick works. The Vickers workforce have suggested two further products that could be used by public bodies. These are fluidised bed boilers, whereby coal is more efficiently burned in power stations, and equipment for dealing with oil spillages at sea. Instead of adopting these proposals, the company prefers to close the works, redevelop the Elswick site as a commercial property asset and move the defence division to the old Scotswood site. The same negative response by Vickers greeted the Barrow workforce's suggestions for alternatives to military production. Although it is claimed that the building of Trident at Vickers Barrow yards is protecting hundreds of jobs, conversion would provide a greater security and quantity of employment.

Shop stewards in shipbuilding on the Tyne are also considering proposals for diversification to avoid becoming too dependent on naval orders. The Falklands war led to some new orders for a time, but few stewards believe that building ships to bolster the illusion of an empire provides a secure future for their jobs. Several of their representatives are working with the Trade Union Studies Information Unit on a number of proposals which could secure their jobs.

One proposal is to make coal-fired steam-driven ships. The new coal-burning technology and the rising price of oil have made them an economic prospect. Another idea is to make floating factories for products such as ammonia which are inconvenient to produce in highly populated areas. Shipyards in Sweden are already working on such factories.

The conversion from military to socially useful production cannot be carried through on a national basis alone. The political co-ordination of NATO's strategy is reflected in the integrated production of weapons across national boundaries. And already the interest in conversion sparked by the Lucas Aerospace workers is spreading to other European countries. John Palmer, the Guardian's European correspondent, reports:

> "The British movement has made a distinctive and, on the Continent, influential contribution with the so-called Lucas plan for alternative social-use production. At last week's demonstration in Bonn, references to the potential of this idea and the related issues of industrial democracy, workers' control and economic internationalism were common in leaflets and pamphlets."

And international activity is not limited to pamphlets. Already shop stewards from the different aerospace factories throughout Europe involved with the Tornado project have made contact in order to put forward a proposal for alternative products.

A new economics

As we list these developments and the new relations and connections they are trying to make, it becomes clear that we are in effect describing the foundations of a new economy, a new form of production. Economics is the practical science of production; an economy is the way in which productive resources are organised and used. These various campaigns based in production but spelling out new directions for consumption, or based in consumption and usage but spelling out new directions for production, in fact constitute an attempt to organise resources according to different economic laws from those that now predominate. Karl Marx talked about the relations of the new mode of production taking shape in the womb of the old. During the transition from feudalism to capitalism this took the form of actual capitalist enterprises emerging, buying labour power as a commodity, extracting surplus value and accumulating money capital. These could survive and spread to a certain point under feudalism. Under capitalism, however, because of the nature of the capitalist market, isolated enterprises based on production for social need and workers' control cannot sustain themselves sufficiently to become the basis of a new mode of production, though they can illustrate the possibility of an alternative. A new socialist economic order, therefore, has to grow through workers both as a producers and as consumers collectively struggling for plans for production and services based on social need.

Rebuilding our strength

The Trade Union movement faces enormous problems if it is to struggle for its own plans for production and services. For example, in manufacturing industry unemployment has undermined the confidence and organisation of shop stewards' organisations. Management have driven home their advantage with a direct attack on trade union organisation.

An indication of what active trade unionists are up against came in an article in the *Financial Times* at the beginning of 1981. The article reported a seminar for senior management from many major corporations and small businesses on 'Options and Controls for Negotiations with Trade Unions'. The convenor of the meeting, Len Collinson, a Director of Duple Coachbuilders, United Gas Industries and Courtauld International Holdings — the owners of the engineering company Mathew and Platt — told the 21 senior managers:

"Managers for 20 years have had a buffeting and bashing from governments and unions and have been put into a 'Can't Win' situation. Many have been fire-fighting and many have given in. We have an opportunity now that will last for two or three years. Then, the unions will get themselves together again; and the government, like all governments, will run out of steam. So grab it now."

In a previous meeting, run on similar lines, Collinson said:

"We have had a pounding and we are all fed up with it. I think it would be fair to say that it's almost vengeance. But take your revenge carefully, most of us have procedure agreements and they (the unions) have established the mechanism for challenging management decisions."

Whether or not "carefully" is the right description, management have certainly taken their revenge deviously and ruthlessly. In several of the

171

companies covered by this inquiry management have used the general atmosphere of crisis to get away with massive redundancies and/or low pay settlements even when the company's profits and share value were in a perfectly healthy state.

While the unions are still reeling from the shock of redundancies, managements have often introduced new technologies and new working arrangements which weaken the unions even further. The experiences of workers at Lucas Electrical, at Dunlops and at Metal Box are classic examples of this offensive. In some cases management have gone further and even refused to negotiate over wages, thereby challenging the most basic function of the trade unions. In Lucas Industries, for example, management have for three years presented the unions with non-negotiable wage offers, well below the rate of inflation.

This concerted offensive has not only reduced workers' living standards and increased the insecurity of their future, it has also seriously weakened the workplace organisations which must be the foundation of any genuine socialist industrial policies. At Lucas Aerospace and NEI Parsons, for instance, the joint shop stewards combine committee and the joint union corporate committee are now in no position to fight for alternative policies. In both cases management have succeeded in sacking leading militants under the cover of a wider rationalisation. Harry Blair, the secretary of the corporate committee at NEI Parsons was sacked in this way, as was Mike Cooley of Lucas Aerospace. They tried to get rid of Ernie Scarbrow, the secretary of Lucas Aerospace Combine Committee in the same way; they did not at first succeed but they harrassed him to the extent that he felt he had no option but to take early retirement.

Both committees could have sustained the loss of these leading activists had they been able to retain their greatest strength: the unity of shop floor workers with technical, office and supervisory staff. However, the changes in managements' tactics and workers' morale opened up old sources of division and suspicion. The break-up of the corporate committee at NEI Parsons illustrates this well.

At first the unions felt that the corporate committee still had a role. The Drax B order had been won and, for the moment, jobs were secure. Work on Drax B would only last two years. So the corporate committee took up a campaign to press the company to take on orders for combined heat and power systems and to make the necessary investment. Barney MacGill, an AUEW member, described their approach:

> "We told the company, 'You've got two years to put your house in order, and get ready for combined heat and power'. We knew that there were orders in it from Scandinavia and other countries and very likely from the government here."

The company did respond in a small way to this pressure and in early 1979 put a manager on to looking into the possibilities of combined heat and power. At this time, and during the Drax campaign, the company was willing to meet the corporate committee almost whenever it asked. The Committee had a room of its own with a telephone. Arrangements were easily made when the corporate committee wanted visitors, and its members were allowed to take time off to carry out the committee's work. After May 1979 and the change of government things began to deteriorate:

> "We were no longer politically useful for them. The company began to get difficult,"

said Matty Straughan, the AUEW convenor:

> "They'd tell the likes of Ken (Ternant) and Harry (Blair) 'Get back on to your drawing board'; they took away the room and the telephone and they refused to meet us as the corporate committee, only as separate unions."

The unity built up during the Drax Campaign was not deeply rooted enough to maintain the corporate committee in the face of company opposition. Matty Straughan again:

> "So long as there was no immediate threat concerning everyone, each union tended to be inward looking. Individual unions started worrying about their own autonomy. Without the momentum provided by a winnable campaign of benefit to everyone, the old suspicions came to the fore."

Another manual worker commented:

> "There's always at the back of our minds a suspicion of *staff* (white collar workers). Some staff — not so much TASS — find it difficult to decide whether they are management or unions."

Sometimes negotiations would take place with the corporate committee (the committee bringing together representatives of staff *and* floor unions) and not with the works committee (the manual shop stewards committee only) and that made the manual shop stewards feel that their problems were not being catered for. The personnel director would play on this and encourage resentment among the works committee towards the corporate committee.

Management's next move deepened these divisions. At the beginning of 1981 management announced over 100 redundancies — primarily affecting staff. By this time the effects of redundancy threats on one group of workers was not to rally others into a united front, it was rather to increase the sense of insecurity which leads those not immediately affected to lie low. The redundancies were successfully carried through but the manual workers do not feel any more secure as a result. At the time of writing they are working on an order which will be ready by the end of the year. They hope that an order will come from the Middle East. Have they got any contingency strategy in case the Parsons tender fails?

173

"A prayer, man," answered one of the manual stewards, laughing, half realising the hopeless situation they had drifted into.

Joking reference to prayers are a long way from the confident proposals made by a united trade union committee in the late '70s for the power engineering industry. The same kind of decline can be seen in the recent history of the Lucas Aerospace Combine Committee. The problems facing the Lucas Aerospace shop stewards have been documented elsewhere*, but one of the shop stewards provided a useful summary of the present state of the combine. John Routley, secretary of the electricians group in Lucas, pointed both to the weakness of the Combine and to a source of strength which indicates an important development among labour movement activists elsewhere. In October 1981 he said:

> "It is fair to say that the last twelve months has seen a growing commitment to the combine from electricians. We see the combine as it stands as a 'Think Tank' which draws on its members at all levels to work out any strategy that is necessary to deal with any problem no matter what it may be. But what it does not have, is the ability to carry out that strategy. The fundamental problem is lack of industrial strength."

John Routley's description of the Lucas Aerospace Combine Committee as a "Think Tank" which draws on its members at all levels to work out a strategy but does not have the ability to carry out that strategy to its full potential, summarises both the strengths and weaknesses of a new kind of trade unionism which is emerging from the experience of the last five years. It is a trade unionism whose leading activists have been bowed but not defeated by the erosion of their industrial strength. These activists are learning lessons not only from industrial defeats but also from the political failures of post-war Labour governments. There are many signs that these activists, many of whom have been involved in this inquiry, are thinking strategically rather than becoming demoralised by the present disarray of the labour movement. An increasing number of shop stewards' committees are investigating their company, industry or service in order to anticipate rather than react to management's plans. They are trying to develop alternative policies — including the technology involved — based on an assessment of social needs both of the workers in that workplace and of the wider community; and to relate these policies and this understanding of management's strategy to issues under collective bargaining, e.g. wages, new technology, health and safety, and sub-contracting in the public sector. They are also trying to extend collective bargaining to cover investment, product choice and design, work organisation, machine tool design and control over services. In these attempts workers acknowledge the need to link with other trade

*The Lucas Plan: A New Trade Unionism in the Making, H. Wainwright and D. Elliott, Allison & Busby 1982.

union or community-based organisations in the development of alternative policies for their industry, locality, or service.

A specific example of these developments as far as trade unionists in manufacturing industry are concerned is the formation and work of the Joint Forum of Combine Committees. In January 1980, at a time when the severity of the Tories' offensive was becoming apparent, shop stewards from fourteen different combine committees — including Thorn EMI, Lucas Aerospace, Vickers, Rolls Royce and British Leyland vehicles — met to create a forum through which they could discuss their common problems and to provide an informal source of support for combines which are just getting off the ground. From these discussions, and from their own experiences, they have suggested some guiding principles for the creation of company-wide and industry-wide shop stewards' committees.

We will paraphrase these here because the growth of multi-plant, multi-union committees which can develop and fight for socialist proposals in their industries is going to be central to any powerful movement for socialism and workers' control. The Joint Forum has also produced work on trade union strategies for new technology and on how to organise a combine committee (see Bibliography).

Multi-union Combine Committees: some suggested principles

1. *Multi-union Involvement*

   In order to build a strong organisation and create unifying policies, it is vital to seek the involvement of all sections of the workforce, staff as well as manual, women as well as men.

2. *Rank and File Involvement*

   The most important problem facing a combine committee, like any other trade union organisation, is that of convincing the membership of the need to act collectively, even when in the short run such action might involve sacrifices. This means the combine committee has to gain practical credibility in the eyes of the membership. For this it is important for combine-wide attack to produce small gains right from the start, if only through exchanging information, e.g. on sickness benefits, pension funds, or through blacking work and collecting funds in support of a dispute. The combine needs a newspaper or bulletin to report back these successes to the membership.

3. *Solidarity and Plant Autonomy*

   In order to build trust and solidarity across plants, it is important that plant organisations do not feel dominated or manipulated by the wider combine. On the other hand, in any campaign or struggle

175

initiated or spread by the combine, the fight must come from the plants or else the combine is nothing. So, while the combine cannot instruct plants to carry out decisions, its delegates should be prepared to campaign within their own plants for the majority recommendations of the combine committee.

4. *Winning the Argument: Policies for Social Need*

In a period of recession where, according to management's arguments, each plant is competing for resources, a combine committee will be very difficult to sustain unless it developes its own clear alternative policies for the industry: policies which directly counter management's forecasts about falling markets by pointing to the social needs which remain unmet.

So long as production and distribution is organised on a capitalist basis we will never win complete victories with these policies. But, by preparing the ground with alternative policies which working-class people can see are rational and moral and which should be possible, we can gain the support which is necessary to win at least some defensive victories (e.g. holding back management's rationalisations). In doing so we steadily erode the credibility of management and question the priorities of private profit; and we prepare ourselves, one day, to take control.

5. *Research and Information Resources*

The ideas for such policies will come from within our own organisations. But to develop them and to be fully informed about management's strategies we need to work with researchers who have the time and background information to go into problems in more detail, in ways described in an earlier section of these conclusions.

6. *Co-ordination between Combine Committees*

One feature of the increased power of top management is their greater co-ordination and mutual support.

As this inquiry has tried to show, the problems trade unionists face in different companies are not only very similar, but are increasingly inter-connected. For example, if workers in the 50 or so major corporations looked at the portfolios of investment of their pension funds, they would find that their companies virtually owned each other!

For these reasons, combine committees need to build links between each other if only, at this stage, to exchange information and ideas and become better prepared to support each other when necessary.

7. *International Contacts*

The first practical objective of combine committees is to develop sufficient solidarity, and sufficient understanding of top-management's plans and manoeuvres, to be able to block off the range of options which give management their power. However effective our means of achieving this at home, most of our efforts can be undermined by the options available to management internationally; unless, that is, we build up an international network. It sounds difficult and out of reach of an unofficial organisation like a combine committee. But it has been done. In the motor companies, in telecommunications and in Lucas Aerospace, contacts are gradually being built up. The National Aerospace Shop Stewards' Liaison Committee already has well-established international links.

Such contacts and the information gained through them can help to overcome a feeling of helplessness in the face of 'mysterious international economic forces'. Finally, when shop stewards and members know something of the problems faced by workers in the company's plants abroad, when they can put human faces and familiar problems to management's statistics, it is more difficult to play the international plants off against the domestic ones.

Combine committees and other organisations built up in this way are not alternatives to the existing trade union institutions. They are a way of extending trade union institutions. They are a way of extending trade union power to confront the new powers of the multi-national corporations. Moreover, as multi-union organisations with the capacity of fully understanding their industry they are the ideal vehicles for helping to develop and fight for policies which match the resources of their industry and the skills of the workforce with unmet social needs. They have, therefore, a vital political as well as trade union importance.

It is important to emphasise here that as *principles* we would expect most democratic trade unionists to agree with them. However, as *proposals for new activity within existing trade union organisations,* we would acknowledge just how difficult they are to put into practice.

In part this is because were are developing arguments for quite new forms of organisation and levels of activity within the unions at a time when the Tories' political and economic offensives make even the most traditional means of organising and bargaining extremely difficult to sustain.

Some of these established forms — like the plant-based 'convenor kingdoms' so familiar to workers in the car industry — grew out of the extraordinary capacity which stewards organisations developed for delivering the goods at plant level. But this tended to be in 'boom' times and did not require the detailed involvement of the membership in devising policy or tactics. Bargaining could go on over the local top table, with the membership being consulted only at key points during negotiations to endorse, or reject, stewards' recommendations.

In other words, widespread popular experience of trade union planning and strategic thinking has not been built into the trade unions — even at their most democratic levels. Yet this — amongst other things — is what we see to be a vital task in the creation of a new kind of trade union power.

In the locality

At a local level trades councils could play a central role in creating this new kind of trade union power; a power to take on the issue of controlling and planning production and services.

This is partly because, as organisations which bring together trade unionists from different companies, sectors and backgrounds, they have a wider horizon than single union-based organisations and they are more likely to feel a responsibility for the common needs of working-class people in their locality. Such a responsibility leads them to take up political issues. At present, however, their constitutions severely limit their ability to follow these issues through much beyond passing worthy resolutions and organising propaganda. One problem behind this is the way that affiliation to trades councils is limited to trade union branches. If trades councils are to develop their potential to help unify different sections of the working class movement, they need to be able to encourage the involvement of representatives from shop stewards' committees, tenants' and women's groups, anti-racist organisations, student organisations, the organisations of the unemployed and pensioners' groups.

If this cannot be achieved in the near future by changing the constitution of trades councils, then it can be achieved by welcoming representatives of these organisations on to sub-committees of the trades councils and by creating centres for the unemployed. This is already happening in many areas.

Coventry Trades Council has organised sub-committees on housing, health, cuts and unemployment, women, education and international issues, in which people unable to participate in the trades council as a trades union branch delegate play an active role through their women's, tenants' or other campaigning group. Coventry has explicitly adopted the principle of using these sub-committees to overcome the barriers and divisions between people as workers, consumers, users of the social services, tenants, and so on. The experience gained from such local work, together with lessons learned from this inquiry, have enabled Coventry Trades Council to begin developing a workers' plan for Coventry. We include in Appendix 5 an outline of this initiative in the hope that it will be helpful to others interested in doing something similar. This is not intended as a 'model' for all to follow, but as a local example of popular planning experiments in practice.

Newcastle Trades Council operates on similar principles to those adopted in Coventry. And North Tyneside Trades Council is moving in this direction through, for example, a very active housing sub-committee. It has also carried out an economic and social audit on the costs of redundancy and closure, in conjunction with Yard Committees from all the shipyards north of the river Tyne (see 'Shipbuilding — the Cost of Redundancy', September 1979).

Liverpool Trades Council has a long tradition of involvement in organising around the social services, race and unemployment. In the very near future this work will be strengthened considerably by an ambitious trade union and unemployed centre supported by a wide variety of trade union, unemployed, feminist and educational groups. This initiative seeks especially to extend and co-ordinate the work of those on Merseyside who have taken on the desperate but daunting task of organising the unemployed. Most notable amongst these organisations of the unemployed is the 6/612 T&GWU branch based in Speke. After the closure of the Speke Standard Triumph No.2 plant this branch turned itself into a branch for unemployed workers in the Speke area. It is now probably the only trade union branch on Merseyside whose membership is growing! In Newcastle, too, unemployment has been the main focus of trades councils' work. The Trades Council in Newcastle has helped to project the idea of centres for the unemployed. Like the Liverpool centre, the one in Newcastle provides printing, meeting facilities and organisational support and advice for the unemployed and for workers resisting closures. The centre has helped to establish an unemployed workers' union in the Tyneside area as a focus for fighting unemployment.

A popular socialist newspaper or involvement in such a newspaper is another vital arm of an effective trades council. Newcastle Trades Council, for example, have their own 'Workers' Chronicle'. Others have worked with a variety of local trade union and socialist organisations to sustain local papers.

Trade Union/Community Research and Resource Centres

We have already referred to the role of labour movement research and resource centres in providing support for the new trade union and community initiatives which this chapter has described. It is worth now describing their work in more detail.

There is now some kind of labour movement centre similar to TUSIU, CAITS or Coventry Workshop in almost every major city. They vary in the kind of research, educational and campaigning activities which they emphasise because they have grown in response to different problems faced by local trade union and community organisations. Whether intentionally or not, they have provided for many groups of trade union activists a base independent of the company and in more close contact with local experiences than a national union research department is able to. Information and research materials for local campaigns have been developed from these bases. The people working full-time at these research centres and those active on their management or advisory committees are themselves deeply involved in local trade union or community organisations. The centres have in many cases come to provide an important point of exchange and joint work between different parts of the local trade union movement on issues of a longer term nature than the day-to-day problems of collective bargaining.

Two centres, both initiated in part by the Lucas Aerospace Shop Stewards, have carried out work on prototypes of alternative products. Both centres, the Centre for Alternative Industrial and Technological Systems, (CAITS) and the Unit for the Development of Alternative Products (UDAP), are based at polytechnics with access to engineering workshops, but are under joint trade union and polytechnic control. The objective of these two projects is to develop products with a clear social usefulness which could then either be used to strengthen the positive bargaining position of trade unionists resisting redundancies or be made in co-operative or municipal enterprises.

A number of resource centres have now formed a joint national organisation to share information, discuss common problems and strategic political issues (The Network of Labour & Community Research and Resource Centres). It would be useful to summarise the principles by which this joint organisation seeks to work:

— The way that many of these resource centres provide services is as important as the services themselves. Many of them state their aim as being to help working class organisations gain control collectively over their lives and to understand the political and economic forces which deny them this control. To this end they try to base their work on a number of principles:

— They try to avoid getting involved as 'outside experts' but work as committed advisers with the groups whose aims they share. They work with them and seldom advocate or negotiate on their behalf.

— They attempt to build up the strength of the organisations they work with

180

by passing on the knowledge, skills and experience of how their work is done, the principles on which it is based, where and how information is obtained and so on.

— They attempt to contribute to a fuller understanding of the inter-relationships between workplace, home or community issues, between industry and the community, the economy and the state.

As far as possible, these centres are trying to develop resources within, and accountable to, the groups they work with and other organisations within the local labour and community movements. This applies both to the way in which they carry out their work in close dialogue with the community and trade union groups concerned and to the overall structures of the centres themselves. They are therefore accountable to management or advisory committees elected from affiliated, subscribing or member organisations representing local trade union, community, women's and ethnic interests.

Working with the local state

In the West Midlands, Greater London and Sheffield there is, for the time being, a greater chance than elsewhere that some of the ideas which come out of a popular planning process like that initiated by Coventry Trades Council and Coventry Workshop will be implemented. The West Midlands and Greater London County Councils and Sheffield City Council have put massive resources — compared to local authorities elsewhere and in the past — into employment initiatives aimed at meeting the needs of labour, rather than bailing out capital. This at least is the intention behind the investment strategies of these Labour-controlled authorities. They might seem like Canute trying to roll back the waves of capitalist re-organisation that wash away people's jobs and livelihoods. But there are two ways in which their control over financial resources and their political authority can complement local trade union initiatives. First, these local authorities can contribute to the defence of labour; that is, the defence of jobs, skills and trade union organisation in the face of a fierce restructuring by capital. Second, they can contribute to labour's ability to pose a credible socialist alternative by making possible practical initiatives that exemplify socialist production.

It is important to remember that there is little past experience, in the history of most local authorities, of intervening on the side of labour to save jobs. True, local authorities have increasingly been trying to 'do something about unemployment'. Employment Committees, Economic Development Units, local authority Advice Centres for small businesses and Co-operative Development Agencies with local authority funding, having been popping up everywhere — in Labour- and Tory-controlled authorities alike. But, except in a few cases, interventions in plant closures and redundancies are treated as outside the remit of local government policy. Local authorities see themselves as responsible simply for trying in a small way to clear up the mess left by economic decisions they see as either unavoidable or outside their influence. They might promote their area as a place in which to set up a factory, in the hope of attracting the 'foot-loose' companies that are supposedly wandering round the country. Or they might give special concessions, cheap factories, advice and grants to small businesses. They will seek to ease market mechanisms in the hope that these might then operate in favour of their own locality, but they will tend not to challenge the mechanisms themselves.

Local authorities which support workers facing the threat of redundancies come, then, as a surprise — a sudden light at the end of the tunnel. Clear public political and financial support can help considerably to boost morale and confidence. Certainly this was the case with workers at a machine tool company in Coventry. Their employment prospects had become so gloomy that at one point the shop stewards committee came near to disbanding itself. Financial and political support from the West Midlands County Council, backed up by research and organisational support from officers of the council's new Economic Development Unit and members of Coventry Workshop, helped them to get back into a fighting mood, although it is too early yet to predict the outcome. In London, too, GLC support for the workers at Staffa Engineering, whose multi-national owners, Short and Brown, were closing down their London plant, fed the militancy which resulted in a prolonged occupation. Local authority support, however, cannot provide a way *out* of the tunnel, especially when the darkness is caused by the decision of a large multi-plant corporation. To such corporations, local authority money is chicken feed and not therefore much of a bargaining weapon for the workers. But, in the case of a medium size, locally based company going bankrupt or facing a serious liquidity problem as a result of the recession, local authority money can make a difference: it can also draw in money from other financial institutions. The problem then is to work out with the shop stewards and workers concerned, terms for the financial support which will safeguard their jobs. The GLC is working on several such cases through its Greater London Enterprise Board, which invests according to clearly specified social priorities rather than solely commercial criteria. Again, it is too early to assess the extent to which the Enterprise Board in practice meets these social priorities. But, if they work, the significance of these deals for the labour movement at this time lies in the possibility of labour using its *political* control over finance to provide resources for continuing *trade union* strength throughout periods of restructuring.

In the past, bankrupticies have generaly enabled the more dynamic competitive sections of capital to restructure a sector of industry in their own interests without any pressure from labour. In this way then, the economic policies of a left local authority can be a particularly useful defensive instrument for the labour movement. That, at least, is a hypothesis to be drawn from the first few months' experience and tested against what happens over the next three years.

Local authorities also have funds that can be used to finance projects with a more explicitly socialist content (although the best defensive strategies always contain principles of socialist production). The Greater London Enterprise Board has the following principles written explicitly into its guidelines:

1. The principle of bringing wasted assets — human potential, land, finance, technological expertise and resources — into production for socially useful ends.

2. The principle of extending social control of investment through social and co-operative ownership and increased trade union powers.

3. The principle of development of new techniques which increase productivity while keeping human judgment and skills in control.

The method of putting these principles into practice is closely related to the principles themselves. Two features of this method stand out so far.

First, the importance of popular involvement in identifying the social needs, wasted resources and the choice of technologies referred to in these principles. The GLC is encouraging a popular planning process within trade unions and community organisations which will not simply produce immediate proposals for the GLC to act on, but longer term perspectives to guide struggles against government, management and even a future GLC. By 'encouraging' is meant the funding of research, educational and organisational resources for workplace and community groups to develop their own proposals for socially useful production or services. For instance, the GLC's Economic Policy Group are working with Adult Education Institutes, the WEA and trade union education departments on a programme of education for popular planning. The GLC, West Midlands and Sheffield are also providing funds for local trade union and community research and resource centres. These resources could help to strengthen workers' organisations in a way which cannot be reversed by a change in political control of the local authorities.

The second and related point concerns the GLC's approach to technology. Technological innovation is fundamental to at least two of the principles outlined above. But, in the GLC's view, as in ours, it is not a matter of encouraging the introduction of the new technology. It is a matter of recognising that there are several different directions in which

183

technology could develop according to different social and economic objectives. The socialist objectives of the GLC are defined in a general way but the implications for the choices of technology will be developed through the popular planning process referred to above. For this to be possible, facilities and expertise on technological matters need to be made far more accessible to people who, in the past, have not considered themselves capable of judging between different technologies. An important initiative already under way to meet this need is the creation of several *technology networks,* some based on geographical areas such as North London, others based on product areas such as energy. These networks will make the grossly under-used facilities of London's polytechnics and universities available to trade unionists and others who wish to develop employment plans, either as bargaining positions in their own company or as the basis of a co-operative or municipal enterprise. The networks will, for instance, develop a 'product bank' of prototypes of a socially useful kind that will be available to such groups and draw on the experience of CAITS and UDAP described above.

For these local authority initiatives to succeed it is vital to establish a close alliance between socialists in the local authority, either councillors or councillor-appointed officers, and trade unionists in the workplaces and localities. The lessons of our inquiry apply as much to these interventions by the local state as they do to those which might be made by a future socialist government. The alliance must be one in which socialists inside existing political institutions use whatever limited power is within their grasp to strengthen the extra-parliamentary power of labour.

The conclusions of this inquiry point to the importance of turning that extra-parliamentary power into a political force; that is, power supported by socialists in parliament and in the council chamber with which we can achieve production for social need.

Will you contribute to creating this power?

In a modest way, we and the other trade union, political and community organisations which have discussed the questions raised by our inquiry, are trying to realise this power. We include people from different political parties and from none. We see our joint work as educational and as providing a forum which will strengthen us in our diverse local and workplace struggles. We hope you will join this discussion. We hope it will contribute to a richer, more inspiring vision of socialism than those which have guided the labour movement in the recent past.

The effects of new technology in just one factory

1 **The machine shop** — computerised cutting, milling and grinding displaces skilled workers.

2 **The assembly line** — computer controlled assembly requires fewer operatives and inspectors.

3 **The design office** — the introduction of computer aided design means fewer designers and detail draughtsmen.

4 **The typing pool** — word processors can increase a typist's productivity by three times. The result — fewer typists.

We are all in the firing line. Are *you* the next target?

Produced by Coventry New Technology Network.   Published by Coventry Workshop, 40 Binley Road, Coventry.   Design by Phil Goodall (Jobs for Design and Publicity Work)

JOBS
FOR A CHANGE

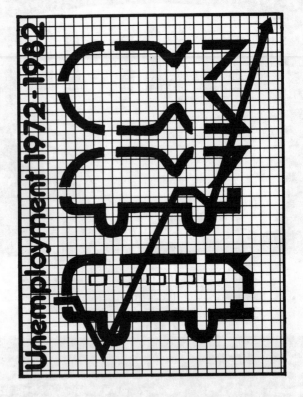

Sponsored by: Newcastle upon Tyne Trades Council, Tyneside Anti-Nuclear Campaign, Tyneside for Nuclear Disarmament

ALTERNATIVE PRODUCTION
ON TYNESIDE

186

Appendices

Appendix 1

The NEB's performance

At the end of 1979, the NEB had interests in 68 companies, *excluding BL and Rolls Royce,* representing assets employed of £202m. The total number of employees of the NEB and its subsidiaries (again, excluding BL and RR) at December, 1979, was 13,152. If BL is, as it should be, included, the total is 172,952. The exclusion of BL from the NEB's detailed review of its activities during 1979 is ominous. Will BL, like Herberts, be broken down and sold off in lots? There is no reason to suppose that such a move would represent a fundamental break with established practice.

Almost from the beginning, the NEB has acted as little more than a very conventional merchant bank filling a gap in the operations of the City. It has, or had, substantial (and, in some cases, 100%) holdings in companies whose managements have followed extremely aggressive restructuring policies, like BL and Herberts. It has also become a nursery for new industries, particularly in electronics and computers, which now look ripe for harvesting by private capital.

NEB members resigned on November 21st 1979 in protest at Sir Keith Joseph's insistence that Rolls Royce revert to Department of Industry supervision. However, changes in the Board were less dramatic than might at first appear. The new Chairman, Sir Arthur Knight, is, like his predecessors, a substantial capitalist in his own right (see Appendix 2 on Board Members and their financial interests in 1977-1980). The NEB's "new role" — as it is called in this year's Annual Report — does not signal a desperate lurch toward dogmatic Tory policies of asset stripping. Changes at Board level reflect a selective shift in the *policy focus* of the NEB rather than a radical revision of its guiding principles. In other words, the newness of the NEB's role under Tory management lies in its *emphasis* and not in its basic objectives or operating criteria.

Knight makes plenty of noise in his April 1980 Statement about the NEB's new functions:

> "Public ownership for the sake of public ownership is no longer a function and, instead, the NEB is to have the function of disposing of assets in order to increase private sector involvement wherever possible . . .

"The key to the new NEB role was expressed in the Secretary of State's statement on 21st November in these words: 'a catalytic investment role, especially in connection with advanced technology and increasingly in partnership with the private sector, as well as its regional and small firms roles'."

New noises, perhaps, but not much news. The NEB's record under Labour speaks for itself (See Appendix 3 on the NEB's investments between 1976 and 1980).

The Record:
Private Sector Involvement

The NEB's portfolio has always included substantial and wide-ranging shareholding partnerships with private capital – including Plesseys, Brown Boveri, Allied Investments Ltd., The Midland Bank, Barclays Bank, The Berec Group, Barclays Merchant Bank, Collinson Grant Associates, plus a number of company directors on incentive shareholding schemes (see, for example, CIC October 1979).

Disposal of Assets

The NEB has never fought shy of disposing of assets where fat profits could be taken or advantages offered to private investors. For example:

Reed and Smith Holdings Ltd.: taken over by a multinational paper company in December, 1977.

Ferranti: half of it sold off in September, 1978, the rest to go sometime in 1980.

ICL: sold in December, 1979 to "a wide range of UK investors" for a profit of £24m.

Fairey Holdings Ltd.: sold to S. Pearson & Son in 1980 for £22m.

Employment

The prospect of creating more unemployment did not stop the Labour appointed NEB from closing or 'rationalising' unprofitable companies – from the smallest to the largest. For example:

Company	Closure/Job Loss
Hivent Ltd.	Liquidated March, 1978.
British Tanners	Liquidated July, 1979.
Herbert Ltd.	Almost 2,000 jobs lost between December, 1975 and December, 1979, with more to go through sales and closures in 1980.
BL	32,800 jobs lost between December, 1975 and December, 1979, with another 25,000 phased redundancies planned for 1980/81.

Investments in Advanced Technology

Appendix 3 makes it clear that, from the beginning, the NEB took on the role of venture capitalist in high technology areas. (Note, in particular: INSAC, June, 1977; INMOS, July, 1978; NEXOS, January, 1979 and LOGICA, January, 1979.) About 20 separate companies in the portfolio over the past five years have been involved in the development of new technology: that is, in micro-electronic 'hardware', control systems and programmes 'software', in consultancy and in marketing.

Appendix 2

Members of the National Enterprise Board and their other interests

Board Members† (1975-1977)   Other interests (as at April 1977)*

With the exception of Caroline Miles, who joined the Board in March 1976, the Board Members were appointed in November 1975.

Chairman
Lord Ryder of Eaton Hastings Kt   Formerly Chairman and Chief Executive, Reed International Ltd.
Employment or office:
British Gas Corporation (part-time member)

Deputy Chairman
Leslie Murphy   Former Deputy Chairman, Schroders Ltd.
Directorships:
Chairman, J. Henry Schroder & Co. SAL, Beirut; Chairman J. Henry Schroder & Co., SAL, Lichtenstein.
Employment or office:
Member of the Royal Commission on the Distribution of Income and Wealth. (Resigned w.e.f. 1 January 1977.)
Payments, etc, from abroad:
(see Directorships above).

Part-time Members
David Basnett   General Secretary and Treasurer, General and Municipal Workers' Union.

J.L. (Bob) Dickinson CBE DL   Formerly Managing Director, SKF (UK) Ltd.
Directorships:
SKF (UK) Ltd; SKF Tools (UK) Ltd; SKF (Steel) Ltd; Sheffield Twist Drills and Steel Co. Ltd; Bofors Companies (UK) Weyroc Ltd. (Swedish Match); Magnatex Ltd.
Employment or office:
SKF (UK) Ltd;
British Rail (Northern Board).
Payments, etc, from abroad:
Director, SKF Tools, Sweden
General Manager, SKF Holding Co. Holland.

---

† Board Members names taken from Annual Reports 1976-1979.
* Members' Interests-Board members' declared private interests were published in an appendix to each of the NEB's Annual Reports for 1976/77, 1977/78 and 1978/79. No such detailed information was published in the 1979/80 report. This has had to be taken from *The Leveller*, No.35, February, 1980.

190

W.B. Duncan CBE	Directorships:
	Deputy Chairman, ICI Ltd
	Payments, etc, from abroad:
	Non-Executive Director of certain
	overseas companies of ICI Group.
Michael Edwardes	Directorships:
	Chloride Group Ltd
	(Chairman and Chief Executive)
	Payments, etc, from abroad:
	Consultant to certain Chloride overseas
	subsidiaries: Sociedad Espanola del
	Acumulador Tudor, Spain.
John Gardiner	Directorships:
	Chief Executive, Laird Group Ltd;
	Courtaulds Ltd;
	British Leyland Ltd.
	Payments, etc, from abroad:
	Director of certain Laird Group overseas
	subsidiaries
John Lyons	General Secretary, Electrical Power
	Engineers' Association
	Trade or professions:
	Occasional radio and television
	broadcasts.
Caroline Miles	Economic and Industrial Consultant
	Directorships:
	Heatherdale Fabrics Ltd;
	Old Chelsea Wine Stores Ltd;
	Scantec Ltd.
	Employment or office:
	Member, Monopolies and Mergers
	Commission
	Declarable shareholdings:
	Heatherdale Fabrics Ltd;
	Old Chelsea Wine Stores Ltd.
Harry Urwin	Employment or office:
	Deputy General Secretary, Transport
	and General Workers' Union; Manpower
	Services Commission; National Freight
	Corporation (Board Member).

Board Members (1977-1978)   **Other interests (as at April 1978)**

Lord Ryder of Eaton Hastings retired on 31 July, 1977 and was succeeded as Chairman by Sir Leslie Murphy (previously Deputy Chairman).

Mr Hugh Scanlon and Sir Jack Wellings were appointed in October 1977; Mr Michael Edwardes resigned from the Board with effect from 31 October 1977; Mr Richard Morris' appointment was announced in February 1978 and took effect from 10 April; Mr W.B. Duncan resigned from the Board with effect from 31 March 1978; Mr Alistair Frame was appointed in April 1978.

Chairman
Sir Leslie Murphy   Formerly Deputy Chairman, Schroders Ltd.
(see also, 1977)

Deputy Chairman
Richard Morris   Formerly Director of Courtaulds Ltd

Part-time Members
David Basnett   General Secretary and Treasurer, General
and Municipal Workers' Union

J.L. (Bob) Dickinson CBE DL   Formerly Managing Director, SKF (UK)
Ltd.
Directorships:
    SKF Tools (UK) Ltd (to 31 December
    77); SKF Steel Ltd; Sheffield Twist
    Drill and Steel Co. Ltd. Bofors
    Companies (UK) Ltd; Weyroc Ltd
    (Swedish Match)
Employment or office:
    British Rail (Eastern Board)
Payments, etc, from abroad:
    Director, SKF Tools, Sweden; General
    Manager, SKF Holding Co. Holland

Alistair Frame   Directorships:
    Director, Rio Tinto-Zinc Corporation
    Ltd.

John Gardiner   Directorships:
    Chief Executive, Laird Group Ltd;
    Courtaulds Ltd
Payments, etc, from abroad:
    Director of certain Laird Group over-
    seas subsidiaries

John Lyons   General Secretary, Engineers' and Managers'
Association

Caroline Miles   Economic and Industrial Consultant
Directorships:
    Heatherdale Fabrics Ltd.
Employment or office:
    Member, Monopolies and Mergers
    Commission
Declarable shareholdings:
    Heatherdale Fabrics Ltd

Hugh Scanlon   Employment or office:
    President, Amalgamated Union of
    Engineering Workers; Chairman,
    Engineering Industry Training Board;
    Board member, British Gas Corporation;
    Board member, Metrication Board;
    Board member, Co-operative Press Ltd.

Harry Urwin   Deputy General Secretary, Transport and
General Workers' Union (See also, 1977)

Sir Jack Wellings CBE   Directorships:
    Chairman and Managing Director, The

192

600 Group Ltd
Payments, etc, from abroad:
Director, La Precision Industrielle, Paris

| Board Members (1978-1979) | Other interests (as at April 1979) |

Mr J.L. Dickinson retired from the Board in December 1978. Sir Leslie Smith was appointed in February 1979; Mr Harry Urwin resigned from the Board in March 1979.

Chairman
Sir Leslie Murphy

Formerly Deputy Chairman, Schroders Ltd
Directorships:
Chairman J. Henry Schroder & Co. SAL Beirut
Chairman J. Henry Schroder & Co. SAL Lichtenstein
Payments, etc, from abroad:
(see Directorships above)
Declarable shareholdings
Schroders Limited
Granville Investment Trust
Whittaker Ellis Bullock Limited

Deputy Chairman
Richard Morris

Formerly Director of Courtaulds Ltd
Directorships:
British Nuclear Fuels Limited
Declarable shareholdings:
Courtaulds Limited
Plessey Company Limited
Bemrose Corporation Limited
Prestige Group Limited
APV Holdings Limited

Part-time Members
David Basnett

General Secretary, General and Municipal Workers' Union.

Alistair Frame

Directorships:
RTZ Group of Companies
The Rio Tinto-Zinc Corporation Limited (Deputy Chairman & Chief Executive)
Anglesey Aluminium Limited
Conzinc Riotinto of Australia Limited
CRA Holdings Pty. Limited
Nuclear Developments Limited
Palabora Mining Company Limited
Riofinex Holdings Limited (Chairman)
Riofinex Limited (Chairman)
Rio Tinto Finance & Exploration Limited
RTZ Aluminium Holdings Limited
RTZ Construction and Development

193

Limited
RTZ Deep Sea Mining Enterprises
Limited
RTZ Development Enterprises Limited
RTZ Oil and Gas Limited
RTZ Ore Sorters Limited
Rossing Uranium Limited
Non-RTZ Companies
The Plessey Company Limited
Declarable shareholdings:
The Rio Tinto-Zinc Corporation
Limited
Davy International Limited
The Plessey Company Limited
RHP Limited
Redman Heenan Limited
William Press Limited
Tube Investments Limited
T.W. Ward Limited
Senior Engineering Limited

John Gardiner — Directorships:
Chief Executive, Laird Group Ltd.
Director, The Laird Group Limited
Courtaulds Limited
Employment or office:
Member of Inquiry into the UK Prison
Services

John Lyons — General Secretary, Engineers' and
Managers' Association

Caroline Miles — Economic and Industrial Consultant
(see 1978)

Lord Scanlon — Formerly President, Amalgamated Union
of Engineering Workers
Employment or office:
Chairman, Engineering Training Board
Part-time Member Gas Board
Part-time Member Metrication Board
Consultant Adviser, Catalytic Ltd,
London

Sir Leslie Smith — Directorships:
Chairman, BOC International Limited
African Oxygen Limited
Airco Inc
BOC (Delaware) Inc
BOC Financial Corporation
Brinsholding Inc
British Oxygen Finance BV
Commonwealth Industrial Gases
Flatco Holding Corporation
New Zealand Industrial Gases Limited
BOC (Europe) Holdings Limited

194

BOC (Europe) Investments Limited
BOC (USA Holdings) Limited
BOC Finance Limited
BOC Holdings
BOC Investments Limited
BOC Limited
BOC Pensions Limited
Cadbury-Schweppes Limited
Member of Foundation Board of the
Centre d'Etudes Industrielles, Geneva
Member of the Executive Committee of
King Edward VII's Hospital for Officers
Member of the Executive Committee of
Industry and Parliament Trust Ltd
Declarable shareholdings:
BOC International Ltd

Sir Jack Wellings
Directorships:
Chairman and Managing Director, The
600 Group Limited
La Precision Industrielle, Paris
Payments, etc, from abroad:
(see Directorships above)

Board Members (1979-1980)   Other interests (as at April 1980)

David Basnett completed his period of service with the Board on 19 November 1979. Sir Leslie Murphy, Richard Morris, Alistair Frame, John Gardiner, John Lyons, Caroline Miles, Lord Scanlon, Sir Leslie Smith and Sir Jack Wellings CBE resigned on 21 November and the new members were appointed by the Secretary of State for Industry. Ian Halliday was appointed a Board member following his appointment by the Board as Chief Executive on 1 February 1980. John Caines served as a Board member from 23 November 1979 until 3 April 1980.

Chairman
Sir Arthur Knight
Directorships:
Chairman of Courtaulds. Member of the
Council of the CBI and various
industrial and industrially orientated
academic bodies, including the Court
of Governors of the London School of
Economics

Deputy Chairman
Sir John King
Directorships:
Chairman, Babcock International

Chief Executive
Ian Halliday
Formerly a senior civil servant at the
Department of Industry (1972-5)
Directorships:
Finance Director of a large insurance
broking firm.

195

Members

Sir Robert Clayton	Formerly Chairman of GEC-Fairchild Directorships: Technical Director, GEC
Alex Dibbs	Directorships: Deputy Chairman and Group Chief Executive, National Westminster Bank Sits on at least six other boards
Jack Emms	Directorships: Chief General Manager and a Vice- Chairman, Commercial Union Assurance Deputy Chairman of the British Insurance Association Sits on the boards of 47 companies, mostly overseas!
George Jefferson	Directorships: Chairman and Chief Executive, British Aerospace Dynamics
Dennis Stevenson	Chairman of Peterlee and Newton Aycliffe New Towns

Appendix 3

Chart of NEB Acquisitions and Disposals

Date Acquired	Company	Main Activity	NEB % Share of Equity[1] (as at April 1980 unless otherwise stated)	Other major share holders	Date disposed	Employees				
						1975	1976	1977	1978	1979
1976										
February	*BL (British Leyland) Ltd[2]	Automotive products	99.1			191,000	153,000	172,000	169,000	159,800
February	*Cambridge Instrument Co. Ltd.	Scientific and medical instruments	93		Oct. 1979 – New company acquired name (CIC) and operating subsidiaries (see CIC 1979)		1,172	1,091	1,032	N/A
February	+Dunford and Elliott[2]	Steel manufacturers			April 1978 – Sold to Lonrho					
February	+Ferranti Ltd.[2]	Mechanical, electrical and electronic engineering	50		Sept. 1978 – Ferranti ceased to be a subsidiary. With certain assets disposed of, it is now an associated co.	16,651	15,576	15,558	16,193	16,464

1. Equity: ordinary shares which normally carry voting rights.
2. Transferred from Dept. of Industry.
* Subsidiary company: in which NEB has a majority shareholding.
+ Associated company: in which NEB has a minority shareholding.
† Other investments.

Date Acquired	Company	Main Activity	NEB % Share of Equity[1] (as at April 1980 unless otherwise stated)	Other major share holders	Date disposed	Employees				
						1975	1976	1977	1978	1979
February	*Herbert Ltd.[2]	Machine Tools	100		1980 – extensive re-organisation begun through sales and closures	6,716	6,017	5,917	5,356	4,855 [1980 – 4,200 (approx) by 1981 less than 1,000]
February	+ICL Ltd.[2]	Computers	1976 – 24.4 Dec. 1979 – Nil	1976 – 24.4% owned by Plessey	Dec. 1979 – sold to "a wide range of UK investors", realising a profit of £24m	24,312	23,350	23,054	24,276	
February	*Rolls Royce[2]	Aero-Engines	1976 – 100 1980 – Nil		Nov. 1979 – Keith Joseph announces transfer back to HM Govt.	62,375	59,758	56,646	56,587 plus 2,200 overseas	59,000 plus 2,200 overseas
March	+Brown Boveri Kent (Holdings) Ltd.[2]	Industrial instruments	20	Brown Boveri (A Swiss multi-national)				4,346	4,247	
July	*Data Recording Instrument Co. Ltd.	Computer peripherals	100			923	1,030	1,184	1,574	1,746
September	+Agemaspark Ltd.	Spark Erosion machines	30			Under 100	Under 100	147	169	210
September	+Twinlock Ltd	Office filing, systems and	33.3			1,780	2,246	2,021	1,962	1,982

Date	Company	Business	%	Notes					
October	+Reed and Smith Holdings Ltd	Paper Mills	1976 – 29.5 1977 – Nil	Dec. 1977 – taken over by St. Regis International, one of the ten largest paper co's in the world	1,634	1,572			
November	*Sinclair Radionics Ltd.	Micro-electronics	73.3	1979 – plans for disposal and run-down begun, NEB's £7.8m investment "written off" (April 1980)	263	244	368	414	261
1977									
January	+R.R. Chapman (Sub-sea surveys) Ltd.	Unmanned submersibles	1971 – 47 1980 – 35.3				Under 100	Under 100	Under 100
January	+Aquilisa Products	Shower heads	40					Under 100	Under 100
February	*Keland Electrics Ltd.	Electrical transformers	100				87	155	164
March	*United Medical Co. International Ltd.	Medical equipment exporter	55	45% owned by Allied Investments Ltd	March 1978 – sold to *UME (see March 78)		Under 100	90	100
April	*The Mollart Eng. Co. Ltd.	Precision engineering	70.6				245	237	252
April	+CAP – CPP Group Ltd (Formerly Computer Analysts and Programmers Holdings Ltd)	Computer software systems	29.5			439	499	631	783

Continued overleaf.

Date Acquired	Company	Main Activity	NEB % Share of Equity[1] (as at April 1980 unless otherwise stated)	Other major share holders	Date disposed	Employees				
						1975	1976	1977	1978	1979
April	†Francis Shaw & Co. Ltd	Process machinery	Nil (but with option to convert shares to 29.8% of equity)						766	N/A
April	†Pakmet International Ltd.	Packaging machinery	1977 – 34 1979 – Nil		Dec. 1979 – Receiver Appointed		Under 100	Under 100	Under 100	Under 100
May	+British Tanners Products Ltd.	Tanning	1977 – 50 1979 – Nil	1977 – 50% owned by Barrow Hepburn Group†	July 1979 – Liquidated			2,025	1,355	
May	†Thermax Ltd.	Glass manufacturers	Nil							212
June	+Hydraroll Ltd	Vehicle loading equipment	48.9					Under 100	Under 100	Under 100
June	*Insac Group Ltd	Computer products and services	100					Under 100	Under 100	Under 100
July	+Pitcraft Ltd	Mining engineering	1977 – 20 1978 – Nil		July 1978 – Shares sold to Booker McConnell Group, realising a 100% profit on NEB's investment		109	149		
July	+Systime Ltd.	Computer Hard- and Software	29.5				111	192	329	657

200

Date	Company	Business	Nil (out with option to convert shares to 29.8% of equity)	Status				
	...Plastics Ltd	Pharmaceutical plastics					Under 100	Under 100
September	+Hivent Ltd.	Air pollution control equipment	26	March 1978 – Liquidated				
September	+Sandiacre Electronics Ltd	Control systems engineering	30			Under 100	Under 100	Under 100
October	*Bull Motors Ltd	Variable speed motors	100			306	316	252
October	+North East Audio Ltd	Audio equipment	49.8			Under 100	168	167
October	*Systems Programming Holdings Ltd.	Computer services	79.9		263	306	307	389
December	+Mayflower Packaging Ltd	Packaging machinery	1977 – 33 1979 – Nil	December 1979 – Receiver Appointed		Under 100	Under 100	Under 100
1978 January	*Fairey Holdings Ltd	Engineering	100	Feb. 1980 – offer of £19.5m made by Hambros Bank. May 1980 S. Pearson & Son offer of £24m; revised offer of £22m accepted			3,057	2,796
January	+Systems Designers International Ltd	Computer software systems	26				121	177

Continued overleaf.

Date Acquired	Company	Main Activity	NEB % Share of Equity[1] (as at April 1980 unless otherwise stated)	Other major share holders	Date disposed	Employees 1975	1976	1977	1978	1979
February	†Barrow Hepburn Group Ltd	Chemicals, engineering and merchanting	4							
February	+Power Dynamics Ltd.	Mechanical and hydraulic eng.	1978 – 33.3 1980 – Nil		Late 1978 – Receiver Appointed			28		
March	*United Medical Enterprises Ltd (UME)	Medical equipment exporter	70	10% each owned by: Commercial Union, London Trust Co. & Orion Bank Ltd.					(See United Medical Co. 1977)	
March	+Vicort of London Ltd	Sports equipment	1978 – 49 1980 – Nil		Feb. 1980 – Receiver Appointed			Under 100	120	
April	+Automation and Technical (Holdings) Ltd	Communications equipment	30%					Under 100	Under 100	35
April	+Computer and Systems Engineering Ltd.	Communications equipment	49.8					205	257	288
April	†Hird Brown Ltd	Photo-electric controls	1978 – Nil (but with option to convert shares	W. Canning Ltd.	Sept. 1979 – Sold to Ransome Hoffman				190	

Date	Company	Business	Stake %	Parent/Backer	Note		
July	+J. & P. Engineering (Reading) Ltd	Electrical & medical engineering	1978 – 33.3 1980 – Nil		Future uncertain; GEC interest in joint financing fails.	100	100
August	† BTB (Engineering) Ltd.	Specialised vehicles	Nil	ICFC (Industrial & Comm. Finance Corp.)	March 1980 – Receiver Appointed	Under 100	Under 100
September	+The Energy Equipment Co. Ltd.	Power systems engineers and contractors	Nil (but with option to convert shares to 42.9% of equity)				Under 100
September	+Negretti and Zambra Ltd	Process control engineering	29.9			1,081	1,079
September	+Newtown Securities (Northern) Ltd	Small firms financing	50	50% owned by Midland Bank Ltd.	May 1980 – Transfer of business to sole care of Midland Bank announced.		
September	+Power Drive PSR Ltd	Power transmission systems	40	Former management of Eaton Ltd's Industrial Drives Divn.		Under 100	Under 100
November	+Monotype Holdings Ltd	Typesetting	37.5	Barclays Bank Ltd		1,261	1,120

Continued overleaf.

Date Acquired	Company	Main Activity	NEB % Share of Equity[1] (as at April 1980 unless otherwise stated)	Other major share holders	Date disposed	Employees				
						1975	1976	1977	1978	1979
December	+Duo Rubber & Engineering Co. Ltd.	Tyre mould engraving and rubber moulding	49							108
December	+Technical Resources (Equipt.) Ltd.	LPG cylinders and pressure vessels	Nil		September 1979 – Receiver Appointed				30	100
1979 January	+Innotron Ltd	Electronic medical equipment	29	Oxford Instrument Group Ltd and "five private individuals"						
January	+Ferranti Resin Ltd	GRP tanks and insulation	49	+Ferranti Ltd						
January	+Logica Group Ltd: Logica Holdings Ltd	Computer software and systems	20.8	Planning Research Corporation – a multinational.					443	504
January	Logica Securities Ltd	Investment holding Co	20	80% owned by "certain +Logica Group Staff"						
January	Logica VTS. Ltd.	Word processing	43	57% owned by +Logica Securities						Under 100
January	*Nexos Office Systems Ltd	Office equipment	79.8							114 Under

Month	Company	Activity	%	Notes		
				Trust Ltd. Post Office Staff Super-annuation fund & National Coal Pension Fund		
February	+George P. Brown (Holdings) Ltd	Welding and metal forming equipment	49		250	258
February	*Burndept Electronics Ltd.	Radio communications equipment	51	49% owned by the BEREC Group		356
February	+Middle East Building Services	Overseas consultancy service	29.6	Barclays Merchant Bank Ltd & The Builder Ltd.		
February	+Sapling Enterprise Ltd	Small firms financing & consultancy	50	50% owned by Collinson Grant Assocs.		
March	*British Underwater engineering Ltd. (formerly part of Vickers Offshore Engineering Group)	Underwater engineering equipment	90	10% owned by Brown & Root (UK) Ltd, a subsidiary of The Halliburton Co. (A US oilfield services group.)		407
March	+Rigby Electronics	Electric high vacuum & sequential control equipment	Nil (but with option to convert shares to 28.5% of equity)			Under 100

Continued overleaf.

Date Acquired	Company	Main Activity	NEB % Share of Equity[1] (as at April 1980 unless otherwise stated)	Other major share holders	Date disposed	Employees				
						1975	1976	1977	1978	1979
May	†Thermax Ltd	Glass manufacturers	Nil							212
May	+Yates Duxbury & Sons Ltd	Paper manufacturers	50	50% owned by by Tootal						440
June	+Microfilm communications International Ltd.	Micrographics	28.3	Norton Warburg Investment Ltd & Touche Remnant & Co						Under 100
July	+James Howorth & Co. (Holdings) Ltd	Advanced air engineering	21.4%							
July	+Sonicaid Ltd	Ultrasonic medical equipment	29.8							252
August	+ASR Servotron Ltd	Industrial servo controls	26.1							
September	+Muirhead Office Systems Ltd	Facsimile systems (offices)	25	75% owned by Muirhead Ltd						N/A
October	+CIC Investment Holdings Ltd (Formerly Cambridge Instrument Co.)	Scientific and medical instruments	25	75% of voting stock owned by CIC Chairman Dr T. Gooding						
October	+Excelarc	Engineering	50	50% owned by P...f. d.H....						Under 100

systems

of USA

December	+Doyce Electronics Ltd	Digital engine testing equipment	25	
December	+Momex (UK) Ltd	Export promotion	28.9	Arbuthnot Latham & Co. Ltd.
1980 February	*Baviscrown Ltd	Electronic test and measuring equipment	94	6% owned by Directors of Sinclair Electronics
March	+Technalogics Computing Ltd	Finance for manufacture & marketing of computer terminal systems	40	Technalogics Ltd, + Sapling Enterprise Ltd. & + Rigby Electronics
April	+Barlin Consumer Products Ltd	Electrical convector heaters & fires	Nil	

Appendix 4

MPs attending national stage of the Inquiry into the National Enterprise Board, Wednesday October 31st, 1979 at the House of Commons

Tony Benn   Secretary of State for Industry March '74-June '75; Secretary of State for Energy June '75-May '79. On Standing Committee on Industry Bill.

Eric Heffer   Minister of State, Department of Industry March '74-April '75; Backbencher thereafter. On Standing Committee for second Bill.

Michael Meacher   Under Secretary of State, Department of Trade & Industry March '74-June '75; Under Secretary of State, Department of Social Security June '75-'78; Under Secretary of State, Department of Trade & Industry '78-'79. On Standing Committee for Bill (previously lecturer in Sociology at University of Essex).

Bob Cryer   Under Secretary of State, Department of Trade & Industry September '76-May '79.

Stuart Holland   Lecturer in Economics, University of Sussex up to May '78; Member of Labour Party Study Group on NEB 1973.

Audrey Wise   MP for Coventry South-West until 1979; Member of Standing Committee on Industry Bill.

Harry Cowans
John Ryman   MPs for the localities involved in the Inquiry.
George Park

In addition, Jack Jones, former General Secretary of the Transport and General Workers' Union, Ian Mikardo MP and Brian Sedgemore MP were interviewed by members of the Inquiry subsequent to this meeting.

Appendix 5

Coventry Trades Council
Joint Activities Sub-committee

17 June 1982

A Working Class Plan for Coventry

It is more than three years since Coventry Trades Council joined with Liverpool, Newcastle and North Tyneside Trades Councils to conduct a national enquiry into the industrial and economic policies of the last Labour government: an enquiry that centred its focus on the operations of the National Enterprise Board and the government's intention of striking planning agreements with the major multinationals.

This work has resulted in the publication of "State Intervention in Industry", a book that draws together workers' experiences from the four areas, and concludes that:

i. without the experience and expertise of working class organisations in the labour and community movements, new policies, however well intentioned, will inevitably reflect and serve the interests of capitalism.

ii. without real working class involvement and commitment behind them, new policies will again be sabotaged because there will be no base of popular support which can be mobilised to defend them.

The importance of this work is now gaining national recognition in the movement as more Trades Councils, Trade Union organisations and Constituency Labour Parties join us in sponsoring the Joint Declaration 'Popular Planning for Social Need'. This document argues the case for a new industrial and political strategy in the Labour movement based on production for need rather than profit.

We are now at a stage when we need to turn the ideas contained in the book and the declaration into solid practice on the ground. In Coventry we want to use the skills and experience of Trades Council delegates to put the lessons learned from this work into practice.

Producing our own plans

It is clear from the last forty years' experience of industrial policies which do little more than stop up the gaps in an ailing capitalist system, that the needs of working class people will not be met unless they determine their own policies and have the power to implement them.

Coventry Trades Council is in a good position to have a go at writing a plan for Coventry. Just think of the industries our delegates represent: health, education, aerospace, engineering, telecommunications, motors, civil service, building and construction, electricity, shops and distribution, social services, mining, entertainment, media and so on.

These industries, services and skills could all be re-organised to answer the unmet needs of working class people. That's why the Joint Activities Sub-Committee is proposing that delegates from as many industries as possible draw up plans for their industries under the headings:

PRODUCTION FOR NEED RATHER THAN PRIVATE PROFIT

USEFUL LABOUR RATHER THAN USELESS TOIL

We don't expect finely detailed planning proposals, but documents that will provide the basis for a Trades Council popular planning campaign in the City. What we'd like you to do is to risk your arm a bit by setting down on paper some ideas about:

1. how your industry or service *could be* organised to meet the needs of its workers and consumers, and

2. the new kinds of organisation which would be required in your industry or service to campaign for and implement those ideas (e.g. inter-union, producer-consumer, workplace-community organisations).

At this stage, we're looking for working proposals and principles which *could* form the basis of real popular planning initiatives, rather than exact pieces in a jigsaw puzzle.

Overleaf you will see a set of guidelines designed to help you write your plan. The sub-committee will require your plans by the delegate meeting after next. These will then be compiled into a single document for discussion at the following delegate meeting.

Drawing up a plan for Coventry from your individual industry plans will be no mean task. The sub-committee will need the help of as many delegates as possible to draw a single plan out of the individual ones. We would hope that other Trades Council sub-committees will allocate at least one of their members to help in this work. It is particularly important that the Cuts and Unemployment and Housing Sub-committees and the Women's Caucus make a contribution to this process.

Joint Activities Sub-committee

17 June 1982

Guidelines for writing workers plans in accordance with the principles laid down in the conclusions of 'State Intervention in Industry' and in 'Popular Planning for Social Need: A Joint Declaration'.

This is a practical exercise in trade union planning. We hope that it will help you and the Trades Council extend:

1. the scope of collective bargaining and campaigning in the workplace and

2. the scope of collective organising both in the workplace and the wider community, by devising alternative policies that we could begin to fight for now.

By alternatives we don't mean policies which look back to the good old days of

210

places like Coventry in the 1960s. The structure of the economy has been so fundamentally changed since then that to think we could ever return to a golden economic age before Thatcher came on the scene is completely unrealistic. Yet much of the policy thinking going on at the top of the labour and trade union movements today is based on the assumption that we can somehow turn the clocks back.

What we are looking for are plans which take a fresh look at the problem. They should be designed to use the experience and meet the needs of working class people as workers and as consumers. As such they will not meet the needs of the capitalist barons by increasing profits and competitiveness. They will re-define industrial success as providing secure, interesting, skilful and useful employment, producing goods and services in the interests of the whole community.

I The state of your company or industry

Before being able to make sense and use of any trade union plans, it will be important to understand the present situation. We would like you to give a thumbnail sketch of the major issues currently being faced in your workplace and industry. Below is a suggested list of topics that we reckon are likely to be of importance. Don't hesitate to add any other issues that we have left out:

Employment trends; New technology; Pay; Demand for product/service; Recent investment; State of trade union organisation/Industrial relations.

Has your company or industry been going through a process of reorganisation? That is, have any plants or facilities been closed or cut back? Have there been any productivity drives? Have any capital assets been sold or bought? Is your company moving into any new markets/product ranges or changing services provided? Have there been any major changes in employment terms, conditions, or working arrangements (deployment of labour, demarcation, work practices, tightening of disciplinary procedures and supervisory practices)?

We would like to emphasise that the above suggestions are not intended as a questionnaire. There is no need to answer all the questions or cover all of the points. Write down what's important about the current state of your company/industry. We have only tried to give some guidelines to help you.

II Management's view of what's been happening in your company/industry

How have management explained the recent changes outlined above?
Lack of orders; cash limits/no money for new investment; over-staffing/high labour costs; world recession; high interest rates; government policies; lack of skilled workers; inability to compete; restrictive t.u. practices/bad industrial relations record; company efficiency.

III Trade union view of what's been happening in your company/industry

How do you as trade unionists explain the recent changes in your company/industry outlined in the first section?
Short-sighted investment policies; excessive profit-taking; government policies; management bungles; crisis in world capitalism/over production.

211

IV Management's future plans

In your view, what future does management hold out for your company/industry? Especially in relation to: employment; pay; new investment; new technology; product range/services provided; working practices; t.u. organisation/industrial relations; company/industry re-organisation.

Does management *have* a plan for the future? Do they really know where they're going?

V Trade union plans for the future

This is the most difficult, but the most important bit. We'd like to see your ideas on how your members' labour, skills and experience *could be used* to create useful work for social need.

We also want some suggestions about what kind of links would have to be made between you as producers and other working class people as consumers of what you produce or provide. If producers can forge such links, there will be an organised basis for determining what working class people really need from industry and services. This would also lay the foundations of organisations in the movement which could mobilise the defence of policies people really believe in.

You will need to consider ways of maintaining and enhancing things like:
— the fullest employment of the available workforce;
— job security;
— worker's control over what's produced or provided and how;
— the quality of your working environment;
— the skills of the workforce;
— the involvement of all workers in their trade union — women and men, black and white, young and old, able and disabled;
— the kinds of t.u. and community organisations needed to mount campaigns which could force managements and governments to negotiate across a much wider range of collective bargaining issues (like industrial production for social need!)

You will also need to consider what demands should be made on existing organisations for support in developing and implementing your plans:
— local authorities;
— labour parties;
— national trade unions/the TUC;
— national government.

There *are* one or two local authorities — like our own West Midlands — which have said they are willing to support local trade union economic planning initiatives. How could/should we use this opportunity (and the money) to develop real plans for real needs?

Appendix 6

Bibliography

T. Benn, *Arguments for Socialism,* London: Cape, 1979.

T. Benn, 'Towards a New Settlement' (Granada Guildhall Lecture), *New Statesman,* May 16th, 1980, 734-35.

Benwell CDP, *Storing Up Trouble,* 1978.

Benwell CDP, *Permanent Unemployment,* 1979.

Benwell CDP, *The Making of the Ruling Class,* 1979.

Benwell CDP, *Adamsez – The Story of a Factory Closure,* 1980.

Benwell CDP and North Tyneside CDP, *Regional Capitalism,* 1980.

H. Beynon, *What Happened at Speke?,* Liverpool: TGWU Branch 6-612, 1978.

H. Beynon & H. Wainwright, *The Workers' Report on Vickers,* London: Pluto Press, 1979.

CDP Inter-Project Editorial Team, *The Costs of Industrial Change,* January, 1977.

CDP-PEC, *The State and The Local Economy,* 1979.

Chrysler Shop Stewards and Staff Representatives Joint Union Delegation, *Chrysler Crisis: The Workers' Answer,* Coventry: mimeo, 1975.

Coventry Machine Tool Workers' Committee, *Crisis in Engineering: Machine Tool Workers' Fight for Jobs,* Nottingham: Institute for Workers' Control, 1979.

Coventry Workshop, *Unemployment and the Multinationals in Coventry,* Coventry: Coventry Workshop, 1978.

G. Craig, M. Mayo and N. Sharman (eds.), *Jobs and Community Action,* RKP, 1979.

T. Forester, 'How Labour's Industrial Strategy Got the Chop', *New Society,* July 6th, 1978, 7-10.

T. Forester, 'Neutralising the Industrial Strategy', in K. Coates ed., *What Went Wrong: Explaining the Fall of the Labour Government,* Nottingham: Spokesman Books, 1979.

J. Haines, *The Politics of Power,* London: Cape, 1977.

S. Holland, *The Socialist Challenge,* London: Quartet Books, 1975.

House of Commons Expenditure Committee, *Public Expenditure on Chrysler UK Ltd.,* London: HMSO, 1976.

Institute for Workers' Control Motors Group, *A Workers' Inquiry into the Motor Industry,* London: CSE Books, 1978.

Labour Party Manifesto: February 1974, *Labour's Way Out of the Crisis,* London: The Labour Party, 1974.

Labour Party Manifesto: October 1974, *Britain Will Win With Labour,* London: The Labour Party, 1974.

Labour Party National Executive Committee Statement, *Labour & Industry: The Next Steps,* London: The Labour Party, 1975.

Labour Party Study Group Report (Opposition Green Paper), *The National Enterprise Board: Labour's State Holding Company,* London: The Labour Party, 1973.

Lucas Aerospace Combine Shop Stewards' Committee, *Lucas: An Alternative Plan,* IWC Pamphlet No.55, Nottingham: Institute for Workers' Control, no date.

National Enterprise Board: Report & Accounts 1977, London: NEB, 1978.
National Enterprise Board: Report & Accounts 1978, London: NEB, 1979.
National Enterprise Board: Report & Accounts 1979, London: NEB, 1980.
Newcastle on Tyne Trades Council Centre for the Unemployed, TUSIU, Search Project: Joint Report, *Life Without Wages.*
Newcastle on Tyne Trades Council: *Annual Report,* 1979.
Newcastle on Tyne Trades Council Centre for the Unemployed: *Agitate, Educate, Organise.*
Newcastle on Tyne Trades Council Centre for the Unemployed: *On the Stores.*
North Tyneside Community Development Project Final Report Vol.2, *North Shields: Living with Industrial Change,* Newcastle: Benwell Community Project, 1978.
North Tyneside CDP, *North Shields: Women's Work,* 1978.
North Tyneside CDP, *In and Out of Work – a study of unemployment, low pay and income maintenance services,* 1978.
North Tyneside Trades Council, *Shipbuilding – The Cost of Redundancy,* September, 1979.
M. Parr, 'The National Enterprise Board', *National Westminster Bank Quarterly Review,* February 1979, 51-62.
Tress Shop Stewards, *The Closure of Tress – A Fairey Story,* 1978.
TUSIU, *The Crisis Facing the UK Power Plant Manufacturing Industry,* December, 1976.
TUSIU, *Workers' Occupations in the North East,* August 1976.
TUSIU, *Machine Tool Report,* 1977.
TUSIU, *British Shipbuilding – What Next,* 1978.
TUSIU, *Direct Labour, The Answer to Building Chaos,* May, 1980.

White Paper, *The Regeneration of British Industry,* Cmnd.5710, London: HMSO, August 1974.
White Paper, *An Approach to Industrial Strategy,* Cmnd.6315, London: HMSO, November 1975.
Wilson Committee: Review of the Functioning of Financial Institutions, *Evidence on the Financing of Industry & Trade: Vol.4, The National Enterprise Board,* London: HMSO, 1978.
H. Wilson, *Final Term: The Labour Government 1974-76,* London: Michael Joseph, 1979.

More recent publications:

Coventry Workshop, *Fighting Fit? How job loss is affecting Coventry,* October 1982, 10p.
Joint Trades Councils/Joint Forum of Combines, *Popular Planning for Social Need – a declaration,* 1981, 30p.
Joint Trades Councils/Joint Forum of Combines, *The Declaration – supplementary information,* 1982, 40p.
Joint Trades Councils/Joint Forum of Combines, *Economic Planning through Industrial Democracy – a socialist alternative,* 1982, 50p.

Joint Forum of Combines, *Trade Union Strategy in the face of Corporate Power – the case for multi-union shop steward combine committees*, 1980, 25p.

Newcastle Trades Council/Tyneside Alternative Production Group, *Jobs for a Change – Alternative Production on Tyneside*, 1982, 60p.

Sheffield Trades Council, *Sheffield – the second slump*, 1982, 75p.

TUSIU, *Direct Labour – the answer to building chaos*, 1980, 75p.

TUSIU, *Jobs From Warmth*, 1981, free pamphlet.

Vickers Elswick Shop Stewards Committee, *A Farewell to Arms?*, 1981, 50p.

West End Resource Centre, *Eveready? A trade unionists' report on the future of BEREC*, 1981, 65p.

Note: For information about Benwell & North Tyneside CDP Publications contact Gary Craig, West End Resources Centre, 87 Adelaide Terrace, Newcastle-upon-Tyne NE4 8BB. Tel: 0632-731210.

For information about TUSIU Publications, contact TUSIU, 'Southend' Fernwood Road, Newcastle NE2 1TJ. Tel: 0632-816087.

For information about Coventry Workshop and its publications contact Jane Woddis, 40, Binley Road, Coventry. Tel: 0203-27772.

PRIVATISATION?
edited by Sue Hastings & Hugo Levie

The aim of this important study is to give a blow-by-blow account of the Tories' programme of privatisation and the responses that so far seem most successful. This volume will be of particular interest to public sector trade unionists who are faced with privatisation, because it helps to set some key special cases in the wider context of the Conservative attack on all public services and utilities. Examples range from the National Freight Corporation, via the gas showrooms, direct labour organisations and refuse collection to British Telecom and the Civil Service.

The book calls upon all those convinced of the need to defend the public sector to stop and think. What have we done wrong in the past, that leads so many people to be confused about the importance of an expanding instead of a shrinking public sector?

Cloth £12.50
Paper £2.95

ISBN 0 85124 359 2
ISBN 0 85124 360 6

SPOKESMAN